Servants of Power
The Role of English-speaking Churches
in South Africa: 1903—1930

Servants of Power
The Role of English-speaking Churches
in South Africa: 1903—1930

Servants of Power

The Role of English-speaking Churches in South Africa: 1903—1930

Towards a Critical Theology via an Historical Analysis of the Anglican and Methodist Churches

James R Cochrane

Ravan Press   Johannesburg

To those whose journey with the holy
  unites their saying and doing
  in the struggle for the healing of all.

And to Thembisa and Thandeka
  Symbols of hope for a new generation.

Published by Ravan Press (Pty) Ltd
PO Box 31134, Braamfontein, 2017, South Africa

First impression 1987

ISBN 0 86975 277 4

Cover Design: Jeff Lok
Set in 9 on 12pt English Times

Printed and bound by Galvin & Sales, Cape Town

Contents

PART TWO: REFLECTION IN THEORY - THE POSSIBILITY
OF A CRITICAL CHURCH

List of Tables

Abbreviations

ALS	Manuscript Letter, signed
APO	African People's Organisation
CCD	Christian Citzenship Department, Methodist Church
CE	*Christian Express* (later *South African Outlook*)
CR	Journal of the Community of the Resurrection, Johannesburg
E & W	*The East and West Review*
GMCSA	General Missionary Conference of South Africa
ICS	Institute for Commonwealth Studies on Southern Africa in the Nineteenth and Twentieth Centuries, University of London
ICU/ICWU	Industrial and Commercial Workers Union
ISL	International Socialist League
IWW	International Workers of the World
JTSA	*Journal of Theology for Southern Africa*
LS	Letter or Document, signed
MCMC	Methodist Church, Minutes of Conference
OX	*Oxford History of South Africa*
RDM	*Rand Daily Mail*
SAMSR	South African Missionary Society Report
SANAC	South African Native Affairs (Lagden) Commission
SAO	*South African Outlook*
TCC	*The Church Chronicle* (CPSA)
TMC	*The Methodist Churchman*
Ts	Typescript
WNLA	Witwatersrand Native Labour Association
WTLC	Witwatersrand Trades and Labour Council

It was the disease, the madness of the age, that
everyone was different from his outward appearance
and his words.

Boris Pasternak, *Dr Zhivago*

Preface

This book manifests more than a dozen years of intellectual and personal struggle to come to terms with the meaning of ministry and mission in a crisis-laden country. This notoriously cruel South Africa, despite vast wealth, remains for its majority a millstone of poverty and prejudice. How many untold thousands have been ground quite literally into the earth? Here power and privilege are outrageous, the questioning of them often offensive. But how necessary! As I too have been a benefactor of South African power and privilege, I have had to question myself over and over again.

That I should find myself on this particular path of questioning owes all to certain 'Significant Others' whose ways fatefully crossed mine. Together with other friends and colleagues, they form the stuff for the inner dialogue of which this study is my temporary report, a moment of arrival on a continuing pilgrimage.

Chief among those who drew me from adolescent innocence, and from a crumbling, teenage, fundamentalist Christianity whose Christ had little to do with the ravages of South Africa, was Theo Kotze. His ministry, both in preaching and practice, allowed a veiled glimpse of another possibility: in a human, broken, bloodied, even abandoned Jesus who painfully reminds me of all the people shattered on the rocks of our broken society. Squirming on the comfortable pews I have known, I confess I never escape this image and its contradiction in me.

Since then, I have had the fortune of friends who have been teachers, and teachers who have become friends; all striving — even in failure — to unite liberating Word with practical deed. They are the inspiration of this study; I cannot name them all.

Among those in whose intellectual debt I especially am, are Mike de Klerk, Bonganjalo Goba, Ted Jennings, Doug McGaughey, Ross Snyder, David Tracy, Herman Waetjen and Francis Wilson.

Others have assisted or supported this project in various ways. They include Shaan Ellinghouse, Mariannne Saddington, Di Scott, Chuck Wannamaker, the Brownes of Elgin, the Dunstans in Johannesburg, the Robertsons in Grahamstown, and Renate. At both the Anglican (CPSA) archives, University of the Witwatersrand, and the Methodist archives, Cory Library, Rhodes University, I received most courteous and willing help. Renate, John de Gruchy (who made it possible to do the research in the first place), Mike de Klerk and Patrick Harries helpfully read drafts of what has become this book, and valuable criticisms were received from Dunbar Moodie, Klaus Nurnberger and David Tracy. In all cases they are naturally excused responsibility for the views of the text published, though I am happy should they feel their contribution to have been worthwhile. The muddiness and gaps that remain I claim entirely.

One learns, I was told, more by teaching than by studying. Indeed, I found this to be true. Thanks go for opportunities offered both at the University of Cape Town and, for a summer, at San Francisco Theological Seminary.

I wish also to express thanks to the Roothbert Fund in New York for financial support at a critical moment, and the Human Sciences Research Council for their assistance towards the costs of research. Of course all opinions expressed and conclusions reached are mine, and are not to be reflected upon these bodies.

Finally, my deepest gratitude to those many friends I have had the privilege to know and work with in my adult years, some of whom have not been treated too kindly for their pains in seeking a just society. They have motivated me to the study this book represents, and helped me to believe there may be value in it. My debt to them all carries far beyond these pages. Their lives never cease to remind me that such study or reflection betrays itself when not grounded in the daily flesh-and-blood battle of those who struggle to survive in the first place; to transform, in the second, the very conditions of suffering and evil as they hope in a renewed world and a healed nation.

PART 1

The Role of the Churches

The most modest task for empirical social research . . .
would be for it to confront all its statements on the subjective
experience, conscious and unconscious, of human beings
and human groups, with the objective factors determining their existence.

Theodor W Adorno

CHAPTER ONE

Introduction

> On the hands of the people
> Callouses will never go away
> For on their hands they depend
> To create the new day
>
> — Wang Hsi-chien[1]

From the first excited person who skilfully wielded a chopping stone to the
fascinated viewer programming a powerful computer, human beings have
quite literally had a hand in shaping history. This is not only true of their use
of the things of the world around them, but also of the work they have done
on the world — not without ambiguous results of course. What is true of our
relationship to nature is equally true of our relationship to each other. We are
the makers of our social history, of its politics, its economics, its communal
life. We are gods of a kind, albeit gods who are continually surprised, startled
and often frightened by our creations.

Those of us with religious views of creation, who suppose that only the one
God creates, are also those who are most dismayed by the march of events and
often least willing to accept our responsibility. The bread of our theological
truths falls into crumbs of earthly fiction easily carried away by the scavengers
of history. Deprived of the life-force of our faith, impotent before others who
call us to autonomy and responsibility, we cry: 'God judges all!' But history
judges us. This is the situation of the Church in South Africa today.

Individual Christians and their churches have been placed in an unusually
vulnerable position by conflicts within the Southern African region over the
last years, conflicts strongly bound up with opposing economic models and
philosophies. The future of the Church in the region is unquestionably at
stake, and within the Church markedly different positions are being adopted.

Moreover, input from the stream of contemporary theology, most impor-
tantly the various 'political' theologies of hope, protest, blackness, liberation

and revolution, has entered into church debate at all levels, finding responsive chords among many. This too, as well as much else, makes it fair to say that the historical ethos within which theology is now being done is specifically characterised by a political exigency.

The growing awareness of the conflicts and polarities within South African society is reflected in the increasing socio-political activity of a number of groups of Christians during the last decade and more, as well as in a wide variety of conferences, meetings, declarations, ecumenical assemblies, and new organisations.[2] To a large extent all of these debates and happenings have been situated consciously in the political context of South Africa. Consequently questions concerning Church and state, Church and society, Church and culture, faith and ideology, and so on, have been and remain paramount.[3]

Moreover, the claim of the leaders of state to religious sanction for their position and in many instances their policy, a claim frequently supported by theologians of the white Dutch Reformed churches in particular, contributes to the political ambience affecting the churches. As one author has expressed it: 'The South African Parliament must be one of the very few such institutions in the world where theological debate erupts from time to time in the discussion of national legislation.'[4] In contrast, many blacks as well as others increasingly question the role of Christianity, and of missionaries especially, in the history of Africa.

This study began as an attempt to explain a particular ambiguity in the South African English-speaking churches: a consistent anti-apartheid record on paper coupled with a generally manifest powerlessness to translate that record into practical policy, except at the least threatening levels.

What is most striking about the 'anti-apartheid' main-line churches is their almost total lack of connection to black labour. Long ago Olive Schreiner — an honoured figure in the liberal English tradition — had already said of black workers: 'They are the makers of our wealth, the great basic rock on which our state is founded — our vast labouring force.'[5] More crassly, Jan Smuts also noticed that 'if he is not much more, he is the beast of burden; he is the worker and you need him. He is carrying this country on his back.'[6] And in her assessment of the role of missionaries, Nosipho Majeke later spelt our more generally the central socio-economic feature of modern South Africa:

> Capitalism has shattered tribalism and destroyed the social relationships that go with it; it has broken the old tribal bonds, but it has created new ties that bind men together in a much wider unity. It brings men face to face with the objective industrial forces, for the whole of society is organised around industry and commerce and men take their place within it irrespective of what tribe or race they belong to.[7]

With these themes no serious economist, sociologist or historian is likely to disagree, even if they might expand on them differently. Yet the Church in all its heavenly wisdom showed little evidence then (now?) of grasping its earthly location. Either that, or it considered such affairs as outside its ambit. In both cases it is necessary to ask why? This is a central problem of the study.

South African Church History Reconsidered

> Those persons who talk most about human freedom are those who are actually most blindly subject to social determination, inasmuch as they do not in most cases suspect the profound degree to which their conduct is determined by their interests.

Karl Mannheim, *Ideology and Utopia*

The year 1948 — the victory of Afrikaner political forces — stands as *the* symbol of disaster for English-speaking whites as a group. But it represents far less a victory of segregationalist views over liberal than a particularly acute moment in a much longer competition for political hegemony between two groups sharing a dominant position in an oppressive society. The historical 'losers' in this competition (English-speakers) then mounted an ideological attack on the 'winners' (the shapers of strict apartheid ideals). Often this attack has not been convincing because it has not been accompanied with self-critical insight into the attackers' own place in the structures of domination.

In order to understand the role of English-speaking churches in South Africa, it becomes necessary to understand (a) the structure and historical nature of domination in South Africa, (b) the relationship of the Church to this reality, (c) implications for interpreting church policy, practice and theology.

Now church histories in South Africa have usually not sought to treat these sorts of questions with much depth at all. On the contrary, ecclesiastical traditions have been recorded almost exclusively as the actions, words and experiences of clerics, church leaders, and subordinate groups of particular denominations or missions, taken more or less at face value. These histories have purported thereby to describe the history of the Church in South Africa. Controversies and conflicts appear as internal battles of the Church itself, or as criticisms of certain state policies or matters of public behaviour. One seldom finds any critical reflection on the structures, practices, and policies of the Church itself, except when the English-speaking churches criticise the white Dutch Reformed churches (often from an overly self-confident point of view). A brief general analysis of a number of works demonstrates these hypotheses fairly well.

JH du Plessis' classic history of missions in South Africa admirably seeks to place Church history within the political history of South Africa.[8] Nevertheless it illustrates the general weaknesses evident in Church historiography. Strongly influenced by George M Theal, who was quite clear that 'civilisation' should conquer African barbarism, du Plessis yet felt that 'civilisation *minus* Christianity, far from being an unmixed blessing to native races, is an unmitigated curse'.[9] Here he was particularly critical of traders, but also of wars upon Africans which had produced 'hurtful results'. He refers to the oppressive effects of colonisation, and to the dispossession of territory. But in both cases he regards any negative judgement of the role of missionaries as uncalled for. For du Plessis the history of Christian missions was by and large positive, producing morality, thrift, industry, and order among the 'savages'. Their pre-eminent aim was 'to capture the strongholds of the enemy', albeit to inspire a new set of (imposed) values.[10] A clearer statement could hardly be made of the controlling perspective of his history than du Plessis' own opinion on the indigenous people of South Africa:

> . . . it is not to be expected that any rights to extensive territories will be acknowledged, which are not 'based on the intention and ability to develop those regions'. This intention and this ability the natives do not possess, and nations of greater culture and virility must show them the way . . . Colonisation, in short, though it has been and still is attended with many evils, has also effected much good, and is destined, in the good providence of God, to bestow inestimable blessings upon the native races of South Africa.[11]

Such views are of course not unexpected. Today we easily recognise the strong biases and prejudices underlying an acknowledged classic of South Africa history, but this should not lead us to assume our own wisdom. It should caution us.

In a follow-up study of the South African mission field covering the period from du Plessis' publication to the 1950s, GBA Gerdener departs little from the earlier approach. His main alteration is to picture recent history from the viewpoint of what he calls the local 'receiving' churches, rather than the foreign 'sending' churches. Accordingly, the first half of the twentieth century he understands to be a period of transition 'from the Mission-Projects of the nineteenth century to the Church-building of this one.'[12]

Like du Plessis, Gerdener points to a possibility fulfilled in only a minimal way, namely the linking of the history of missionary enterprise with the political and economic conditions of the 'target groups' among the indigenous people. Brief introductory comments on the Boer War, the World Wars, the Western pattern of life and the multifold character of South Africa's population; a chapter on separation and independence among African churches; and a further chapter on the state and its legislation (by and large positive) — these constitute the extent of Gerdener's linking of Church history to socio-economic history. Like du Plessis, then, Gerdener indulges in little critical analysis of the Church's role in South Africa, and he too believes a critical attitude to the Church on the part of Africans is something to be disarmed.[13]

This fear of criticism, or as it may be, this resistance to negative judgements on one's beloved institution, is as understandable as it is commonly evident. Other historians show the same tendency, for example, Leslie Hewson in his introduction and tribute to Methodist missionaries, in which he discusses the pioneers who established institutions of worship, study and publication, the threat of independent churches, and the establishment of a national Conference of Methodist churches. Throughout, obviously quite intentionally, the book praises the missionary enterprises but with little attempt to assess its import in other than religious terms. The single exception comes with repeated references to the reconciliatory role played by Methodism between African and settler, between conquered and colonist.[14] Racial peace was a primary aim of Methodism in Hewson's view. Though this noble goal may have been shared by most, it cannot be assumed that the Church understood the necessary conditions and processes required for it. Such questions do not enter into Hewson's history at all.

Similarly, the account of the Anglican Church (CPSA) by Peter Hinchliff, in itself an excellent example of the genre, nevertheless treats church history from an essentially internal point of view. Occasional sections on general South African history function only to set the scene, written as parallel and, to all intents and purposes, unconnected narratives.[15] In his later brief study of the church as a whole in South Africa, Hinchliff does advert to the imperialist critique of missions, regarding it as 'not surprising that most missionaries longed, and even worked actively, for the day when British rule, and British order and justice, would cover all Southern Africa'.[16] Certainly this is not surprising, yet the critique of missions accepts precisely this unsurprising fact and tries to explain it. But for Hinchliff, there it rests.

The above comments are by and large equally appropriate to Brown's work on the Catholic Church (though he treats the 'colour question' more fully),[17] and to Jane Sales' review of Church history in South Africa.[18] Even Verryn's recent history of the Order of Ethiopia places the two problems of racial animosity and denominationalism at the forefront of influences on the Church, without considering in any detail the material conditions of the rise of the Order. While pointing out the role of 'ecclesiastical imperialism', of colour prejudice, and of church discipline in fomenting an independent church spirit, the author somewhat neglects the massive effects of conquest, proleterianisation and land legislation. In fact the concept of urbanisation, understood in essence as an inevitable (natural?) process disrupting traditional tribal life, is as far as any analysis goes.[19]

A substantial part of Hans Florin's look at Lutherans in South Africa is given over to social, political and economic conditions under the heading 'The Setting'. Though his treatment of the setting is by far the most detailed among the authors so far discussed, it falls short in two respects. Firstly, his focus on the 'race issue' (by which he means group prejudice and group relations) as the major problem, effectively conceals economic realities and thereby leaves his analysis superficial. One result of this is his critical attack on the ideological role of the Dutch Reformed churches, without any recognition that other denominations may stand equally well judged of ideological captivity. Another indication of the inadequacy of his analysis may be found in the view that economic interests provide the single most unifying category for common loyalties and shared aspirations among the various groups in South Africa ('economic growth is equally good for everybody'), a position difficult to reconcile with the long and substantial history of conflict between Capital and Labour.[20] Thirdly, the 'setting' is never integrated into the history of the Church. It is parallel history once again, except insofar as some account of the anti-apartheid churches' criticism is included (but there again these churches are treated as institutions in some way apart from the society within which they are irrevocably embedded).

Similar points can be made about two more recent histories, both of which concentrate on the second half of the twentieth century but also treat the longer term. Regehr draws directly on the historiographical tradition criticised above, utilising many of the same authors, but does not seek to go beyond or revise their interpretations to any significant extent.[21] Consequently, Afrikaner nationalism emerges as the bogey, permeating his interpretation of contemporary church history. De Gruchy's work begins somewhat differently, but he ends up in more or less the same place as Regehr, albeit with a less critical stance.[22] However, de Gruchy does at least recognise and in places discuss the manner in which the Church 'is affected by, and often corrupted by, the society in which it is placed'. To that extent church history becomes part of general history and benefits thereby. The deficiencies in his study concern rather his relatively superficial treatment of the general history of South Africa, and his consequent inability to penetrate the multi-various captivities of the Church to the structures and ideologies of its host society.

Two exceptions stand out in church historiography of South Africa. One of those, strictly speaking, addresses not the South African context but the

Namibian, while the other — for the lack of academic procedure — is seldom taken seriously. The former is Lukas de Vries' account of mission and colonialism in Namibia,[23] and the latter Nosipho Majeke's critique of the role of missionaries in conquest.[24] The major difference between the two authors lies in their respective relationships to the Church, de Vries being a leading cleric, Majeke an outspoken external judge. Yet their assessments of the role of the Church in the region coincide substantially, though de Vries' motive in writing is that the Church in Namibia should 'not repeat the past error of the mission', whereas Majeke views the Church as inescapably an instrument of oppression.[25]

While recognising the permanent need for narrative history in the traditional sense, and while noting that every standard history reviewed above had particular aims and limits, it is within this last, socially critical historiographical tradition that the present study is located. As such, an attempt is made to go beyond any previous work by introducing considerably greater detail and analytical specification into an investigation of the role of the Church in South Africa. The methodological problems involved include the need to restrict the field of inquiry without losing the possibility of generating widely applicable results. For that reason certain decisions were made concerning the most fruitful period of study and the specific denominations to be studied.

Framework of Inquiry

The period 1903—1930 was chosen because developments in the political economy of South Africa during this time laid the foundation for the next fifty years. The period saw the development of an advanced industrial and technological base coupled with a marked structure of exploitation and oppression of labour, and of the rural colonised population. Thus any results obtained and conclusions reached in respect of the churches promised to have contemporary theoretical and practical relevance.

From the beginning I was interested in looking at the history of churches today known as 'anti-apartheid' rather than the oft-criticised Dutch Reformed churches. These are the 'English-speaking' churches, a somewhat vague category. I mean it to refer to those denominations whose origin in South Africa may be traced to Britain via its colonial relationship to South Africa, and who for some time at least regarded Britain as their home base. It should be kept in mind, however, that in most cases the majority of members of these churches did not and do not speak English as a home language.

Two denominations characterised as 'English-speaking', the Church of the

Province of South Africa (CPSA, or colloquially, the Anglican Church) and the Methodist Church of South Africa, are the focus of this research. The selection of these two is not entirely arbitrary, but is based on several good reasons:

1   Between them they represent a particularly broad socio-economic spectrum of English-speaking South African society, usually incorporating many leading industrialists, bankers, businessmen and politicians, as well as white- and blue-collar workers.

2   Both were and are numerically speaking strong in South Africa, the Methodist Church having the largest single membership (see Table 8).

3   Both were heavily involved in African missions, and together they included no less than 79 per cent of Africans affiliated to churches defined as 'English-speaking' (Table 8).

4   Both have been clear in their statements against racially discriminatory policies of the state, especially since the middle 1920s; yet both have been, and in some respects still are, dominated by the wealthy and the white, notwithstanding attempts at change.

5   Finally, both were highly visible during the period analysed, being considerably more influential than any other denominations, barring the Dutch Reformed churches.

Where I wish to refer to the Church in its most general sense (meaning no specific denomination) or in the theological sense (the 'Body of Christ'), the word Church is always capitalised. The one exception is when it is is attached to the name of a denomination ('the Methodist Church') in which case the meaning is obvious. Wherever I mean the specific denominations under investigation here, the noun remains in the lower case ('the churches of the Witwatersrand'). The distinction is necessary because at times a descriptive task is in mind, while at other times a generalised judgement of Christian religion *per se* in the South African context is implied.

In this study I assume that the period investigated is characterised by a dominant capitalist mode of production whose principle of organisation lies in a relationship of wage, labour and capital anchored in a system of bourgeois civil law.[26] I take into account that in South Africa capitalism is modified by monopolistic and monopsonistic practices, notably in the mineral industries and in national transport and communication systems.

Within this framework certain other terms are used later which specify particular aspects of the dominant mode of production and its ideological consequences.

'Primitive accumulation' refers to the transfer of value from the traditional African economy and parts of the Afrikaner feudal agricultural sector to the capitalist sector. In the context of the imposition of a capitalist economy from the outside, this 'primitive accumulation' takes the form of conquest and colonisation.[27]

'Imperialism' means the formal or informal control over local economic resources in a manner advantageous to the metropolitan power at the expense of the local economy or of parts of it.[28]

'Dependency' occurs where certain sectors of the economy in the interaction between different modes of production are dependent on others while being unable to survive as independent centres of capital accumulation.[29]

'Hegemonic competition' refers to the political conflict between fractions of a class whose programmes for the direction of economic development are situated within the same system but with alternative choices and visions as to their strategies. In a colonised nation the struggle for hegemony is often a marked feature (as between Afrikaner and Britisher in South Africa).[30]

'National capital' refers to the alliance of the modernising sectors of a national bouregoisie and the middle class with co-opted sections of the proletariat and peasantry against foreign capital on the one hand, and against anti-modernising rural sectors on the other.[31]

In this study as a whole there is a desire to meet the needs of a serious piece of research, but also to challenge the values, choices and actions presently characterising — but no longer considered adequate to — the Church in South Africa. We begin where the churches in South Africa themselves begin — with the nineteenth century and the role of missions, the forerunners of today's established denominations.

Notes

1 From *Fanshen,* William Hinton (Vintage Books, NY, 1966), p428.
2 Among the most important gatherings were: the Assembly of the World Alliance of Reformed Churches (1970); the Reformed Ecumenical Synod (1975); the Nairobi Assembly of the World Council of Churches (1975); the Pan-African Christian Leadership Assembly (1976); and the first interdenominational meeting since Cottesloe in 1961, of all major denominations in South Africa (1979, in Pretoria). Critical projects begun include Spro-Cas I and II (1969—73); the WCC Programme to Combat Racism (1970); the Reformed African Studies Programme (arising out of the Koinonia Declaration of 1977); the black Dutch Reformed 'Broederkring', and later the Alliance of Black Reformed Churches of South Africa (1981). The recent declaration of Apartheid as a heresy by the Ottawa Assembly of the World Alliance of Reformed Churches (1982) has made a par-

ticular impact (much more so than the weaker 1977 declaration of 'status confessionis' in Dar es Salaam by the Lutheran World Federation). Government intolerance of the rising tide of Christian rejection of its policies has been most evident in the Schlebusch—Legrange Parliamentary Commission of Inquiry into the University Christian Movement and the Christian Institute (among others, 1972), the forced removal of the protestant Federal Seminary from Alice and then again from Umtata (1974), the banning of the Christian Institute (1977), the Eloff Commission of Inquiry into the South African Council of Churches (1982/3), and the rise and decline of the government sponsored (secretly) enemy of the SACC, the Christian League. Major issues such as war, liberation movements, relocation of Africans and new constitutional proposals have also been paramount.

3 Surprisingly, despite all this, theological writing as published in established journals does not reflect the same political concern. See *JTSA* vol 17, December 1976, p25ff, an article by C Villa-Vicencio analysing the theological writings of the period 1973—76, in which he shows that among six major theological publications, only 15 per cent of the articles published are relevant to the South African political context.

4 J de Gruchy, *JTSA* vol 9, December 1974, editorial.

5 O Schreiner, 'The Native Question' *Transvaal Leader,* December 22, 1908.

6 Cited in J Stone (1973), p 128, footnote.

7 N Majeke (1952), p 140.

8 JH du Plessis (1911).

9 Theal's interpretation of South African history is often referred to as the 'settler' view, hostile to Africans; see HM Wright (1977), p5.

10 JH du Plessis (1911), pp260—3 *passim*.

11 *Ibid,* pp264—5.

12 GBA Gerdener (1958), p267; also p7.

13 *Ibid,* pp7—24 *passim*.

14 L Hewson (1950), particularly Chapters 6 and 20.

15 P Hinchliff (1963); the one major exception is the discussion of the effects of the Boer War on the Church, p183ff.

16 P Hinchliff (1968), p50.

17 WE Brown (1960).

18 JM Sales (1971).

19 TD Verryn (1972), pp30—48. A very different, more penetrating study of 'Ethiopianism', and a very valuable one at that, is E Kamphausen (1976).

20 H Florin (1967), pp16—25 *passim*.

21 E Regehr (1979); see Chapters 4 and 5 especially. Some discussion of imperialism and colonisation is found in this section, pp132—5.

22 J de Gruchy (1979).

23 L de Vries (1978).

24 N Majeke (1952).

25 See especially L de Vries (1978), pp195—8.

26 See J Habermas (1976), p20—1, for a description of the tasks a state normally fulfils under a capitalist order.

27 See I Roxborough (1979), p64.

28 *Ibid,* p57, citing James O'Connor's definition. This definition leaves open the specification of the content of the imperialist relation, its working, and its operational circumstances.

29 *Ibid*, pp64—9.
30 *Ibid*, pp76—7. also pp20 and 124. Roxborough discusses these aspects in relation to conflicts in modern Chile.
31 *Ibid*, p24: this formulation follows, but does not exactly duplicate the reference, which is in the first place to the definition offered by H Jaguaribe.

The Critique of Missions and Missionaries

> Many South Africans grow up today with the impression that the missionaries were well meaning but misguided men who did not really understand the Native and so were responsible for the racial problems of the present. There is a lot of pathetically ignorant nonsense, a lot of wilfully ignorant prejudice and a certain measure of truth in that idea.
>
> — L Hewson (1950), p25

> Unfortunately wherever the Church went, the State, like Mary's little lamb, was also bound to go. For the Church of England, as by law established, was subject to the Royal Supremacy. Where its bounds spread, its bonds spread also, and a Bishop beyond the seas was no less an official and a servant of the Crown in matters ecclesiastical than was a Governor in matters civil and political.
>
> — H J Kidd, Gray Centenary Lecture, 'The Anglican Church Overseas a Century Ago'. Ts: 1947

The Debate

When southern African tribes first looked upon the strange, pale faces of the Europeans whose nations would come to rule their continent, they surely could not foresee the impact of their arrival. Within short decades the newly emerging African states and kingdoms were shattered; their chiefdoms were undermined until many chiefs were little more than lackeys of the colonial administrations; their pre-capitalist economies were variously altered, and later tugged to pieces though not quite destroyed; their ways of life, usually centred on close kinship communities and the values of 'ubuntu',[1] changed irrevocably and often rudely. All of this served the individual success of others, and the values of progress and profit.

Unavoidably, great forces bore down upon the indigenous people. Superior military technology backed by great wealth sustained the goals of the expansionist free traders of the Victorian empire. In addition, the political tools of annexation and colonisation were applied with varying degrees of success by the representatives of the old European aristocrats and of the new moneyed class to secure order and stability against a restless, often resistant local population. Where this was not possible or profitable, local alliances could be forged with interest-groups in the traditional economic structures, thus exploiting — and often exacerbating — internal divisions.

Among the waves of invading conquerors were the missionaries of the metropolitan churches. They were inspired by a peculiarly Western, post-Enlightenment idea not only that proselytisation and the zealous conversion of the entire human race was the supreme task of the Christian community, but that this goal was also culturally determined, that is, connected to the European meaning of civilisation. About these intrepid explorers and doggedly devoted envoys many legends and fables have been spun. More recently, criticism has been heaped upon their heads in equal measure. These men of the cloth and their work are our concern here.

The hot and long-standing debate over the role of missionaries has raised much battle dust. Some have called for a moratorium on European mission involvement in Africa;[2] other indignant knight errants have rushed to defend the honour of the sullied heroes. No less a doyen than Edgar Brookes felt that the missionaries 'served Africa well, and their denigration is neither justifiable nor even decent'. On the contrary, says Brookes, the nineteenth century 'demanded great self-sacrifice' of them. In his view a disservice is done to the worthy evangelists by those who depict the missionary 'as the agent of "colonisation" and "imperialism"', the servants of capitalistic trade, imbued with a superiority over the Africans, preaching provincial European customs rather than timeless truth.'[3]

In contrast Nosipho Majeke is one critic who indeed adopts just the view Brookes rejects. Fired by the resistance struggles of the 1950s, Majeke presses strong claims that the missionaries 'had acted as agents of "divide and rule" policies; that they had been political advisors to the colonisers; that they had helped to evolve "Native" policy; and that they had been apologists for a ruthless military campaign and eulogists of the governor'.[4] Majeke's work carries with it the stamp of a polemic and the absence of footnotes makes a detailed assessment of her argument difficult. Nevertheless it has been far too easily dismissed. The poignancy of her views derives partly from the perennial nature of the struggle in South Africa between dominant and dominated, and partly from the defensive desire of churches to euologise their founding workers. The evidence she adduces, however, is not countered by academic high-handedness, nor is it fairly treated when the opportunity for self-criticism is missed. We cannot allow the absence of footnotes, for example, to persuade us that Majeke's book may be disregarded.

Brookes and Majeke clearly reflect a distinct disparity in their historical presuppositions and historiographical method. They manifest wide disagreement in their opinions of the Church. Their dissimilarity is of considerable significance: it bears directly on how one interprets the Church and its role in the nineteenth century, the early part of the twentieth, and later.[5] Therefore we now attempt a review of missionary history in South Africa in order to highlight the conflict in interpretations and to draw our own conclusions.

The churches of the Dutch trekboers and the English colonists are a separate phenomenon from the missions run by the London Missionary Society and others, says one contemporary writer. He argues that the conflict between them 'became a dominant issue for church and society at the Cape during the nineteenth century.' On the basis of this distinction, he asserts the now standard view that British missionaries (Philip van der Kemp and James Read in particular) withstood the growing thorns of a racism rooted in Boer exclusiveness and championed the indigenous people whose side they took 'in the struggle for justice, rights, and land'. Thus 'the missionaries . . . regarded themselves as the conscience of the settlers and the protectors of the "natives."[6]

Unquestionably, the discord between settlers and missions reflects an historical dynamic. But this dynamic remains obscured if there is no reference to the economic underpinnings of conflicting viewpoints, the link of settlers and missions with the metropolitan centres, their conquest of land as well as of peoples, and — a matter often inadequately treated — the resistance of the peoples. To regard missionaries as in some sense 'above' the settlers by virtue of their calling would not rescue the position. From an African point of view the differences between the white settler groups often had little significance. Thus, commenting succinctly on the clash between Boer and Brit over the 'Native Question', Selope Thema remarked that 'while this quarrel was going on the African was living his own life', yet 'this kind of life was condemned by both the missionaries and the colonists as a life of laziness and indolence. Both agreed that the African should be taught the dignity of labour.'[7] In short, discord between settlers and missionaries did not often undermine their more or less common view of the economic role of Africans.

We need to look more closely at the issue of labour — and of land as well — to understand the often surprising unity between Boer and Briton, and for that matter between church and government. Until this unity is understood the evidence of discord and dissonance among European settlers is misleading, albeit real. Consequently the issues raised by Majeke have not retreated. They revolve most fundamentally around contending views of the missionary enterprise: (1) as enabling indigenous peoples to enter into and cope with a fateful and irresistible global campaign of free trade and capitalist penetration; or the different parts of the Empire having separate Governments, as to secure that for certain purposes, such as warlike defence, internal commerce, copyright, and postal communication, they shall be practically a single state.[26]

Africa, after a rather poor attempt by Shepstone to annex the Transvaal ~~ublic~~ in 1877, followed two years later by the disastrous British defeat at ~~dhlwana~~ and a simultaneous crisis in Ireland, another blow came as the ~~ch~~ settlers threw off the imperial yoke at the battle of Majuba.[27] But a turn-~~point~~ came with the Suez Canal crisis in Egypt (1882). The British occupa-~~of~~ Egypt 'triggered off at last a secondary rivalry for possession of ~~ical~~ Africa' among the European powers, and 'began its partition among ~~Powers~~ at the Berlin Conference of 1884—5.'[26] The earlier attempt at con-~~al~~ politics through annexation of the Transvaal Republic was modelled ~~e~~ Canadian experiment of dominion. This followed the idea that

~~such~~ a dominion would be strong enough, without British military or financial aid, ~~o~~ keep internal law and order and to absorb any African chiefdoms that had ~~previously~~ remained independent; that the British navy would protect it from ~~foreign~~ aggression; that British entrepreneurs would dominate its foreign trade; ~~nd~~ that British government would control its foreign relations and, perhaps, have ~~ome~~ financial say in its treatment of African inhabitants.[29]

~~goals~~ continued to shape imperial concerns in southern Africa. Direct ~~ts~~ in recently discovered diamonds, soon to be inflamed into overt ~~by~~ the glitter of gold, raised the stakes immeasurably.

~~t~~ a genuine interest in the indigenous peoples remained part of British ~~is~~ sure, but as de Kiewiet puts it, 'British humanitarianism was stronger ~~timent~~ than in guiding principles . . .'[30] More important were the ~~ic~~ interests that would ensure passage to the East and ready access to the ~~mineral~~ wealth. In the colonies strong and well-established settler com-~~es~~ were the most convenient allies, especially as commercial experience ~~pressed~~ upon the Victorians that 'all their most successful trading ~~ions,~~ with the exception of the Indian Empire, were with Europeans ~~nted~~ abroad.'[31] (In southern Africa earlier attempts at building low-~~ances~~ with various chiefdoms too frequently foundered on a multiplici-~~nflicting~~ factors within and between chiefdoms, and between Africans ~~ders~~ generally. Moreover Africans too easily resisted control over their ~~en~~ withdrawing supplies when prices or terms were unfavourable.) ~~quently~~ the invention of responsible colonial government in the form ~~inions~~ created a 'structure of Empire unique in the history of the ~~It~~ was a 'device for achieving financial economy at Home without in-~~commercial~~ expansion, and for reconciling imperial unity with col-

(2) as itself a tool of domination and a demand of submission.

The argument here is that any attempt to find the middle path between the two views is insufficient, for the two perspectives reflect discrete positions in society, respectively that of the dominator and that of the dominated. In other words, the truth about the role of missionaries must include their presupposi-tions and pre-selected values. It is not simply determined by compiling and correlating supposed facts. Arguments such as the following reveal this quite clearly.

> Marxists often argue that the missionaries, or at least those who provided them with funds, were actuated by economic motives. They see the missionaries as emissaries of capitalist powers seizing the land . . . But it is a false interpretation which does not fit the facts when they are examined in detail. The men whose names are cited did not become missionaries to get rich, or powerful, nor is there evidence that those who subscribed to the Societies which sent them out were seek-ing wealth or power by this means.[8]

The writer of this comment confesses to be concerned with true historical in-terpretation. He is aware that 'every society, even the most primitive, has a view of its own history', and that 'this view is closely linked to its structure'.[9] Ironic then, that he should so completely miss the point of the Marxian criti-que, perhaps forgetting that the histories of missions cannot be understood merely by reference to the good they tried to do.

The issue is not whether missionaries and their societies sought wealth or even conquest (though proselytisation may be seen as one form of conquest). It is whether the view that the missions were closely linked to the dominant structures of the society is valid, and if valid, whether the insights gained by an analysis of the links are not already the source of a profound criticism in the best sense of the word. This connection of structure to a view of history in relation to a specific society grounds the critique of missions and missionaries. The blatant disregard of its import in the annals of the church is not suc-cessfully dealt with by defences built uncritically on another particular but unacknowledged view of history. Thus Edgar Brookes is not correct when he called the critique of missions 'superficial thinking, with little knowledge of history and inspired by materialistic anti-Christian thinkers' whose thinking is merely designed to 'deprecate the Church as being a purely European Church linked up with the European capitalism and imperialism which ruled Africa.'[10] In contrast, I accept the critique as an industrial diamond capable of cutting deep into the rock of the established Church, thereby revealing its failings to itself. In this way critique may become self-critique in the best possible man-ner.

Victorian Expansionism and the Missionary Ethos

The missionaries who began work in southern Africa did not arrive in a vacuum. They carried with them the mentality of their time and place of origin. Thus it is useful with respect to the churches of British origin to explore briefly the nature of the Victorian Empire.

In a petition to Parliament in 1820 the London merchants, probably influenced by both Jeremy Bentham and Adam Smith, wrote that 'the maxim of buying in the cheapest market and selling in the dearest, which regulates every merchant in his individual dealings, is strictly applicable as the best rule for the trade of the whole nation.[11] Richard Cobden, the apostle and missionary of free trade, believed that the London merchants required a broader vision. He wished to 'instil in the minds of the labouring classes the love of independence, the privilege of self-respect, the disdain of being patronised or petted, the desire to accumulate, and the ambition to rise.'[12] 'Commerce,' he proclaimed, 'is the grand panacea, which . . . will serve to inoculate with the healthy and saving taste for civilisation all the nations of the world.'[14] Thus was the spirit of early Victorian free trade and its expansionist desires declared. Its political bench-mark, the Reform Bill of 1832, helped transform Britain from 'an agricultural nation ruled by squires, parsons, and wealthy landowners into an industrial nation dominated by the classes produced by industrial expansion and commercial enterprise.'

Within this milieu the London Missionary Society had begun work in South Africa at the turn of the century.[14] By 1814 (the same year that Holland ceded the Cape Colony to Britain) the Weslyan mission was under way: and ten years later the Church of Scotland established the Lovedale Mission Station, destined to be of considerable importance.[15]

The slogans of industry, civilisation, and progress rang as loudly in the sermons of the period as they did in the chambers of Whitehall, promulgated with a sense of 'moral duty to the rest of humanity', and 'suffused with a vivid sense of superiority and self-righteousness' based on the self-evident utility and rapidly growing power of industry and commerce. 'Economic expansion . . . seemed not only natural and necessary but inevitable' in the centrifuge of the machine revolution. 'The trader and missionary would liberate the producers of Africa and Asia' and the indigenous people 'would respond to the gospel and turn to legitimate trade', it was believed.[16]

At the height of this period, while Karl Marx at his desk in the British Museum was exposing the heart of the industrial revolution and showing it to be cold-blooded, John Stuart Mill began to criticise his previous attachment to free trade principles. The ills of the system were becoming evident and Mill, 'that peculiar product of the nineteenth century, a professional reformer',

began to modify the reigning notion of 'a natural harmony tween entrepreneur and worker which automatically prom good.[17] Thus the beginnings of social democratic thought Mill's later writings; they signify the shift from early Victori later Victorian insecurity. But even for Mill, real democrac for those who have developed sufficiently to accept it and sibilities: it is to be protected 'against the domination of inf and the selfish interest of the numerically superior Class'.[18] class were of superior intelligence and less selfish than any been taken for granted. Missionary opinion appears to ha agreement on this point.

One author has noted that 'Mill's attempts to absorb, ar truths alike of the utilitarian and idealist positions is, after very large part of the subsequent history of English think of the colonial churches and their missionaries as well as Socialists in Britain, Kingsley, Maurice and Ludlum, who ly, but who later were to have considerable influence o South Africa.[20]

At this time, however, Africa was of far less concern India, and 'if the papers left by the policy-makers are to ed into Africa, not to build a new African empire, but pire in India.[21] The strategic importance of protecting East remained even after the Suez Canal was opened i

Imperial expansionism, gaining strength through th Australia and later in California, soon required the u the Crimea.[23] And in southern Africa, policies of incr tion were occasioned firstly, by the threat to the sec from other European powers, and secondly, by the republics inland. Thus the traditional strategic doctri Africa came to be restated by the all-party Commiss of 1879—1881.[24] As we shall see later, when the ge 1870s came to recognise 'that the duty of British for never before the duty of protecting the vital econ terests of the nation,' the missionaries were not lack

The shift in later Victorian polices from free tr control of widely flung territories is no more clearl ford Dictionary entry of 1898:

> In recent British policy, 'Imperial' means the prin
> at least not refusing an extension of the British Em
> interests and investments require the protection o

onial aspirations for independence'.[33]

In South Africa the required alliances lay more and more with the European settlers, but the independent Boer republics posed a problem and attempts to gain control over them followed. Several mistakes were made, among them Rhodes' sponsorship of the abortive Jameson Raid, which is acknowledged to have had the imprimatur of Joseph Chamberlain. Following on that, the economic and political necessities behind a policy of 'settler colonialism' united Cecil Rhodes, prime minister of the Cape Colony, and Jan Hofmeyr, leader of the Afrikaner Bond, in seeking local autonomy and expanded influence. It came to flower in the Union of South Africa which did not injure in the least British economic and strategic interests.[35] In effect, 'Great Britain transferred . . . its prerogatives as a colonial power to the white settler minority.'[36]

With these changes came a significant alteration of policies in respect of the indigenous people who were by then doomed to exclusion from the most critical alliances. The earlier desire to create of them stable producers, traders and consumers with the hallmarks of English gentlemen and gentlewomen gave way to an ideology of separation, fuelled by an increasingly typical colonial racism born of Victorian superiority and still widespread cultural strangeness. Economic interests which had found political expression in responsible government and dominion status were given social expression in the language of Herbert Spencer's Social Darwinism, and of 'Manifest Destiny'.[37]

Social Darwinism viewed Africans as 'racially handicapped and facing a long evolutionary struggle before being able to aspire to parity with Europeans'.[38] A belief in 'Manifest Destiny' provided divine sanction for the dominance of European people and the British in particular, by arguing that providence reigns in the affairs of nations. Rule is therefore a providential matter, as is privilege. Rule was further legitimated by the notion that privilege carried with it responsibility for ruling the unprivileged.[39] The Newtonian cosmology of an ordered physical universe governed by mechanistic laws and originating in an omnipotent God lay behind the doctrines mentioned above. For the missions, largely influenced by British Evangelical Christianity, this cosmology was united with biblical revelation. As MJ Ashley notes,

> This committed missionaries to certain key theories regarding race and education. Their position on human origins was thus unequivocably monogenist. Explicit reference to the common origin of all races can be found in the writings of early missionaries in South Africa.[40]

But 'fallenness' was also a central point of their anthropology, simultaneously grounding a distinction among persons and societies (Christian versus heathen) and a theory of redemption (conversion from heathenism, culturally, politically and economically, as well as religiously defined via a contrast with 'Christian' nations of western Europe). Equally important was the 'biblical injunction to spread the Gospel and also apparently a belief among Evangelicals that the second coming of Christ was dependent on the Gospel being sounded among all nations'. On a more mundane level, elements of Victorian morality mingled with claims derived from scripture, including the condemnation of nudity, initiation ceremonies, feasting, dancing and promiscuity (which round huts apparently encouraged, according to John Philip).[41]

These various beliefs correspond with practice in the colonies. They helped rationalise conquest and privilege, later assuaged consciences through the logic of segregation, and finally provided a satisfactory intellectual argument for dominance through the theory of social evolution. The intimate union between Empire and Church could not have been stated more directly than in the words of the Bishop of Grahamstown who wrote in 1897 that

> . . . missionary work, viewed under the light of the Eternal Purpose of God (is) the inner meaning of history, . . . the 'far-off divine event to which the whole of creation moves.'
>
> (It is the call) as citizens of our British Empire, and as sons and daughters of our British church, to rise up, in furtherance of this end, to their truly imperial responsibility and their imperial mission and destiny.[42]

All the dynamics and the ideological terms of Victorian expansionism are reflected in the South African missionary literature of the nineteenth century and the first years of the twentieth. With the economic changes that followed the discovery of gold, this is then transformed into the language of the captains of industry and of the financial plutocracy as the early Victorian aristocratic gentry faded from the scene (leaving behind a slightly bitter smile?). The effects of this transformation are the subject of later chapters. For the moment we turn to the connnection of Victorian expansionism to missionary endeavour.

The Critique Affirmed

Soon after the turn of the century JH du Plessis, referring to the earlier Dutch East India Company, wrote in his *History of Christian Missions in South Africa* that 'the way in which the material interests of the Company and the spiritual interest of the natives were inter-twined . . . must sound somewhat strangely to our modern ears.' Others who have given their attention to the later British trading empire find the same connection there. Perhaps this is not at all strange to modern ears.

Military campaigns and political programmes by which the South African territories were progressively won from the fiercely resisting local people often obscure 'the story of trade and labour, of measles and typhus, of Sheffield hoes and greasy cotton clothes, of crop shortages and imbalanced diets, of cattle disease and the collapse of tribal discipline, which were the signs that these men of opposite race were doing more than quarrelling with each other.'[44] Yet they do represent the expropriation of land by which European settlers accumulated the capital to sustain conquest, and by which the destruction of African independence was guaranteed. The struggle for land was manifestly unequal. With rare exceptions the settler 'with his superior weapons and his notion of individual ownership, his theodolite and his title deed, and his greater awareness of the market generally gained at the expense of the black.'[45] This asymmetrical contest pulled or drove many Africans out of their pastoralist-cultivator economy into various forms of labour, it radically altered the foundations of their society and it severely reduced their long-term competitiveness.

These dynamics so profoundly mark the nineteenth century political economy of South Africa, and their consequences are so weighty, that no genuine understanding of the role of the missionaries is possible without considering the interconnections of religious, political and economic concerns. The way in which colonial missionaries engaged with the indigenous people; their hand in the subjugation of chiefdoms; their relation to the forces of economic expansion and to the creation of labour; their specific part in the emergence of a black elite with advantageous connections to the colonies and metropolis — all these themes come to the fore.

In his study on the roots of segregation in Theophilus Shepstone's Natal administration, David Welsh uproots the myth that segregation-policies in South Africa were born of Dutch prejudice and isolation. The missionaries in Natal he interprets not only as agents of change and critics of policies either outdated or inhuman, but also as the carriers of conscience which the colonists could not ignore.[46] Elsewhere he comments that the divines were 'targets for brickbats from both sides', for not only were they resented by white settlers, but 'Africans, *kholwa* and *pagan* alike, saw them as instruments of racial and cultural domination'.[47] This last admission is, however, rather revealing, not of the men as such but of the role of missions in general. The implication is that Africans in general, converted or not, saw the missionaries as part of the forces of conquest. In this respect, John Philip, one of those whom Welsh mentions, was manifestly undisguised:

While the missionaries have been employed in locating the savages among whom they labour, teaching them industrious habits, creating a demand for British manufactures, and increasing their dependence on the colony, there is not a single instance of a tribe thus enjoying the labour of a missionary making war against the colonists, either to injure their persons, or to deprive them of their property. Missionary stations are the most efficient agents whcih can be employed to promote the internal strength of our colonies, and the cheapest and best military posts a government can employ.[48]

Controls

Not suprisingly, Philip provides a major source of ammunition for Majeke's critique of missions. Attacked by the settlers in his own time for his crusade against the feudal relationships between Afrikaner landlords and their African serfs, Philip remained a valuable servant of the free trade principles of early capitalism. Most liberal commentators sympathetic to Philip have seen him predominantly from the view of the twentieth century revulsion against racism.[49] Majeke more clearly perceived Philip's close ties to the rising industrial elite and their imperial ambitions, and cites him appealing for a liberal native policy in most disabusing manner:

'By adopting a more liberal system of policy towards this interesting class of subjects,' he declared, 'they will be more productive, there will be an increased consumption of British manufactures, taxes will be paid and the farmers will have no cause to complain of lack of labour.'[50]

Philip, it should be noted, was not exceptional. Van der Kemp was a somewhat misguided disciple of Rousseau in du Plessis' opinion,[51] in Sales' mind a possible 'hero-saint' for the 'tiny group of rebels' who want 'integration and a new deal in politics for the non-white population.'[52] But he was also a most useful agent of the government, Majeke believes, utilising the Bethelsdorp Mission Station (in co-operation with Resident Commissioner Maynier) to draw Khoikhoi away from the leadership of the rebellious Klaas Stuurman; to provide a military outpost which assisted the fight against Ndlambe's Xhosas; to collect taxes; and to set the pattern for providing reservoirs of labour for neighbouring farms.[53]

There are also other examples among the best-known missionaries. On behalf of the colonial administration, John Ayliff unsuccessfully approached the troublesome Hintsa (who would later be defeated in the 6th War of Resistance in 1834)[54] and then wrote back to the Governor that Hintsa 'viewed us in the light of agents of the Colonial government and nothing more than colonial spies.' Of the Wesleyan, the Rev Mr Boyce, Colonel Harry Smith remarked that 'the man of the gospel is after all a worldly fellow . . . more full of dragooning our new subjects than a hundred soldiers.' Shrewsbury, another Wesleyan, recommended to a military officer that blacks should be made to wear a tin identity plate around their necks to enable identification of, and an estimation of, the number and strength of frontier tribes.

The Rev Henry Calderwood became the first of several missionaries to take on as well the colonial role of commissioner-magistrate which eventually included the task of recruiting labour; Calderwood himself instituted a system of taxation and 'locations' that Sir George Grey was to continue. And William Shaw, superintendent of Wesleyan Missions, was instrumental in depriving Moshweshwe of parts of his people's territory in favour of missionary proteges.[55]

The subjugation of the African kingdoms and chiefdoms, despite long resistance, is well attested.[56] It was achieved not only by military means (for which missionaries provided much useful intelligence), but also by administrative measures such as dividing territory into magisterial districts, making the magistrate the chief legal functionary of the region, and thus subordinating chiefs and their communities to magisterial rule.[57] Or, just as frequently, treating more amenable chiefs as official representatives even when this was not so, and thus exploiting available divisions within tribes. Moreoover, notes Bundy, 'the role of the missionary as standard-bearer for the commercial economy and western manners was one which missionaries themselves were not slow to point out, and they left no doubts as to the overriding influence of missionary endeavour, precept, and enterprise.'[58]

Missionaries, on the other hand, needed the government, as was recognised by the 'Commission Appointed to Inquire into the Past and Present State of Kafirs in the District of Natal' (1852—3), whose considered opinion was that the success of the missionary was directly proportional to the extent to which the government could reduce the size of African communities, break up their social systems, and bring them as 'free servants' into the colonial orbit.[59] Several scholars have in recent years pointed out the relative lack of success (often almost none) of the missions in winning converts. Ulrike Kistner argues that, with some exceptions,[60]

> . . . it can be maintained that the various missions could only establish themselves in South Africa in cases where clan and tribal loyalties were being undermined through warfare, through land occupation by white settlers, through the subjugation of blacks and their employment as wage labourers, through annexations and labour legislation.[61]

Some have claimed that it was 'order, police, Imperial sovereignty and the Pax Britannia, which have destroyed the sanctions of the old social system,' and that 'missions could do nothing to preserve or abolish them.'[62] But this is only partly true.

As Selope Thema has pointed out, missionaries did divide villages into two camps: *Kholwa* (the converted) and traditional.[63] Yet this division contributed rather than gave rise to political divisions deriving more fundamentally from conflicts over issues of production and reproduction. Moreover, in some areas the cleavage between converts and others played no significant role.[64] Misisonaries did advocate increased trade and commercial activity, as well as contribute to class formation in African society through relatively greater access by 'mission natives' to the market and its rewards. And what is more, they played a significant role in the penetration of the market system into the traditional economy. So, for example, Wesleyan missionaries introduced the first ploughs in some areas, opened the 'first store in all Kaffirland for necessary reputable trade' at Wesleyville, and planted the first South African cotton at Morely Mission Station.[65] This does not, of course, prove that missionaries were mere imperial agents. Often, in fact, at least some things were done at the request of a chief who sought his 'own' missionary as a kind of go-between in dealing with both the new pressures and the fresh opportunities.

At this point it is worth investigating more closely the double deprivation which marks the history of most (though not all) indigenous peoples at the height of the missionary period: the loss of land and the loss of political power. In actuality the two elements are inseparable. However, for the purposes of analysis they are treated here as distinct emphases, together describing the alienating impact of European settlement.

Land

Cattle may have been the visible sign of capital accumulation among the African tribes, but land was the economic base. As one Zulu made clear in a comment to a white official critical of overgrazing, 'It is not that we have too many cattle for our land, we have too little land for our cattle.'[66]

With the settler conquest of the territories and the later introduction of individual tenure (signalled by the Glen Grey Act of 1894), the stratification of African society was ensured on the basis of relationship to land. 'Cleavages exist between landowners or those with recognised land rights, and "squatters": and people from reserves generally look down on farm-labourers as "landless wanderers",' writes Monica Wilson. In this regard, she describes the significant role of missionaries, as well as of Sir George Grey and Rhodes, in motivating the allotment of land under individual tenure, a major structural factor in altering the pre-colonial economy.[67] Similarly, de Kiewiet notes that

Nowhere can the unintentional collusion between the genuine humanitarian desire improve the condition of the natives and the selfish motive of exploitation be more interestingly observed than in the policy of substituting individual tenure for tribal land tenure.[68]

This process was uneven, varying according to the local context, and in some cases never carried through (thus the 1913 Land Act demarcated non-ownable tribal lands in the reserves, usually where colonial penetration had been rather incomplete; but by then new policies were in mind).

In the Afrikaner republics the same dynamic occurred, though here it was not, at least initially, the policies of individual tenure that applied, but the activities of the Boer farming household and the speculation of land companies, both appropriating large areas of land that remained unused or worked by labour-tenants.[69]

Mission stations also became important centres for the transformation of traditional land relationships and at least one author believes they did more than any other institution to alter the relations of production. Frequently the 'demands of the missionary were much greater than those of the Boer farmer'. Besides taxes to the state, tithes were often required for church buildings, educational facilities, ploughs, new seed, symmetrically constructed villages, and European clothes.[70] All of these items required surplus value and combined to drive those who could not produce enough, as well as those who had no means of production, into the labour market in search of wages. Moreover, many Africans preferred to use their wages to re-establish their own holdings, particularly in the form of cattle. Given the pressures, only some succeeded.

One rather interesting account may illustrate this sort of dynamic. In the Transvaal, by the law of the Raad, African peasants were in effect barred from purchasing land in their own names, and a common procedure was the use of a missionary as 'dummy' purchaser.[71] But this often unsatisfactory arrangement depended overly on the continuing goodwill of the clergyman concerned. Thus in 1873 Johannes Dinkwanyane rejected his lengthy ties with the Berlin Missionary Society project at Botsabelo. He broke away to enable himself and his followers to purchase land in their own right, and to establish an independent Christian community at Mofolofolo where life was possible 'without attendant heavy demands for tithe, labour and tax'. The exploitation involved at Botsabelo was probably unconscious and almost certainly understood to be in the best interests of the black community. But the fact of the exploitation was clearly articulated in the redoubtable Dinkwanyane's letter to missionary Nachtigal. 'Do we have no land?' he wrote in referring to lack of black control over the mission zone and the relative absence of participatory decision-making. 'We helped to build a mill and were not paid and the school and churches. Further, we have worked the land for him (Merensky, the other missionary at Botsabelo) in the form of the tithe.'[72] Here then Africans had no formal control over decisions affecting the community, nor over the fruits of their labour.

In the Eastern Cape, Natal Africans displaced by the Mfecane were settled on the frontier with the permission of the colonial administration and the help of interested Methodists.[73] For these Mfengu there was a *quid pro quo*: they were to be the human buffer between the colonists and the Xhosa foe. Their incorporation into market relations was encouraged and stimulated, and they 'were hastened along their path to fuller involvement in a capitalist economy by their close association with the Methodists, a group of missionaries who keenly favoured the spread of peasant agriculture.'[74]

European impact upon African societies usually began with the growth of trade. Part of a trader's offering might include firearms, often out-dated, sold to numerous groups of Africans who thereby acquired a greater ability to defend themselves. But at the same time this first arms trade in southern Africa inevitably helped to alter traditional social and economic relationships among Africans, both by virtue of the implication of the technology and by reason of the attraction of the objects of trade.[75] The acquisition of European manufactured artifacts, from 'really good descriptions of clothing', articles of furniture, crockery, spades and forks, to soap and jewellery, was also equated by missionaries with 'rapid strides in the matter of civilisation'.[76] The point is made clear in a recent study of a Zulu community, which concludes that 'the English-speaking churches . . . have tended to pass on to Africans a high appreciation of and desire for things English and American.'[77]

Missionary interest in stimulating peasant agriculture was well-intentioned, and it undoubtedly enabled some Africans (such as many of the Mfengu) to cope more easily with an otherwise daunting situation. But its effect was much wider:

> . . . missionaries believed a whole constellation of beneficial results would flow. These were: a stimulated demand for the consumption of British goods, the increase of commerce, of civilisation and of learning, the spread of Christianity and the defeat of heathenism, polygamy, and barbarism — in short, the extension of British control, protection, culture, economy, religion and language.[78]

The decisive point is the last. Missionary enterprise, remaining always beyond radical self-criticism, could normally do no other than transmit the values and structures embodied in British imperial colonialist expansion. An ability was missing to distinguish firmly between what was intrinsically worthwhile and what would lead to long-term destructive consequences for precisely those people whom many believed themselves to be championing.

Besides trade, individual tenure also played a major role in the transformation of African society, and in particular, of land relations. A further strain on traditional patterns of land usage was the expropriation of large tracts as Crown land, subsequently redistributed in favour of eager settlers. In Natal, for example, as Crown lands were released, colonists were 'assigned the richer and more cultivable portions' as well as much land still uncultivated and unoccupied, whereas 'for the use of the native population a much smaller portion' was reserved, this comprising 'the more broken tracts . . . fully occupied.' Thus, as early as 1882, fifty-five per cent of the African population in Natal were already either tenants on private land or squatters on Crown land.[79] Nothing demonstrates more clearly the impact of colonisation than this massive change in status.

A further legal infliction came in the form of taxation: hut taxes and marriage taxes at first, later the poll tax which produced more revenue. Little of this income returned to Africans in the form of services; but then its primary purpose was control and 'a way of simultaneously and indirectly curbing polygamy'.[80] This latter item, to which we shall return, had its economic implications as well.[81]

The traditional settler view on African land management was negative. Settlers were convinced Europeans could do far better, a convenient ideology supporting the various forms of land expropriation. But several recent studies show that 'traditional African techniques of agriculture and animal husbandry were well adapted to soil and climactic conditions, and much less wasteful of natural resources than many of the European techniques of intensive exploitation.'[82] Yet the nexus of forces embodied in colonisation — military conquest, land loss and land control, labour supply measures, technological innovations such as plough and wagon, and political pressure — combined eventually to defeat the traditional order in most areas and to polarise or divide further the indigneous population.

Nevertheless resistance, sometimes violent, has never ceased. One form of resistance to full incorporation on disadvantageous terms, namely the ability of many black homesteaders to seek and find an alternative to wage labour in the capitalist economy, created an early prosperity for some. Missionary ventures, as has already been noted, sometimes significantly affected this development. But hardly a missionary understood the implications of the economic, political and cultural domination over Africans by outsiders in the wider society, or their incorporation into relations of coercion and obedience.[83]

To be sure, this was not an inevitable process. In the interaction between indigenous modes of production/reproduction and those introduced by settlers and colonists (what some have referred to as an 'articulation' between modes) many configurations were possible. What actually happened in any one area depended not only on exogenous forces but also on the interplay of conflicts and interests within an indigenous group, an interplay predicated upon differentiation, stratificiation and the partial formation of classes within the tribal society.[84]

In some areas, for example the Herschel district (documented by Bundy), incorporation of Africans into wage labour and a relatively rapid destruction of tribal society came quicker and often harshly. In other areas (eg among the Xhosa), the penetration by settlers/colonists proved very difficult, chiefs and commoners being sufficiently independent to exploit new opportunities without being controlled.[85] Similarly in Zululand white settlers for long made little headway against resistance to incorporation and removal of land, particularly as the metropolitan power was not keen to expend large sums of money in backing up annexation of the whole area. This was not then regarded as a profitable region.[86] In Pondoland it was even more difficult to force people onto the labour market or to keep them there once they had earned sufficient for their needs. Pondoland was '. . . one of the last annexed areas of South Africa, it was not conquered by force of arms, and little land was taken for white settlement.' Here as elsewhere, the 'rhythms and relationships of pre-colonial society, as much as the momentum of penetration', shaped the response of Africans and in turn the possibilities and choices facing settlers and colonials.[87]

The impact of missionaries has also to be situated within this context. They were as often used by chiefs and others to gain particular ends, as much as they tried to convert Africans to Christianity and 'civilisation' (many traders too found their clients to be shrewd and selective bargainers). Consequently, for long only marginal social and economic changes resulted in most chiefdoms and kingdoms, and missionary activity did not usually deeply threaten the political power of the chiefs. As Peires points out,

> The chiefs agreed to receive the missionaries for a number of reasons, all of them secular. Political prestige, the provision of a regular channel of communication with the Colony, and fear of the consequences of a possible refusal all played their part. But these benefits were offset by suspicions of the missionaries' secular motives. Some were even viewed as spies (which, in a sense, they were) or, even worse, as part of a plot to destroy the Xhosa by drought and disease. . .
> More concretely, the mission stations were seen as an invasion of the sovereignty of the chiefs. The mission people considered themselves British citizens under the protection of the British Government.[88]

In Pondoland even as late as the early 1930s mission churches could count fewer than five per cent of the population as members or adherents.[89] Suspicion remained widespread. Thus a chief like the Xhosa Sandile regarded the

Wesleyan missionary HH Dugmore as 'a man who came to teach the truth to Caffers: but he does not know the truth himself. Such men from the Colony speak lightly of war: they delight in the grass and water of Caffaria and make strings of lies to secure it.'[90]

But whatever may be said about individual missionaries, it remains generally the case that their ambiguous role within chiefdoms, the effect of their connections to the colony, their tendency to split converts away from their fellows, and their reliance upon colonial force or power in crisis or conflicts, all contributed to undermining chiefdoms in the long run, or at least to making it much easier for settlers and colonials to exploit existing divisions and tensions. As time went by the great majority of indigenous groups were finally forced to capitulate to colonial control, especially after the discovery of diamonds and gold. Thereafter Africans increasingly found themselves unable to avoid being drawn into the colonial economy as a reservoir of cheap, rightless and largely migrant labourers, to meet the sharply increased demand for workers.[91] Many tribal farming areas deteriorated rapidly in the wake of extended controls and overpopulation, especially after the Land Act had come into force, but the swift deterioration went largely unnoticed by the churches in these areas until Dr Henderson of Lovedale belatedly recognised the calamitous results in the late 1920s. Church solicitude meanwhile shifted blithely but pointedly from 'Europeanisation' to 'the dignity of labour' as large number of Africans were transformed into a landless, rightless mass of cheap, wage-earning labours.

The baneful process of underdevelopment, by which the indigenous peoples were more or less speedily incorporated into market relations and the capitalist economy with deleterious consequences for themselves and ruinous impact on their land and pre-colonial economy, thus characterises the present century in South Africa.[92] 'Within less than a century the Natives had changed over from a subsistence economy to a money economy, and consequent upon the loss of their land and cattle from a position of independence to one of dependence.'[93]

One author comments that the indigenous population 'could not be exterminated or driven away altogether for, following close on the first step of settlement, came the demand for cheap black labour.'[94] But this is not the whole story, for complete conquest of the chiefdoms was not always possible. The great difficulty of establishing settler or colonial control over many areas, the high costs involved in maintaining what had already been achieved, is thoroughly attested in recent scholarship. Moreover, there were moments when, as happened in other parts of Africa, the imperial lords might well have chosen to back an amenable black chief with widespread popularity rather than settler groups.[95]

But once mineral and strategic interests in the South African territories became strong enough, the patterns of resistance which made co-operation

with tribes difficult, led the British to take the easier route of joining with settler demands as far as was necessary, while seeking to draw Africans (and also
Afrikaners) into wage labour. For this purpose, strong legislative and political
controls were necessary, annexation proceeded apace, and local authorities
were entrenched. At this point the missionary became a more valuable ally,
one by now sufficiently informed about tribal politics and situations to assist
in the exploitation of weaknesses and divisions in the African communities.
This included the protection and support of client chiefs who saw in the colonial power a force for their own interests against other contenders for power
within the tribes. Also significant, as Peires notes, 'was the growth of a
"school community" within and without the mission stations, a community
which saw European culture and technology as desirable acquisitions.'[96]
Moreover, the drive of settler communities, assisted by determined, local administrators like Theophilus Shepstone, Melmoth Osborn, Sir Bartle Frere, Sir
Benjamin D'Urban and others, to expand into and take control of uncon-
quered areas could not ultimately be held back. With the empire behind them
their logistical resources became strong enough to grasp hold of most of South
Africa, even eventually forcing the Boers into an alliance.

The peculiar nature of rural underdevelopment in South Africa was sealed
by certain early decisions, first given full formulation by the Lagden Commission of 1903—1905, to leave large sections of the black population — especially women and children whose labour was less valuable — confined to 'native
reserves'.

Indeed, such legislation was regarded relatively positively by some chiefs
who were able to use their position and contacts to secure some land and accumulate cattle, or to play an administrative role on behalf of the colonists,
thereby retaining at least some semblances of their earlier power and rights.
This set patterns for the later entrenchment of chiefs and headmen in the administrative and political structures of South Africa, and the introduction of
salaried positions in the local bureaucracy.[97] The transformation of land from
being 'the instrument of labour of the group' to being, firstly, a 'means of production of surplus value' for private accumulation, and, secondly, a commodity within the market itself (freehold land), contributed to radical changes
in the traditional African political economy.[98]

But in general the majority of Africans increasingly found their situation in
the rural areas an unhappy one. And with direct state intervention in African
cultivation which largely followed the original Lagden proposals over the next
decades, the fate of the South African rural lands was sealed.[99] Here industrialists could be assured of a reserve pool of labour based on a subsistence
economy which saved entrepreneurs the costs of maintaining and serving
workers' families left in the reserves. These important developments will con-

cern us more fully later.

Political Power

It remains to consider the broad assault on the structures of African society which played so influential a part in the destablisation of its pre-colonial economy.

Kinship structures, the basis of hierarchy and political obligations, bound tribal systems together, though in some cases the political structure was dominated by a network of districts and wards under sub-chiefs and headmen.[100] Polygamous relationships, 'a system with which of necessity, all their laws, customs, habits and ideas are bound up,' commonly shaped family structures.[101] Thus in southern Africa production and reproduction were generally linked to the household and extended family. Despite local variations the total political economy of southern African chiefdoms is thus sometimes analysed as a 'lineage' mode of production; yet each economic identity had its specific characteristics, differentiations and strengths and weaknesses.[102] Moshweshwe's kingdom, for example, 'was not an autocracy, but a loose confederation held together by two kinds of bond, the maintenance of family ties within a large ruling house, and the consent of subordinate chiefs.'[103] Multiple wives, often transferred, bound groups together in the same way as European monarchies sought political ties through inter-marriage.

Production was usually in the first instance by and for the family, while the division of labour was 'not between families but amongst the members of a family . . . based primarily upon the sexual division in each family.' This tended to limit production to goods that could be directly utilised by the producers themselves.[104] Kingdoms varied in their manner of organisation. Tswana society, for instance, was a 'tribal estate', organised into three distinct areas: 'one for residence', usually a 'settled town of perhaps 25 000 people known as the *metse*; . . . one for the growing of crops; and one for grazing and hunting,' but they retained the basic features of kinship.

Social coherence on the other hand depended largely on the chief. Chiefdoms 'all were concerned with the control of power, the rationalisation of decision-making, and issues of distributive and natural justice.' As Davenport indicates, the chief was

> the 'father' of his people, expected to govern conscientiously, wisely, and generously. He was the judge of all serious misdemeanours, the lawgiver, the war leader, the distributor of land, and the universal provider, in time of need, from the royal herds, which were largely composed of beasts levied as fines or tribute. As a Zulu proverb expressed it, he was the 'breast of the nation'. He might also be the organiser of the hunt, controller of labour, and ritual rainmaker as well.[105]

Gatherings for consensus decision-making (known among the Sotho as *pitso,* among the Nguni as *imbito* or *imbizo,* and among the Swazi as *libandla*) meant that widespread participation in government was a basic feature of African society. Thus contemporary observers of Moshweshwe's *pitso's* noted that 'discussion . . . was keen, great freedom of speech allowed, and great weight attached to the opinion and attitude of the people.'[106] These observations are general and should not lead one to forget that a hierarchy of chiefs often existed. Within this hierarchy and between chiefs and commoners dynamic relationships were involved in the resolution of conflicts and contradictions.

Central to the economic role of the chief were the redistributive tenets and mechanics of the tribe, with communal property rights formally vested in the chief.[107] The European notion of land individually owned was alien to a conception of the land as a neutral resource avaible for use by those who occupied it, a resource to be redistributed according to need with property rights accruing to no-one. These values made the European settler idea of land-cession treaties both ludicrous and open to serious misunderstanding. In addition, Europeans viewed cattle as consumption goods whereas Africans saw them primarily as capital goods.[108] Thus ownership and power revolved around cattle, which 'represented not only the accumulated product of past labour', but 'also served as the key to all future production and reproduction' (thus their role in bridewealth as well).[109]

As a whole, in traditional African economies and societies, 'economic relations of coercion and exploitation and the corresponding social relations of dependence and mastery' were not created, and where they tended to emerge, they were constrained by generally accepted rules and practices of redistribution (cattle-loans, for example). In these ways, 'in tribes production, polity, and piety are not as yet separately organised, and society not as yet a holy alliance of market, state and church.'[110]

How were missionaries viewed in this context? In an address to the Natal Missionary Conference of 1920, Dr DDT Jabavu, himself a beneficiary of missionary education, complained about the growing 'socially distant attitude of master to servant' as compared with the great friendship to black people that missionaries had shown.[111] There is reason to believe that Church attitudes did in fact shift with the industrialisation of South Africa, as will be seen. Assuredly, missionaries were concerned to befriend the indigenous people. But their desire was conversion, the dynamics of which were by no means politically, economically or ideologically neutral. This religious onslaught reinforced the confusion, breakdown and victimisation — even inferiority — that land loss and political pressures created. 'Africans', warned the insightful missionary Colenso, are men, shrewd, intelligent, inquiring: but they dread any closer contact with Christianity which is to tear up at once their families, rend asunder the dearest ties which connect them with one another, and fill their whole tribe with anarchy and confusion.[112]

Thus one learns that chiefs were concerned with missionary impact upon traditional discipline, resenting the removal of converts from their jurisdiction, and the loss of their services in time of war.[113]. Many chiefs in fact actively opposed the work of evangelisation. Mission stations forcibly abandoned in the resistance wars of 1835, 1846 and 1851 were destroyed (though Calderwood, ironically, interpreted this as positive testimony to the disturbing influence of 'true' missionaries on the 'injurious power of the chiefs and of heathen customs').[114] No wonder that chieftainship, 'the greatest barrier in the way of Africans emerging from the traditional society', according to Lt Governor Pine of Natal Colony, was the institution Shepstone believed should give way to the magistracy as customary law was abolished.[115] It was also a sometimes unwitting, sometimes conscious, missionary target. Resident missionaries in particular'

. . . were a revolutionary influence; because they condemned African customs and institutions and taught the social norms of nineteenth century Europe as though they crystallised a moral code of universal validity.[116]

What was true of chieftainship was true of the kinship structure. Christianity where it took effect had the effect of destroying 'the ritual and ceremonial bonds which bind the traditional kinship group'. Consequently, in later years and in many places, 'the church as an institution . . . soon took upon itself most of the functions which had traditionally belonged to the family, the kinship group and the tribe. Moreover, the nineteenth century Christian emphasis on the individual person rather than the group, an emphasis admirably suited to the ideology of capitalism, 'meant that single members of the kinship group were taken out of the fold and . . . considered themselves quite separate and different from the rest of the group.' Equally significantly, if the single member was male the whole family was committed too, 'even the property which is not really his but belongs to the members of his family which may be polygamous.'[117] Against this, it should be pointed out that conversions were very hard to come by, they often occurred among a people already disintegrated (in Xhosaland, for example, the majority of early Christians appear to have been among the misfits and refugees), and even converted chiefs (such as Khama and Dyani Tshatshu among the Xhosas) could not always bring their families let alone their followers with them.[118]

The distinction between converts (*kholwas*) and those not absorbed (often called 'reds' by Eastern Cape missionaries), combined with access through mission stations to secure land and to the market (perhaps a reason for conversion sometimes), frequently also played a part in the stratification of African society.[119] This was particularly true where chiefs and others, in conflict or competition with their peers, saw advantage in binding themselves to colonial resources and power. The acceptance of Christianity also led most converts as a matter of duty to accept submissively the government, the institutions and the laws of the white man.[120] It comes as no surprise to learn that *kholwa* Africans were sometimes the first targets of attacking tribes.[121]

Among the customs that fell prey to missionary (and government) assault was polygamy with its attendant bride-price (*lobola*) system. The latter was regarded by whites as a form of slave purchase. Yet whatever its drawbacks, *lobola* in fact played an important part in the manners of social relations as well as in the redistribution of wealth.[122] Polygamy was sufficiently anathema to the Church that 'most missionary bodies upheld the rule that polygamists were not to be admitted to church membership unless they put away all their wives save one.'[123] In contrast, Moshweshwe, as well as Sekhukhune, Selshele, Kgama and others, found it almost impossible 'to reconcile the commands of the Church, in particular Christian monogamy, with those customs of his society which held it together.'[124]

Issues of morality, education and organisation also affected the traditional society. Christianity introduced new and usually disruptive definitions of social morality, while what remained of the old was modified and made to suit the new conditions and situations. But this was no universal morality, it was that of the Victorian Evangelicals and the declining gentry, but shaped by the values of the rising commercial and industrial elite. Moreover, in an African context, the new morality would often have been viewed as imbalanced and ignorant. Peires thus notes that among the Xhosa, missionary hostility to 'witchcraft' was in fact an attack on witch-finding: 'For the Xhosa, this was like denying the existence of a disease and suggesting the elimination of the medical profession.'[125]

Education offered by missionaries was an additional lure to conversion, because it allowed easier access to the market and a place in the new industrial society. Certainly, missionary education made its contribution in enabling many Africans to cope with and master the totally new conditions now irrevocably upon them. It also allowed others a channel by which they could selectively utilise new opportunities to their own benefit. But it nevertheless carried its own ideological impetus, for which reason, on the whole, many chiefs remained opposed to education and Christianity.[126] For the few privileged Africans, many of whom were the early leaders of African Nationalist protest and the dialogue partners of the churches, education became the principle means to breach the citadel of white privilege, and a key element in the self-identification of an aspirant petty bourgeoisie. It was also a means into better paid or subsidised jobs, often salaried, in growing local administrative apparatuses (mission churches too began to employ African evangelists and ministers).[127] Thus education was the major demand in the agitations of 1918—1920.

Mission activity often has been lauded for its educational efforts. To be sure, much of value was done, but this should not obscure the two-edged sword education was (is) in a conflict-ridden, ideologically overburdened context. Education played its role in the subjugation, co-option and stratification of Africans in what became increasingly an oppressive society. So, for example, work was made a key concept in education, but by work was not meant cattle husbandry. On the contrary,

> cattle were seen as a means of subsistence whcih enabled the people to live in idleness except for the occasional diversions of fighting and raiding. Real work was agricultural work and the missionaries encouraged the men to undertake it by paying them themselves at the beginning and securing them contracts for forage and other produce.[128]

Thus, comments the same author, 'physical labour became a moral virtue rather than a simple necessity, and indolence became a sin.' Education, from the 1870s onwards a cornerstone of missionary activity, thus fulfilled a larger role: 'it was playing a part in determining what place Africans were going to occupy in society.' This function was increasingly emphasised in the twentieth century once control over education came fully into state hands.[129]

Finally, it is worth pointing out that missionary penetration of African society, and the subsequent establishment of local churches, introduced unfamiliar styles of organisation. Bureaucratic methods, commonly initiated by missionaries, contrasted with the participatory *pitso's* etc, and eased the way for magisterial rule: 'and this, in the case of families like the Ayliffs, Brownlees, and Shepstones, meant literally a transfer of responsibility from fathers to their sons.'[130] The principle of voluntary association too found its way in through the Church — a principle inseparable at this point in history from the individualistic ethic and a bourgeois perspective, and one which disrupted the group discipline of traditional African life.[131] Lastly, and of considerable significance in the later development of African indpendent church life, the denominationalism so characteristic of western church life tended to provoke black disunity, with both communal and political impact, as was recognised by an insightful early African nationalist:

For the Black man makes the fatal mistake of thinking that if he is an Anglican, he has nothing to do with anything suggested by a Wesleyan, and the Weslyan also thinks so, and so does the Presbyterian . . . (But) we must be united on political matters. In fighting for national rights, we must fight together. Although they look as if they belong to various churches, the White people are solidly united when it comes to matters of this nature.[132]

Conclusion

In conclusion and much to the point, we cite the tell-tale anecdote of a well-respected missionary. In it one may discern, in microcosm, an early apprehension of the liberal judgement upon colonisation, a ready capitulation to prejudice, and an uncritical confirmation of colonial mentality on the part of the missionary. It comes from an influential and esteemed work by a missionary who wishes to explain the South African situation to his readers:

> It is also but fair to notice here, that it is much easier to love and maintain a deep and right interest in the heathen at a distance from them, as in England, than it is seeing them in their true state, and coming into contact with them in everyday life. I was once travelling with a friend, who was in the habit of extolling rather too highly the good qualities of the native African, and denouncing rather sweepingly the colonist as oppressor. It happened, however, in the course of the journey, that he got into a violent passion with his wagon-driver, or leader, and said everything that was bad against him, excepting swearing at him. I laid my hand upon his arm, and playfully said, 'My dear sir, don't forget! *That* is a native — a black man — one of those whom you have painted as innocents, whom all good men must love and pity.' 'Oh,' said he, 'they are *so* trying.' 'Yes,' I replied; 'just remember this when you draw your next picture, or are disposed to denounce too strongly the poor farmer, when he gets angry, as you have been.' He good-humouredly said, 'You are right, you are right.'[133]

The integrity, the character, the genuine charity and the contribution of the missionaries are not the moot points. Rather, 'it is essential to analyse the effect of colonialism in the making of the social structure . . . Colonialism involves conquest with its concomitant of dispossession, the introduction of a new mode of production, and the imposition of a new status hierarchy involving differential treatment of the colonised group.'[134] The issue concerns the historical role of missionary endeavour in the colonisation process. At least one famous missionary, John Philip, known for his championship of the 'natives', was candid enough to provide a clear description of that role:

> Wherever the missionary places his standard among a savage tribe, their prejudices against the colonial government give way; their dependence upon the colony is in-

creased . . . confidence is restored; intercourse with the colony is established; industry, trade and agriculture spring up; and every good genuine convert . . . becomes the friend and ally of the colonial government.[135]

In so saying, Philip may well have been concerned to put in a good word for missionaries (often under attack from settlers). Nevertheless, in an important sense Philip spoke the truth. Of course the incorporation of African societies into market relations does not on its own explain much, for this could occur in multiple ways, and not necessarily by coercion, control or with a loss of relative independence.[136] Moreover, 'with Christianity, as with the rest of Western culture', Africans were usually 'not passive recipients, but chose what they wanted and discarded the rest.' But once the triple relationship between chiefdoms, settlers and metropolitan power began to resolve itself through a whole variety of conflicts, contradictions and accommodations, into a determined, systematic policy of coercion and control over the indigenous peoples, the disadvantageous incorporation of Africans into a white-dominated South African political economy became easily the most prominent feature.[138] In this whole process, the role Philip ascribes to the missionaries had its place.

The matrix of forces which characterised colonial conquest and economic penetration did not represent self-conscious missionary ambitions. Yet these forces did enfold the missions and to them, in the stamp of Victorian self-assuredness, they made their contribution. They did so not because they were scheming, half-witted or malicious, but because they were of their time, of their place, and in an advantaged position in an expanding political economy increasingly characterised by a capitalist hegemony. Many of those who came to South Africa were influenced by the powerful and influential British Evangelicals who 'gave to the island a creed which was at once the basis of its morality and the justification of its wealth and power, . . . and, a sense of being an Elect People.'[139] Whatever their theological opinion, they 'inclined to the view that the social order from which they came *was* the Christian one,' and on the whole 'did not think of African culture as anything other than the work of the devil to be rooted up'.[140] As a prominent Methodist put it, 'the ultimate victory over savagery was to be won by the use of weapons of warfare not carnal but mighty through God to the pulling down of strongholds'; and in less rhetorical and more precise fashion:

The Flag has followed the Cross. The missionary opened the way, first for the trader, then for the magistrate. Both trader and magistrate should be among the foremost friends of the missionary . . . Our injunction to the natives, 'Fear God,' has ever had its complement in the other injunction, 'Honour the King'.[141]

Thus, to interpret the missionaries primarily either as the carriers of racial prejudice or the prophets of racial tolerance glosses over a necessary insight into the structures which they were part of and which they helped create. We require a proper comprehension of the changes in history in the broad sweep beyond matters of private conflict, personal idiosyncracies, or individual decisions. Here the missionary role was sometimes small, sometimes quite direct, but always of significance. But only when it is fully situated within the broader context will we have an adequate basis by which to explain the transformations in Church thought and policy that were to occur in the first decades of industrialisation.

The positive contribution of missionaries has recently been defended by Monica Wilson against the kind of critique here affirmed. She lists an impressive collection of facts and makes clear that, in a society inevitably undergoing change as it interacts with a larger world outside its control, old structures and practices must crumble, or be radically altered. Moreover, she believes (as I do) that an acceptance of the gospel probably must drive us 'to question *any* existing structure'. On this basis, she believes the missionary attack on certain African institutions and behaviour is not automatically reprehensible, or even negative if one believes the Christian task is to change 'such laws and customs as deny or impede the expression of love.'[142]

This defence does not, I believe, undermine the argument of this chapter. For the argument is not based on a Rousseau-like glorification of the 'noble savage' and his/her culture, but on a peculiar absence of precisely the self-critique Monica Wilson concedes as necessary. The missions and missionaries did question the existing structure of the African kingdoms and, consciously or not, sought to undermine them. It cannot be said, however, that they were anywhere near as thorough, if they even had such thoughts, in reflecting upon the existing structures from which they came and which they in part extended, namely those of the metropolitan colonial powers. On this point the critique rests.

What requires elucidation is why missionaries (and the Church) did their best to 'inculcate a way of life which bears no necessary relationship to biblical Christianity', and what this had to do with three important principles advocated by most missionaries: the 'dignity of labour' as an end in itself; the importance of obedience to constituted authority (meaning British and not the African authority); and, economic individuation.[143]

That the conquering colonials of South Africa were self-interested; that on a large scale their interests were the British national interests; that the colonial administration and their military arms helped expand and protect those interests; and that the missionaries and leaders of the Church were generally unable to distinguish all this from their own self-proclaimed task — these things cannot be easily gainsaid, notwithstanding any legitimate evidence of humanitarian behaviour or racial tolerance in missionary relations to the indigenous peoples, or their positive contributions. Thus when Anglican historian Peter Hinchliff writes of missionary theologies that 'in the last resort they can only be defended on the ground that what one is taking to other parts of the earth is better than what is already there', he admits the intimate connection of the missionary to the Empire. But while defending the missions, Hinchliff refrains from judging the contrary evidence in the disastrous impact upon the indigenous peoples of a systematically applied racial (colonial) capitalism from which the missions cannot be abstracted.

Its ideological captivity, rather than the failings or the disingenuity of its workers and leaders, characterises the Church and its missions in the nineteenth century (and not only then); exactly here the critical dissection of the Church's role is needed for its own sake. And if not for its own sake, at least for the sake of veracity. Only then can one empathetically understand the representative claim made in April 1876 by Dinkwanyane, the black Christian who resisted domination at Mafolofolo, in a letter to the Landdros of Lydenburg: 'I say: the land belongs to us, this is my truth, and even if you become angry I will nonetheless stand by it.'[145] What applies to land, applies equally to the products of labour.

Analytical Implications

> Oh, for that historian who, with the open pen of truth, will
> bring to Africa's claim the strength of written proof. He
> will tell of a race whose onward tide was often swelled with
> tears, but in whose heart bondage has not quenched the fire
> of former years. He will write that in these later days when
> Earth's noble ones are named, she has a roll of honour too,
> of whom she is not ashamed.

> Pixley ka I Seme

The foregoing review of the impact of missionaries and mission churches on the traditional African society is intended not only to bring to light certain themes that continue into the industrial period but also to indicate the validity of a critical interpretation of missionary history. The Church, overfond of eulogising its own, is too ready to defend itself on the assumption that by divine origination it stands exempt from criticism which seriously calls its history into question. Solid social criticism, however radically opposed to the

Church and its aims it seems to be, is not only worthwhile in its own right, but vital to the Church's self-purification. Where it is neglected or angrily rejected without being given serious attention, there the Church is most likely to reflect rather than illuminate its historical context.

The quotation by Pixley Seme which heads this section asserts a presupposition that colours my earlier critique of missions and lies at the base of my subsequent analysis of the Church in the early industrial period: history told by conquerors and their allies — by the power elite in any social structure — is both deficient and ideologically overburdened. Conversely, history which attempts to understand and articulate the view of the conquered and the dispossessed people not only balances the picture, but requires emphasis for two reasons. Firstly, it is hard to come by in the very nature of oppression. Secondly, it directs one's attention more clearly to the processes by which history is transformed.[147]

The ability of the radical critical tradition to uncover structures and ideologies of domination — to bring them to consciousness, one may say — is its major advantage. Within this perspective concepts and terms are not always clear enough, agreed upon, or understood. For a better understanding of the subsequent analysis of the role of the churches during industrialisation in South Africa, it is therefore worthwhile spending a little space on some of the more important assumptions made here. These concern issues of race and class, and of rural underdevelopment.

Liberal Historiography and the Question of Class
Liberal ideas influenced missionaries like Philip, Read and van der Kemp, all often unwelcomed by Cape rural conservatives. Nineteenth century liberalism was neither monolithic nor static. But the impetus by which it was 'expanded and elaborated into a general philiosophy of life' came from early Victorian commercial and political principles born of a new notion of wealth: liquid capital and mercantile wealth, free trade and its global expansion (made possible by the industrial revolution).[148] These elements combined to give visible credence to the belief in the power of individual enterprise and progress. The exuberant self-assurance of the Victorians entered the African scene, fused with the necessary bourgeois emphasis on the right of the individual above all and spurred by Renaissance ideals and Enlightenment practicality. It hesitated and often stumbled in the face of resistance from both settlers and the indigenous people; it then acquired later Victorian imperial ambitions; and finally it capitulated before economic interests, leaving the field wide open for nationalist ideologies.

Certain features of liberalism emerged in the process, and these concern us in our later analysis:

1   the importance of gradualness in political change;

2   the motive power of the moral will in effectively sustaining society (acts should be well-intentioned, obligations honoured);

3   the participation of an educated public to guarantee a progressive government (hence the frequent assertions in the history of South African liberalism of the need for a qualified franchise as was practised in the Cape colony);

4   the belief that ideas rather than material forces change the world (thus reasonable discussion, persuasion and negotiation must be pursued rather than policies of active, even militant resistance, in the conflict between dominant groups and subjugated people).[149]

These ideas are treated in this study as relative to their time and origin in European industrial capitalism, and thus as indicative of a particular worldview not to be taken as self-evident but itself to be criticised. In particular we turn at this point to the 'liberal' school of South African historiography.

Davies contends that liberal analyses of South Africa begin with the view that the principal contradiction is racism (white versus black), and that racism found its political home in the National Party.[150] It supposedly gestated in the pre-industrial agricultural milieu of the trekboers to grow into a full-blooded worldview with the emergence of Afrikaner nationalism. Thus liberal historians, writes Garson, generally presuppose that:

> . . . the British, through the politics which produced the Jameson Raid and the Anglo-Boer War, unleashed a new force in reaction, the emergent Afrikaner Nationalism which has come to dominate the country since Union.[151]

Whether or not this is entirely fair, van den Berghe is one example of a liberal historian who deliberately tackles the race-class opposition, concluding that class struggles play an 'almost insignificant role' in South African power conflicts.

On the surface van den Berghe's assertion seems just — that 'any interpretation of Apartheid other than that of a system of oppression and segregation based on race clearly conflicts with objective evidence'.[152] It finds support among others, including Stone:

> Ethnic or 'racial' groups determine the life chances and life-styles of their members to as great a degree as classes in other societies. This is not to deny the reality of class in the South African social system, but to emphasise its secondary importance.[153]

But there is a great deal of contemporary research which seriously undermines such perspectives. Taking a different point of view, Foszia Fisher points out that:

> A society is a structured whole, and to refer to a person as being a member of a particular class is to situate that person within the structure. Irrespective of the question of consciousness, certain shared interests and certain conflicts of interest can be derived from this fact.[154]

Within this framework an adequate explanation of the power of racism to inflame minds and hearts remains necessary, as does its connection to interests (analytically some authors have thus begun to define modern South Africa as a form of 'racial capitalism'). In Memmi's view,

> . . . colonial racism is built from three major ideological components: one, the gulf between the culture of the colonialist and the colonised; two, the exploitation of these differences for the benefit of the colonialist; three, the use of these supposed differences as standards of absolute fact.[155]

Thus Fisher (using Memmi) defines South Africa as a class society 'in which different individuals have differential access to the means of production and distribution of costs and benefits', and analyses the concept of ownership of the means of production in relation to colonialism. She regards it not only as an economic but also a legal category, such that ownership in any particular society 'is mediated by the politico-legal institutions and the actual relations of power'. Within this framework 'property' must be considered in terms of 'a set of rights or powers, and these rights can be disaggregated and distributed in odd ways.'[156]

Correlating these distinctions, Fisher draws the conclusion that exploitation by the owners of the means of production (initially acquired by means of conquest and subjugation) cannot straightforwardly be analysed as a dynamic between capital and labour without the role of settlers being considered. It was necessary for colonial settlers to maintain loyalty to the metroploitan power. In order to ensure their alliance the rights and powers contained in 'property' were disaggregated and distributed in favour of the settlers rather than of the indigenous people. Racism, inevitably present in the clash of cultures, proved to be a sound ideology for articulating the presumed rights of power and privilege. Thus in the long run a dual distinction was created between capital and labour on the one hand, and between coloniser and colonised on the other. The latter is the structural basis for the experience of racism which marks conflict in South Africa, whereas the former is the overriding generator of this conflict. In Fisher's mind this requires a three-fold distinction in the South African context: 'colonist-capitalists; colonist-workers; and colonial workers.'[157]

Some evidence supports her point. In particular, one may cite Rhodes' views on African policy (not much different from Shepstone's), that 'there must be class legislation, that there must be Pass Laws, and Peace Preservation Acts, and that we have to treat natives . . . in a different way to ourselves. We are to be lords over them.'[158] Moreover, the administrators of state and empire were predominantly of the aristocratic gentry,[159] of whom one historian has written that 'it was not so much, originally, that Europe felt itself called to govern the rest of the world as that the upper classes of Europe felt themselves called to govern.'[160] The aristocracy's influence on colonial mentality would fit neatly with the structure of colonialism, especially reinforcing a racial explanation of that structure. Elaine Katz has picked up the same theme at a different level in her description of the influence of British and Australian craft unionism on the organisation and attitudes of white labour in South Africa.[166]

The combined evidence of many studies highlights the political economic basis of South Africa's racist society and is more than sufficient to gainsay van den Berghe's belief that any interpretation not based on race 'conflicts with objective evidence.'[162] Understanding class interests, even where racial ideology is strongest, adds important and necessary correctives to traditional liberal historiography. 'Talk is cheap, but money buys the whiskey', notes Hermann Giliomee in reviewing Dan O'Meara's study of Afrikaner nationalism, which he regards as demonstrating the need to 'concentrate less on ideological and ethnic divisions and give proper weight to the important class forces that are influencing the situation.'[163] At the same time the newer, more critical historiography is in flux. Many issues are under heavy debate. Criticism of many works has focussed on an often too static, determinist use of political economic theory. Cooper comments on recent studies of African peasantry that

> one cannot understand the nature of social structures and social movements in rural areas if one forgets the difficulties of establishing direct control over production, the consequences of allowing cultivators to have access to land, or the different ways in which production can be organised and controlled. . . . Change has proceeded more by jerks — at which the basic nature of class power and labour control was contested — than by progressive incorporation.[164]

The point is this: because of the clear, dominant role of capitalism in South Africa in the last decades, one can fall easily into regarding its dominance as an inevitable (therefore deterministic) development of colonisation, a 'natural' mechanistic process of history, a 'fate' to which the indigenous people could ultimately only succumb. Thus one may view history as a teleological process: fixed, pre-determined sequences with prior ends. Actual class conflicts and relations are thereby obscured, for they define a struggle which has to be analysed in respect of specific, concrete modes of production and reproduction and their contradictions. Thus, Ranger agrees with Robert Brenner that 'the historical emergence of any given class structure is not comprehensible as the mere product of a ruling class choice and imposition, but . . . represents the outcome of class conflicts through which the direct producers have, to a greater or lesser extent, succeeded in restricting the form and extent of ruling-class access to surplus labour . . .'[165]

So one cannot finally accept Fisher's three-fold distinction between colonist-capitalists, colonist workers and colonial workers as sufficiently nuanced. While it designates the privileged position of white workers vis-a-vis black, as a description of the South African political economy it is only partial. There are significant groups in the 'gaps', eg chiefs and headmen absorbed into local administrative roles or a so-called 'Homeland legislature'; or black professionals (one thinks especially of clergy here, but also of teachers, social workers, etc); or people who have homesteads, cattle and access to land in one area while a member of the family supplements income through wage labour in another. In the complexities of local and regional interactions, in the attempt to rule and control against an ever-present variety of forms of resistance, such groups have had no small part.

In sum, the current revising of our understanding of South African history, often in its detail full of the necessary richness, still strains the theoretical frameworks it adopts. This must lead one to caution. But not to ignorance. For despite all criticisms, some fundamental insights are being established. One of them is that the particular form of capitalism now dominant in South Africa emerged because of specific struggles connected to colonial conquest and capital penetration of the region, itself driven in particular directions through confrontation with the traditional societies it encountered, their use of its opportunities, and their resistance to total incorporation over long periods of time. Moreover, it is now clearer just how diamond and gold discoveries affected industrialisation, labour policies and legislative decisions in general, and how capital itself was restructured in the process. Finally, at every point one observes the fruitfulness of analysing events in respect of class relations and the modes of production and reproduction which underlie them.

Consequently, the analysis of the role of the Church undertaken in this study attempts to take account of the Church as a collection of people involved willy-nilly in the political economy of South Africa as individuals and groups. This role is not exempt from the dynamics of colonialism (or the 'articulation' of differing modes of production) or of industrialisation. It must therefore also be understood within the framework of class conflicts and relations. Market interactions in themselves are in turn not the focus of the analysis; but the political and ideological struggle that occurred within and without the market and which shaped its trajectory are. These struggles can be recognised as a battle over and between differing material interests on the part of the actors in the South African drama. In this sense, the concept of class adopted here specifies interest differences. It thus describes structures of political economy and their inner connections and contradictions, rather than consciousness, attitudes, or behaviour (a point especially forgotten by those who brush aside class analysis).[166]

On this point, it must be made clear that such an approach is primarily looking for 'hidden' connections, ones more often than not hidden to the historical actors themselves. Put differently, the analytical goal (to see if any dynamics not immediately obvious are occurring, and which) is not to be confused with a descriptive statement (eg 'Church leaders deliberately hid their interests or motives'). For this reason, as should become clear, the deeply critical look at the Church manifested here, perhaps offensive to some, is not an apportioning of blame for anything in particular, but a task of self-criticism out of which may arise a greater responsibility and sense of accountability on the part of the Church in relation to the people it claims to serve.

'First World—Third World': Rural Underdevelopment

The Methodist and Anglican churches in South Africa, from their beginning, developed close connections with what today would be called the rural reserve areas. Missionaries of course paved the way, but eventually local congregations were developed almost everywhere. The social cohesion and economic status of the rural areas has altered markedly since industrialisation began. The articulation of the traditional economies with the invading market economy, and the later impact of rapid industrialisation coupled with extensive coercive legislative and administrative controls, have eventuated in a situation which places these rural areas at a severe disadvantage. This reality shaped and continues to shape important facets of South African history, but the interpretation of the process is not uncontroversial.

Hobart Houghton, for instance, considers nineteenth century South Africa to be a text-book example of a backward country slowly developing into a modern economy, thanks to the impact of colonial enterprise aided by the educational role of missionaries. Diamond and gold finds, *the* vital stimulus to development, accelerated the incorporation of Africans into urban life and modern industry. This Houghton regards as probably the most important cultural, social and economic consequence of the mineral discoveries.[167] The

South African economy is therefore understood in terms of a divide between 'old' and 'new', between a persisting low-subsistence economy and a much higher productivity exhibited in the modern market-oriented sectors — an economic dualism consistent with the ideological terms 'primitive' and 'civilis-ed'.[168] Similarly, van den Berghe believes 'one may speak of two parallel economies: subsistence agriculture on the one hand, and an industrial wage economy on the other.' Thus conflict in South Africa, in his view, results from 'imbalances' between these parallel economies which are 'not necesarily con-nected except by geography.'[169]

Such 'dual economy' typologies, however, are singularly unsatisfactory. They neglect, for example, the crucial role of political and ideological deci-sions through which white rulers have pursued a rather coercive, constrained set of economic policies. Thus in a dual-economy framework one cannot really explain the wholesale dispossession of tribal land. Land loss is then simply at root the giving way of an out-dated economy to a new, superior one. The con-nection of land dispossession to the need for a supply of labour, and policies to force Africans into wage-labour are inexplicable in this model.

By contrast, de Kiewiet is much closer to an adequate interpretation:

> . . . a true and full understanding of South African history . . . lies ever in the understanding of the process that . . . produced during the course of a century a single society in which the main line of division was not one of race and culture, but of possession and authority.[170]

The fact that 'nowhere else in Africa has so large a part of the population been dispossessed of land and absorbed in the capitalist economy' forces a recogni-tion of the integrated character of the South African economy, and requires an acknowledgement that the process of underdevelopment in the reserves is directly connected to the enrichment of the capitalised developed sectors of the economy.[171]

In this study I assume that the central emphasis of the theory of underdevelopment — namely, the mutual interaction of African and Euro-pean economies and the incorporation of the former into the global market economy — is correct. But some of the corollaries of the theory cannot be ac-cepted as they are. So for example, the implication that underdevelopment (eg in South African rural areas) is an inevitable process of capitalist penetration creating an inescapable dependency upon the 'centre core' economy, has been widely and correctly criticised. Such an interpretation is too mechanical (ie deterministic), and too teleological (downplaying actual causes and processes which vary considerably from area to area). Moreover, it is too crude for it does not penetrate the conditions and possibilities of class differentiation in either the 'centre' or the 'periphery', nor the real struggles that determined outcomes.[172]

Given the limitation of underdevelopment theory, one must make restricted claims for it. Thus in the South African context we must allow for the three criticisms noted above, particularly remembering the forms of resistance and exploitation of opportunities displayed by indigenous peoples, the difficulties of control encountered by colonists and settlers, the incomplete penetration of some rural areas, and the coercive policies developed in the twentieth century to deal with all these dynamics.

Yet it may still be said that the process of underdevelopment in the reserves is a reality, and that it occurred to the benefit of the core industrial economy as the form of the resolution of problems of control, production and reproduction. Thus, especially since the 1913 Land Act, 'there exists a vast and depressing body of evidence as to the nature and the extent of underdevelopment in the reserves' in the details of 'infant mortality, malnutrition, disease and debility; of social dislocation expressed in divorce, illegitimacy, prostitution and crime; of the erosion, dessication and falling fertility of the soil; and of the ubiquity of indebtedness and material insufficiency of the meanest kind.'[173]

Conclusion

The various arguments outlined above provide a preliminary description of the presuppositions informing the analytical approach adopted throughout this investigation of South African society and the Church's role within it. The decision to employ categories of class rather than race, conflict rather than interaction, political economy rather than culture, underdevelopment rather than the dual-economy typologies, is made because of their greater promise of meeting two relevant analytical principles outlined in general terms by Durkheim:

(1) The determining cause of a social fact should be sought among the social facts preceding it and not among the states of the individual consciousness.
(2) The function of a social fact ought always to be sought in its relation to some social end.[174]

In this study stress is laid upon economic forces, though without implying any strict economic determinism (a positivist error more than an historical materialistic error). I accept Rayomnd Williams' warning against a rigid methodology by which a phenomenon is unilaterally interpreted in terms of its economic history, perhaps arbitrarily, 'for, even if the economic element is determining, it determines a whole way of life'. On this reasoning, the socio-theoretical terms 'structure' and 'superstructure' are 'the terms of a suggestive analogy' rather than mechanical descriptions of reality.[175]

It is nevertheless possible to claim that:

> . . . the South African economy is not a 'market economy' in which goods are allocated solely by the forces of supply and demand. It is a 'labour repressive' economy in which the rapid accumulation of capital and the high standard of living of the white working class is made possible by the political machinery of repression which assures the continued subservience of the black workers.[176]

The following questions therefore arise. What is the Church's position with respect to

1 the creation and control of the labour force,
2 the institutionalisation of the power relationships embodied in that process,
3 the resistance of the working class to its domination and exploitation.

These question lay behind the earlier discussion of missionaries; they also inform the following investigation of the early industrial period.

Notes

1 'Ubuntu', meaning the human person, signified key values closely related to the contemporary rubrics of 'humanisation' and 'solidarity'. In practice this usually meant that members of any society could normally expect their basic social and economic needs to be fairly met even in times of general poverty such as when severe drought occured.
2 See M Nash (1977).
3 EH Brookes (1974), pp196—201 passim.
4 N Majeke (1952), p54.
5 A more moderate critique of missionaries than Majeke's may be found in Lawrence Zulu's 'Nineteenth Century Missionaries: Their Significance for Black South Africa', in Essays on Black Theology, ed M Motlhabi (University Christian Movement, Johannesburg, 1972).
6 J de Gruchy (1979), p2 & p13.
7 Selope Thema, 'Thinking Black: the African Today', Umteteli wa Bantu, as published in 'Advance', April 1929, p71.
8 BB Burnett, memo to Cottelsoe Conference, 1960, mimeograph, p12.
9 Ibid, p17.
10 EH Brookes, 'The Universal Church in its South African Setting', mimeograph, 1966.
11 D Thomson (1950), p77.
12 Cited in DJ Manning (1976), p96.
13 D Thomson (1950), p32 & p73.
14 J Sales (1971), pp32—3.
15 JH du Plessis (191), p464 & p184 respectively.

16 J Gallagher and R Robinson (1968), pp1—4 *passim*.

17 D Thomson (1950) , pp49—50 *passim*.

18 DJ Manning (1976), p127.

19 R Williams (1961), p65.

20 A Armstrong (1973), pp183—4.

21 J Gallagher and R Robinson (1968), p464.

22 OX: p290 — L Thompson, 'Great Britain and the Afrikaner Republics'.

23 GM Young (1964), p80.

24 J Gallagher and R Robinson (1968), pp59—50 *passim*.

25 CW de Kiewiet (1937), p139.

26 GM Young (1964), p170.

27 TRH Davenport (1977), pp131—2.

28 J Gallagher and R Robinson (1968), p162.

29 OX: p291 — L Thompson, *op cit*.

30 CW de Kiewiet (1937), p9.

31 J Gallagher and R Robinson (1968), p7.

32 D Thomson (1950), p29.

33 J Gallagher and R Robinson (1968), p55.

34 OX: p307 — L Thomson *op cit*. The term 'settler colonialism' is a modern one and in intended to designate rule by proxy through an allied group of settlers who serve metropolitan interests. Control by the imperial power is thus not direct, yet the political economy of the colony is indirectly structured to protect regional interests of the great power. Additionally, of course, it is the settlers and not the indigenous people who rule, and they in turn rely on their metropolitan connections to maintain power and privilege. Within this relationship, necessarily a dynamic one, there are of course many permutations, any particular one being the outcome or resolution of current local interests and their conflicts.

35 D Denoon (1972), p208.

36 P van den Berghe (1967), p73.

37 HJ Schultz (1972), p61.

38 In A de Villiers (1976), p255: Michael Ashley, 'The British Infleunce on Education in SA'; see also OX: p306, L Thompson, *op cit*.

39 Rev W W Rider, 'A Wonderful Century', p 20, nd.

40 MJ Ashley (1980), p29.

41 *Ibid*, p32 & p34.

42 Bishop AB Webb, 'Principles of Missions', SPCK, London.

43 JH du Plessis (1911), p21.

44 CW de Kiewiet (1941), p49.

45 TRH Davenport (1977), p116 & p97.

46 D Welsh, 'English-speaking Whites and the Racial Problem', in A de Villiers (1976), p221.

47 *Ibid*, p272. 'Kholwa' is the Zulu or Xhosa word for African converts.

48 *Researches in South Africa,* vol 22, p227, cited by P van den Berghe (1967), p27.

49 A recent example is J Sales (1971), p55.

50 N Majeke (1952), p19; also pp14—15.

51 JH du Plessis (1911), p128.

52 J Sales (1971), p52.

53 N Majeke (1952), pp10—11 & 21.

54 E Roux (1964), p32—3.

55 N Majeke (1952), pp36—46 & pp60—3 & p99 *passim;* see also M Ashley. *op cit*, p254.

56 See for example, OX: pp245—86, L Thompson, 'The Subjection of African Chiefdoms: 1870—98'.

57 OX: p281 — L Thompson, *op cit.*

58 C Bundy (1979), p35.

59 D Welsh (1971), p45.

60 Moshweshwe, for example, readily accepted the Paris Evangelicals and Roman Catholics.

61 U Kistner, 'The Growth of the Mind and the Body in the SA Climate', *Africa Perspective,* no 13 Spring 1979, p59.

62 PN Waggett, 'Church Affairs in SA', *Journal of Theological Studies*, nd (but probably 1st World War).

63 *Advance*, April 1929, p71.

64 For example, W Beinart (1982) argues this case for the Pondoland area, p152.

65 Rev WW Rider, 'A Wonderful Century', p12, nd (but probably the turn of the 19th century).

66 P van den Bergh (1967), p220.

67 M Wilson, 'Growth of Peasant Communities', OX: p98 & p60.

68 CW de Kiewiet (1937), p159.

69 TRH Davenport (1977), p119.

70 S Trapido (1977), pp21—23.

71 C Bundy (1979), p202.

72 P Delius (1981), pp14—18 *passim*.

73 'Mfecane' means 'the Great Hammering' and refers to the early wars between African kingdoms which left central South Africa temporarily relatively unpopulated owing to the flight or death of the resident people. Shaka's rising kingdom, militarily organised, was particularly instrumental in generating the 'Mfecane'. As it happened this time coincided with white Dutch migration into a supposedly 'empty' interior, claims since then having been made that the land was free for European occupation and possession.

74 C Bundy (1979), p33 & p74.

75 See W Beinart (1982), p25.

76 C Bundy (1979), p74.

77 A Vilakazi (1962), p96.

78 C Bundy (1979), p38.

79 D Welsh (1971), pp178—9.

80 *Ibid,* p77.

81 U Kistner, *op cit,* p63.

82 P van den Berghe (1967), p220.

83 C Bundy (1979) p9 &pp32—60. Among the missionaries who had some grasp of the issues and did something to support African struggles, Bishop Colenso is the only notable figure.

84 The point here is, of course, that African chiefdoms were dynamic social structures characterised by varying modes of production and relations of production. Moreover, internal trade, external trade with other tribes and nations, competition for material and human resources, specific political and social practices and traditions — all these factors differently characterised any one area or group of people, This in turn necessarily meant that colonisation, or the 'articulation' of the tribal

and the exogenous modes of production, resulted in patterns and structures determined not only by capitalist or mercantile market relations, but also by local conditions and context. In short, 'an analysis of capitalist markets can contextualise the processes of change but not explain the shape of rural communities, the political conflicts within them and their response to absorption into a capitalist world' (W Beinart, 1982, p5).

85 See J B Peires (1981). He points out, for example, that 'as long as they still had an independent subsistence base in Xhosaland, the Xhosa as a people could not be forced onto the labour market, whatever the fate of some individuals. They could still opt out when the wages were too low. Before 1846 proletarianisation was still partial, temporary and to a certain extent voluntary' (p106).

86 See J Guy (1982). Guy argues persuasively that the British invasion of Zululand in 1879 which led to the battles of Isandlwana and Ulundi, did not terminate Zulu political independence nor free Zulu labour. In fact, he shows this to have been only a 'first stage in a prolonged process during which metropolitan and colonial forces undermined the strength of the Zulu by exploiting divisions within their society' (xxii).

87 W Beinart (1982), pvii & p4.

88 JB Peires (1981), p76.

89 W Beinart (1982), p138.

90 JB Peires (1981), p128.

91 C Bundy (1979), p3.

92 An excellent study on Lesotho documenting similar processes there and their impact on a once proud kingdom, has been done by C Murray (1981).

93 RH Godlo, 'Urban Native Conditions', 5th National European-Bantu Conference, 1933.

94 RK Cope, Ts, Papers, 1941—50.

95 In some parts of Africa the evidence is that the impact of colonialism and a market economy was small enough to judge that the people 'stood aloof' from it, finding that it had little to offer. T Ranger (1978), p113ff, refers for example to the case of the Ila in Zambia, studied by K Rennie. F Cooper (1981), p289, furthermore points to another dynamic not really under colonial control, as evidenced in the studies of farmers in Ghana and Senegal, which show that 'peasants can indeed secede from the world economy if the marketplace remains the primary means through which capital and the state exercise power over them.'

96 JB Peires (1981), p164.

97 See for example comment by W Beinart (1982), p129ff.

98 See P Kallaway, 'Tribesmen, Trader, Peasant and Proletarian', in P Bonner (1981), p19.

99 The details of this story are quite well known, the Land Act being the most obvious place of controlling legislation; but a full analysis of the dynamic of 'direct state intervention', as called for by T Ranger (1978), p120—1, has still to be done. The necessity of brutal, systematic intervention of the state and landowners in engineering controls over African agriculture and labour is also pointed to by F Cooper (1981), p299ff. Thus he points out that '. . . for all the tendencies — in many cases decisive tendencies — to do what was cheap or to grab what was to be grabbed, there is much evidence that imperialism involved a rethinking of production processes as industrial capitalism demanded access to commodities and labour that was both more regular and more intensive' (p304).

100 TRH Davenport (1977), p44.

101 D Welsh (1971), p71.

102 A fuller description of the lineage system, in this case amongst the Zulu, may be found in J Guy (1982), p22f.

103 TRH Davenport (1977), p51.

104 C Bundy (1979), p15.

105 TRH Davenport (1977), pp44—49 *passim*.

106 *Ibid,* p46.

107 C Bundy (1979), pp16 & 21.

108 P van den Berghe (1967), p219. A valuable discussion on this point, elaborating the role of cattle in the traditional economy, may be found in W Beinart (1982), p14.

109 JB Peires (1981), p4.

110 C Bundy (1979), p15.

111 T Karis and G Carter (1972), p123.

112 D Welsh (1971), p74. Of Bishop Colenso himself, Chief Singana, son of Mpanda and brother to Cetshwayo, proclaimed: 'The thing which we admired in Sobantu was that he resisted the devices of Satan for deceiving other people, for eating up their strength, and oppressing them that they may become like dogs for ever' (J Guy, 1982, p199). Conversely, as is well known, settlers and even his own church took an all too dim view of Colenso's position and activities.

113 TRH Davenport (1977), p117.

114 Rev H Calderwoord, *Caffres and Caffre Missions,* 1858, p211.

115 D Welsh (1971), p25—8 & p29.

116 L Thompson, *op cit,* p25.

117 A Vilakazi (1962), pp31, 94, 27 & 12 respectively.

118 JB Peires (1981), p77.

119 M Wilson gives a description of the differences between 'reds' and 'kholwas' in 'The Growth of Peasant Communities', OX: pp74—6. 'Kholwas' are often also referred to as 'school' Africans, an indication of the role of Western education in the missionary enterprise.

120 A Vilakazi (1962), p143.

121 C Bundy (1979), pp99—100.

122 One exception to the general church views on such practices was Bishop Colenso. For a more detailed study of the impact of Christianity on traditonal family practices, see E Krige's 'Traditional and Christian Lovedu Family Structures', in *Religion and Social Change in Southern Africa,* eds MG Whisson and M West (David Philip, Cape Town, 1975). It should also be noted here that traditonal practices are not neccesarily in themselves always the best for all concerned — pressures on women in many African societies appear for example to have been one reason why many women in particular converted to Christianity, thereby gaining a different status in some respects on the missions.

123 D Welsh (1971), p73.

124 TRH Davenport (1977), p51.

125 JB Peires (1981), p75.

126 D Welsh (1971), p279.

127 See W Beinart (1982), p137ff.

128 JB Peires (1981), p107.

129 M Ashley, 'The British Influence on Education in SA', A de Villiers (1976), p255.

130 TRH Davenport (1977), p56.
131 See M Wilson, 'The Growth of Peasant Communities', and D Welsh, 'The Growth of Towns', in OX: p97 & p217 respectively.
132 Statement by SM Mvambo, *Imbumba*, Dec 1883, cited in T Karis and G Carter (1972), vol 1, p12.
133 Rev H Calderwood, *Caffres and Caffre Missions*, pp11—12, 1858.
134 EC Webster in P Bonner (1979), p9.
135 J Philip, *Researches in South Africa*, cited in C Bundy (1979), p39.
136 See for example. JB Peires (1981), p95ff; J Guy (1982), p15—17; W Beinart (1982), pp3 & 27ff; T Ranger (1978), pp102 & 107ff.
137 JB Peires (1981), p78.
138 Clearly this was a process that occurred unevenly, and up to a certain point in time in any one place, it could not be said to be inevitable. Thus, the overview given here should not be interpreted schematically, but descriptively. However, once a critical point had been turned, it can be claimed with considerable backing that the dynamics of racial capitalism in South Africa came to determine virtually everything else, even as its specific features were shaped by the earlier conflicts, choices and conditions. Thus, by way of example, J Guy (1982), p243, concludes that the historical forces that led to the Zulu civil war in the time of Cetshwayo, forces initiated by invasion, led to a fundamental difference in Zulu ways of life after 1884: 'In the former period they were in possession of their land and largely in control of their labour and its products; after 1884 they were losing this possession and control.'
139 GM Young (1964), p4.
140 P Hinchliff (1963), p67.
141 Rev WW Rider, 'A Wonderful Century', pp3 & 12, nd (but probably at the turn of the 19th century).
142 M Wilson, 'Missionaries: Conquerors or Servants of God?', address on the opening of the South African Museum, King Williams Town, 30 Jan 1976; first published in *SAO*, March 1976, reprinted *SAO*, Jan 1983.
143 F Fisher, 'Class Consciousness among Colonial Workers in SA', in L Schlemmer and E Webster (1977), p209.
144 P Hinchliff, 'The English-speaking Churches in the 19th Century', in A de Villiers (1976), p172.
145 P Delius (1981), p21.
146 Pixley ka I Seme, 'The Regeneration of Africa', *The African Abroad,* April 5, 1906, cited in T Karis and G Carter (1972), vol 1, p70.
147 The widespread recognition by contemporary historians that fact and value cannot be neatly separated in history or history-writing, and that there is therefore no such thing as a 'neutral' perspective, is nicely illustrated by the so-called 'liberal-radical' controversy in South African historiography. Thus HM Wright's book, *The Burden of the Present*, after reviewing the two positions (and having subsequently been criticised by both for failing to understand them) calls for a mediatory position within this controversy. But although academic scholarship deliberately seeks a privileged realm of objective truth whereby ideological stances are nullified, it is certain that no general interpretation of history can be neutral, nor two opposing perspectives necessarily reconcilable.
148 D Thomson (1940), p226; also EJ Hughes (1944), p21.
149 DJ Manning (1976), pp22, 17 & 145.

150 R Davies (1979), pp2—3.
151 NG Garson, 'English-speaking South Africans and the British Connection: 1820—1961', in A de Villiers (1976), p22.
152 P van den Berghe (1967), p100; see also p72 & p154.
153 J Stone (1973), p3.
154 F Fisher, *op cit*, p197.
155 A Memmi (1965), p71.
156 F Fisher, *op cit*, p197.
157 *Ibid, loc cit.*
158 Cited in D Welsh, 'English-speaking Whites and the Racial Problem', in A de Villiers (1976), p224.
159 GM Young (1964), p168.
160 P Hinchliff, 'The English-speaking Churches in the 19th Century,' in A de Villiers (1976), p173.
161 E Katz (1976), especially Chapter II.
162 Relevant studies have been made by Johnstone, Legassick, Wolpe, Davies, Trapido, Bundy, Webster, Bonner, Bozzoli, van Onselen and O'Meara, among a number of others. A useful bibliography may be found in HM Wright (1977).
163 Review in the *Cape Times*, 11 June 1983, of D O'Meara, *Volkskapitalisme: Class, Capital and Ideology in the Development of Afrikaner Nationalism,* Cambridge University Press, 1983.
164 F Cooper (1981), p309.
165 T Ranger (1981), p124.
166 E Webster in P Bonner (1979), pp2—4.
167 H Houghton (1967), pp215—6; also 'Economic Development: 1865—1965', in OX: p19.
168 H Houghton (1967), p19.
169 P van den Berghe (1967), p92 & p183.
170 CW de Kiewiet (1937), p14.
171 Quotation from HJ Simons and RE Simons (1969), p611.
172 See for example, comments by F Cooper (1981), p288ff, and T Ranger (1978), p124ff.
173 C Bundy (1979), p221; see also p161.
174 E Durkheim (1938), p110—11.
175 R Williams (1961), pp272—3 *passim.*
176 L Schlemmer and E Webster (1977), Inrtoduction, p12.

CHAPTER THREE

Exploitation, Segregation and Union: 1903—1910

> These people, in the providence of God, are brought into immediate contact with an energetic, enterprising, progressive race. Time can scarcely be afforded for the ordinary and slow process of civilisation. If then, we are to have peace, and the uncivilised nations are not to be destroyed, efforts on a great scale . . . must be made to impart to them the more useful arts of civilisation, and that speedily.
>
> Rev H Calderwood[1]

The end of the nineteenth century more or less coincided with the transition from a pattern in which traditional missions dominated church affairs to the pre-eminence of local congregations and a greater centralisation of church organisations. Mission societies themselves felt this need, so that in 1904 the first General Missionary Conference including the majority of missions in South Africa was held in Johannesburg to consolidate the results of previous work and to plan for a new era.[2]

Synods, conferences, councils and other similar meetings; bishops, presidents, superintendents and other clergy — these became the major sources of power and control within the halls of the South African churches. Alliances with one or another politician or industrialist were common. At the same time the churches contained the largest black, colonial membership of any institution under the direct control of settlers and colonists. The relatively non-coercive nature of this membership, in a structure more or less defined by voluntary association, led to a special sensitivity and concern for those who had been subjugated. Otherwise any tenuous hold over them would have been forfeited to the Independent churches or to none.

The following dissection of the Anglican and Methodist churches as representative of the broad base of non-Afrikaner and non-Independent churches attempts to discern their particular characteristics and role in relation to the political economy of South Africa during the first stages of industrialisation. The critique developed here is not moralistic but involves the hermeneutical task of deciphering appearances which are otherwise opaque, usually even to the actors and speakers themselves (though not always: conscious manipulation, deceit, and so on, are also part of history).

An initial assumption is that the Church in general does not necessarily belong to any particular class. Moreover, the Church as a social institution is not directly involved in processes of production. Thus within the framework of means and relations of production whereby class determination becomes possible, the Church is an enigma. Its membership and professional hierarchy may have differing class positions, some being capitalist or bourgeois, others peasant or proletarian. This leads to the judgement that the primary social role of the Church *as an institution* must be defined at the political and ideological levels (including its functions in the structures of family and community). At any rate, its role cannot be deduced directly from economic processes and relations.

At the political and ideological levels, class determination dissolves into questions of alliances and dependencies whereby social institutions take up roles either for or against one or other class, or alternatively play an ambiguous role. These questions define the arena within which our discussion is situated. The Church itself claims and proclaims much more than is likely to emerge from such an investigation. The true value of its proclamation, therefore, is not at this point under question. But the contradictions, illusions and uncritical subterfuge which blind, distort or destroy that proclamation are very much at issue — these are not unrelated to wrong theory and practice in the Church's own terms.

The Politics of Dominion

> 'I am in favour', said Mr Theron of Richmond, 'of
> teaching him (the native) what is necessary for him to know
> in order to become a good subject during life, and to enter-
> tain the expectation of better things hereafter: further than
> that I would not go.'[3]

The first decade of this century laid the legislative and constitutional foundation upon which South African society today still rests. In this respect, two foci were especially significant, one near the beginning of the period, the other at the end. Respectively, they were the Lagden Commission on Native Affairs and the National Conventions on Union. A brief sketch of what happened around and through these events will provide us with the preliminary backdrop for an analysis of the role of the churches.

With the end of the second Anglo-Boer War (1899—1902) came the need for reconstruction along the lines of some federation of the British colonies and the Boer republics. An alliance between the more feudal Afrikaner settlers and the imperially connected English and others still needed working out. Alfred Milner, a keen imperialist with considerable experience in Egypt of the need to develop a settler colony favourable to the Empire, vigorously sought the correct grounds for co-operation. The first tool, the Treaty of Vereeniging, achieved this through its well-known article 8 by distinguishing clearly between settlers as a whole and the indigenous population. 'The question of granting the franchise to natives will not be decided until after the introduction of self-government', it said, effectively proclaiming the disinheritance of the colonised people.[4] The aim of British policy was clearly stated by Bryce:

> . . . to reconcile the races . . . and render the prosperity of each the prosperity of both, and so pave the way for the ultimate fusion of Dutchmen and Englishmen in a common Imperial as well as a common Afrikaner patriotism.[5]

Talk of 'race' here, of course, does not refer to black and white pigmentation or culture, but to two groups both originating from Caucasian Europe. Why, after a century of comparative lack of interest in Afrikaners ('Dutchmen'), did the British now seek a fusion of the two groups — or more correctly, a fusion of the Cape and Natal colonies with the Boer Republics? The answer lies not in Cecil Rhodes' personal ambitions, but in strategic and mineral interests on the part of the Imperium. How these are defined has been a concern of recent historical writings. The results of this research help us to situate the role of the Church more clearly, more penetratingly.

The initial interaction of African pastoralist-cultivators with the market economy was through trade, ramifying north and east into the South African interior. But for long this meant access to an exchange economy without the basic structure of traditional societies being seriously affected. Later, however, dispossession and coercive legislation led relatively quickly to the creation of a labour force through the need to seek wages — on farms, in colonial homes, and on capital projects such as railroads.[6]

There were two sides to this process. On the one hand settlers claimed that the indigenous people needed the benefits of 'more intimate and regular contact with Europeans', which really meant that their labour was needed. On the other hand the supposedly 'simple wants of the natives' allowed serious underpayment practices, and taxation 'disproportionate to their wealth, their income, or the benefit they derived from government expenditure'.[7] Thus the structuring of wages around differential 'wants' and 'needs' became the rationale of the exploitation of the colonised peoples.

The fact that a rurally based agricultural economy could sustain many of the costs inherent in maintaining a labour force strengthened the role of migratory labour and enhanced the tendency to develop a dual wage structure — one level for the settlers who sought labour and had 'relatively greater wants and needs', and another much lower level for African employment-seekers. The great demand for labour on the diamond mines raised these practices to the level of convention, particularly as settlers flowed into the country.[8]

Finally, the unique gold-bearing reefs of the Witwatersrand, low-grade and difficult to mine but holding riches in and of themselves sufficient to provide the foundation for a major industrial economy, placed the seal upon the structure of the twentieth century South African political economy. Moreover, the economic revolution resulting from the exploitation of this mineral wealth has few parallels both in the speed of its accomplishment and in its far-reaching consequences.

With the discovery of gold, Britain in the full flower of late Victorian imperialism was suddenly playing with high stakes. Not only were 'foreign' Dutch settlers in control of the northern gold-bearing districts, but gold might be their source of strength to challenge British regional and strategic interests. Moreover, Britain by this time stood at the heart of the international money market, but had been experiencing problems of modernisation and competition with American and German producers just when its gold reserve was in a precarious situation and very narrowly based. Consequently, 'the transformation of the international monetary system into a gold exchange standard which took place during this period was therefore of the utmost importance to those statesmen concerned with Britain's imperial position.'[9]

Thus, the British High Commissioner, Lord Selborne, could write a memorandum in March 1896 to Cecil Rhodes saying: 'I take as my postulate the fact . . . that the key to the future of South Africa is in the Transvaal. It is the richest spot of earth.' In similar vein, with dramatically clear motives that foreshadow the second Anglo-Boer War, Colonial Secretary Chamberlain wrote on 5 April of the same year:

> If we ever were forced into it against our will I should try to seize and defend the gold-bearing districts. This is the key of South Africa. . .[10]

The colonial governor, Alfred, Lord Milner, a man at the centre of the British financial establishment, had learnt in Egypt to equate civilisation with good government. He coupled this view with the 'chauvinistic assumption that the British race had unique imperial gifts and a moral right to rule other peoples, whether Asians, Africans or Afrikaners.'[11] On 6 July 1898 he wrote to Chamberlain that the last chance to gain mastery in South Africa without resorting to war required Britain to 'obtain practical control of Delagoa Bay', the rail outlet for the Transvaal. But the Portuguese stood firm. Thus the strategy that was to precipitate war — compelling Kruger to admit the British 'Uitlanders' to political power — was chosen instead. Consonant with the concept of an imperial dominion held safe by an autonomous but allied representative government, Milner indicated in November 1899 that 'the *ultimate* end is a self-governing white community, supported by *well-treated* and justly governed black labour from Cape Town to Zambesi'.[12] Nothing states more plainly than this, albeit benignly, the structural economic basis of colonial racism and politics.

The Anglo-Boer War of 1899—1902 needs no discussion here save to refer to the succssful outcome for the British, not so much in terms of military honours as of a political solution amenable to their economic and strategic interests. Britain by this stage regarded the granting of self-government to large established settler groups in the colonies as an effective and perhaps the only 'way of retaining influence short of the uneconomical use of force, in a part of the world where Afrikaner power was bound one day to reassert itself.'[13]

Milner would have preferred a conclusive surrender on entirely British terms including an extension of the proven, safe, Cape franchise system. He also desired an influx of British immigrants. But as neither of these objectives proved realistic, they were easily jettisoned. The Treaty of Vereeniging signalled the consignment of blacks into the political wilderness, and the constitution of Union sealed their fate. Milner, no less than others, felt that blacks should not have political equality, but should be taught 'habits of regular and skilled labour' and kept severely 'away from strong drink' — themes loudly echoed by clergy of the time.[14]

In the alliance between foreign and national capital, the first major breakthrough came with success in the hard-fought battle to establish a Customs Union in 1903. But all was not plain sailing. The war had precipitated a recession that would continue for six years, creating considerable difficulties in the labour supply position; severe drought from 1903—8 made rural recovery difficult; and the lack of a sure labour supply and adequate control of policies necessitated action.

The latter need was met by the appointment of the South African Native Affairs (Lagden) Commission, whose recommendation foreshadowed so much in contemporary South Africa.[15] Sir Godfrey Lagden's Commission provided basic formulae for labour controls in accordance with already well-developed practices. The great majority on the Commission were English-speakers representing capitalist interests seeking to promote the accumulation of wealth in a settler colonial framework. Thus their report was 'mainly the natural product of well-to-do land and mine-owners, representatives of an acquisitive society hardened by pioneering experience and eager for economic development.'[16]

All sectors of the industrial world now began to seek regularisation of labour policies and a separation between colonists and colonised, though attitudes differed towards the rigidity of suitably qualified colonised people. It was a 'rethinking of production processes'.[17] In the outcome, these 'changes in the organisation of production and a realignment of class forces' gave great impetus to segregationist policies which protected settlers, delineated the source of cheap mass labour (Africans), and contained a credible ideology based on cultural strangeness and estrangement. The Lagden Commission dealt with these issues, creating an appropriate labour control structure just when the gold-mining industry was at the beginning of its eleven year expansion of outputs and profits, and as the manufacturing industry was getting into its stride (by 1904 the four territories contained 4 778 factories producing goods valued at £19,3m).[18]

If one understands by white supremacy the power of European capital operating through a colonist oligarchy, then the following sympathetic comment of the journal, *The Nineteenth Century*, is a fair summary of the intentions dominating the Lagden Commission:

> The Commissioners . . . devised a scheme the adoption of which will safeguard white supremacy almost as effectively as wholesale native disenfranchisement (sic), and be free from the difficulties attending the execution of such a project.[19]

While the Lagden Commission sat (1903—1905), the four South African territories experienced a burst of political activity. The Transvaal Progressive Association (Chamber of Mines interests), the Transvaal Labour Party, and the Transvaal Responsible Government Association (diamond interests) were formed in 1904, a short time before the Het Volk and Oranje Unie parties of the Boers in 1905. Black political opposition emerged that year in the form of the African People's Organisation (Dr Abdurahman) in the Cape, but already 1904 had seen the establishment of the Natal Native Congress, the Orange River Colony Vigilance Association, the Transvaal Congress, the Bapedi Union and the Basuto Association.

Also of relevance to South Africa, December 1905 saw the coming to power of the Liberal Party in Britain for whom an accommodation with the Boer generals was almost an article of faith. This led fairly quickly, after Smuts had lobbied in London, to the granting of self-government to the Transvaal in 1906, followed the next year by the Orange Free State. In both areas the Boer parties came to power, providing the basis of negotiations for Union of the four territories and for an alliance between Afrikaner farmers and mining magnates.

Much support emerged for the segregationist policies advocated by the Lagden Commission. Additionally, a variety of economic changes, together with the need to unify the vital and expanding railway network, all combined to lend force to negotiations for a union of the four territories which would secure alliances and firmly establish patterns of policy and practice now well-tested. Thus in 1908 and 1909 National Conventions were held in Durban, Cape Town and Bloemfontein to work out the terms of a union which would ensure the creation of a 'common market of nearly a million people', but under conditions in which capitalist interests would gain.[20] A memorandum by Lionel Curtis, Assistant Colonial Secretary of the Transvaal, written to Lord Selborne in January 1907, published in July that year, and widely taken up by South African politicians in the national conventions, provides a keen insight into the nature of the union proposals:

> Union was also desirable so that a uniform 'native policy' could be devised and applied. Only then would white South Africans be secure against African uprisings and only then would the labour potential of the African population be rationally distributed. A united South Africa would be a strong and prosperous state and in due course it would extend its authority over the territories to its north.[21]

In this context, the Lagden Commission's proposals clearly played a strong though not uniform role in defining segregation policies (already largely in practice) and controls over African labour supplies. As Davenport puts it,

> if this meant deliberately depressing wages, or preventing the growth of labour's bargaining power, or playing off white against black workers, or keeping land for Africans in short supply to force men on to the farms, or down the mines, the power balance arrived at in the South African Act made it possible to do these things.[22]

Opposition to the majority trend came from some Cape liberal politicians who saw the Cape franchise system as the best, perhaps the most vital measure to meet the aspirations and utilise the leadership of an emerging group of educated, moderate blacks. But their own interests were clear in a generally explicit rejection of any mass struggle for the rights of the colonised, and in an implicit belief that 'the Natives should be prepared to remain in a minority in the electorate, if not permanently, at least for a very long time.'[23] In fact Selborne, though hoping for the extension of the Cape franchise, found acceptable the decision to maintain the status quo in the four territories. He even declared that 'he did not think the British Government would object to a provision making non-white people ineligible for membership of parliament, if the constitution was otherwise acceptable.'[24]

He was right. Britain washed its hands when Prime Minister Asquith addressed the House of Commons on the South African Act: 'Any control or interference from outside,' he said, 'is in the very worst interest of the natives themselves.' Yet British interests were clear: in 1909 in the Cape, whites (23 per cent of the population) had 85 per cent of the votes; in Natal, the figures were 8 per cent and 99 per cent respectively. No-one had any reason to fear that a transfer of political power to a white minority in the colony would threaten the British position of economic and strategic dominance.[25]

Africans, however, perceived well their situation and the importance of Union. First reactions from those already co-opted into the colonial system were cautious, but these grew into a chorus of protest, motivated a delegation to petition the Crown, drew the churches into the fray, and eventually, after defeat became obvious, culminated in the formation of the South African Native National Congress (later the African National Congress) in 1912.

In reviewing the period 1903—1910 it becomes apparent that the aftermath of the Anglo-Boer War, itself an attempt by foreign capital to establish control over the mineral-rich republics following the Jameson Raid debacle, represents the period during which national and foreign capital came to a competitive alliance over labour, in particular colonised (black) labour. As we have noted, the policies of labour control, the maintenance of the exploitative wage bars, and the segregation of the indigenous people found their first full formulation in the Lagden Commission and their political life in the Act of Union which established South Africa as a national state governed by a white settler oligarchy. This pattern in turn influenced the place of white labour, entrenching a privileged labour aristocracy with significant economic and therefore political clout. The period also saw the fairly rapid transformation of African resistance from military encounters to political and labour actions.

With these things in mind we proceed to investigate the Church's place in the events of the period.

Exclusion

Though the generalised system of capitalist exploitation was broadly accceptable to all settler groups and their churches, no popular consensus existed as to the direction in which it should develop. Segregation, the dominant political emphasis in colonial policy at the turn of the century and after, could be viewed in a number of permutations, from virtual total exclusion on the one hand to partial exclusion with a relatively high degree of inter-group mobility on the other. These two tendencies reflected the commonly perceived differences between Boer and Brit respectively. The debate between them has dominated white politics in the twentieth century though neither group has seriously disagreed about white dominance of the society as a whole. Within this framework one may locate the political and ideological debates beginning with the Treaty of Vereeniging and culminating in the Act of Union.

Well before the mining ventures it had become clear that settler and indigenous populations were to face a common, inextricably linked future. By the end of the nineteenth century social stratification was part of the equation, described by one churchman as a pyramid: 'the great coloured population; Kafir and half-caste at the base, being first in order and number; above that is the next stratum in order and number, the Dutch; and the English element comes in last and fewest at the apex'.[26] However, the Dutch and English together may be seen basically as at one with each other against the colonised groups. The division by colour was in effect a class division, somewhat imprecisely described by Co-Adjutor Bishop Gibson in a sermon as follows:

> . . . the average white man feels as if, by a law of nature, by some inherent superiority, he has a right to the land: and the native has no right to be there, except as his (the white man's) servant.[27]

The same distinction appeared in different language in the Lagden Commission report's discussion of 'Christianity and civilisation'. It affirmed the important role of religion in the 'great struggle between the powers of good and evil, of light and darkness, of enlightenment and ignorance, of progress and tradition, of Christianity and heathenism.' But the Lagden Commission, as its terms of reference make clear, intended neither more nor less than a common policy of settler domination through a federation of the colonies in a capitalist economy.[28] The then current debate over segregation came to a focus in the work of the Commission. It concerned the right formula for maintaining a good labour supply now essential to the process of industrialisation, but without according effective power to those who laboured. Control over their potentially threatening presence in the towns was also necessary.

On the whole the general tenor of the Commission Report found much favour with the Church, especially as the Commission had warmly commended the Church's role in educating blacks to their place in white society while moderating their resistance through moral suasion. 'No more satisfying justification of the missionary work of the churches has ever been penned', the South African Missionary Society proudly noted in reference to the Lagden Report.[29] The general verdict of the *Christian Express* was that the Commission had 'done its work well' and produced a sane, moderate Report, which *taken as a whole*, 'is neither unfair nor unfriendly towards the great Native interest with which it deals.'[30] Bishop Gaul went further: 'It might well be called the prose edition of Rudyard Kipling's *White Man's Burden*,' he charged, 'and will be a Guide Book to the Statesmen of South Africa for many years.'[31] *The Kingdom* (Anglican) read it as a 'great document', for

> what work in the world is more worth doing than the guidance of savages into civilisation, by the gradual imposition of responsibilities, the teaching them of the value of such responsibilities by a share in the consequent burdens, the exercise of a firm and just control from outside, while habits of self-control are being formed within, and the implanting in the native of a confidence and trust in the justice, the integrity, and benevolence of the white man.[32]

Still positive though a little more critical, the president of the Congregational Union Assembly regarded the work of the Commission as 'encouraging to the negrophilist', but felt that it should allow Africans greater mobility into the dominant society through the right freely to purchase individually titled land, and through a qualified franchise with stringent education and income tests. Many blacks could then be made allies rather than a menace. This was the view of limited, 'porous' segregation:

> . . . a certain proportion will accept and profit by industrial, technical, and theoretical education; that this proportion, to whom it is our very present duty to offer it — that this proportion may be very much increased through wise encouragement, so that the people instead of being a menace, as some fear, will prove a help to the state, taking their proportion of the burden and of responsibility.[33]

Another solution to native policy, one which moved towards total political exclusion and in many respects anticipated the intentions of aparthied (though in different form), was proposed by the *Christian Express*. The best answer, the editors thought, would be to group together existing native reserves, in the form of small Protectorates, thus providing a 'homeland' for Africans where they would be 'free men (sic) in their own country' and 'free to go and work on the mines when they liked.'[34]

But whatever political ideas might have come forward, the fundamental structures of control and exploitation were not up for auction, a realisation rather quaintly expressed as early as 1903 by the Bishop of Lebombo. Comparing the existing government to a company run by directors charged to produce dividends for the constituent shareholder, he wrote: 'Does not our political difficulty with regard to natives arise very largely from the natural desire not to admit more shareholders into the Company?'[35]

The various reactions noted above characterise the churches' response to the new exigencies of the South African political economy. The debate in the

Church paralleled that among settlers and colonists, a debate that arose, as has been pointed out, as a result of new economic forces and class realignments. Despite the manifestations of black protest and resistance in the rapid sprouting of political organisations and independent churches, there is little evidence that the churches took their point of view or position any more seriously than did whites in general.

After the Lagden Commission, attention naturally turned to the planned federation of the colonies. At a very early stage it was clear that the British prefered a general extension of the Cape franschise rather than the status quo or total exclusion. They believed that no threat to settlers rested therein, whereas black opposition would be considerably reduced through the incorporation of the most articulate, moneyed and educated blacks.

In these matters the Anglican and Methodist churches by and large concurred. The franchise issue had already raised its head in the Lagden Commission report. It had recommended limited access of blacks to the vote, 'not more than sufficient to provide an adequate means for the expression of native views and the ventilation of their grievances, if any. . . .'[36] To this the Johannesburg Evangelical Church Council gave assent, adding that those suitably advanced 'should receive special consideration, and should be exempt from all special laws applying to natives.'[37] A desire to see 'the rights of the Natives secured in the framing of the 'new constitution' was expressed at the General Missionary Conference of 1906, but along the lines laid down by Cape liberals, including WP Schreiner and John X Merriman.[38]

A while later, Bishop Gaul wrote to the *London Times*, possibly to influence leading British opinion prior to a planned visit of a black protest delegation. By now the issue of African franchise rights had focused on whether the Cape limited-franchise system would be extended throughout the Union or not. The plan was to leave the matter for later, that is, for the decision of the proposed Union parliament. In protest a black delegation went to Britain. In this context Gaul argued that the Act of Union would permit eventual extension of citizenship, and should not be unduly interfered with, for

> any attempt to raise final issues on the native franchise question will arouse local state prejudices, local traditional enmities, and endanger the honourable, but somewhat delicate understanding arrived at . . .such discussion would even injure the best native interest and welfare . . . and would encourage a fictitious political Ethiopianism, a deadly foe to the slowly but surely growing sympathy between the races.[39]

But Gaul's hope of 'growing sympathy' was somewhat misplaced. Even the liberal Merriman, using precisely Gaul's argumentation, treated as 'agitators' an imposing delegation from the Evangelical Church Council which urged a rethink on the proposals of the National Convention and their political exclusion of Africans in the northern republics.[40]

As the compromises of Union became clear, church protest gathered. Fifty clergy in the Cape Peninsula signed a protest against the political colour bar clauses. Leaders of all the main Protestant churches, including the Anglican, Methodist, Presbyterian, Unitarian and Baptist, and the Evangelical Church Council addressed a letter to the National Convention expressing 'very widespread regret' at the exclusion of blacks from the franchise clauses.[41]

But even the segregationist views remained prominent, as is evidenced in a rather equivocal letter from newly-enthroned Archbishop Carter. He confessed that the position publicly expressed by Lord Milner, Lord Selborne and Cecil Rhodes in favour of a qualified franchise should be upheld, recognising that 'citizenship is one thing, if men are qualified to exercise the rights of citizenship, but social intercourse is another thing . . .'[42]

On the other hand, calling it 'the shadow that haunts us', the Anglican provincial newspaper strongly criticised the Union constitution, pronouncing that 'self-interest and self-preservation have compelled the unification of the European rulers.'[43] The Methodist conference of 1909 too called for 'the fullest consideration of the interests of colonised groups, though it regarded comment upon the details within the sphere of ordinary politics and thus not its business.[44] The picture one gets, then, is of a Church at last developing a position strongly in support of the majority of its membership, at least potentially. The words are sharp and often remarkably clear.

Yet, notwithstanding all these criticisms, talk proved to be cheap. The actual fact of Union, once realised, was remarkably easily accepted by most who had warned against the general political exclusion of the indigenous population. The Methodist Conference of 1910 about-faced. In a special address to Gladstone, the new High Commissioner, the Conference spoke of the new hope that 'to the various races of South Africa would come all the blessings of peace, prosperity and progress which it is confidently expected may result from Union of these colonies.' And to the British Conference it wrote that 'with you we pray that this Union may give to our land political stability, permanent peace, as well as commercial prosperity . . . to the furtherance of the Kingdom of Christ.'[45] Similarly, in his charge to the Diocesan Synod, the Bishop of Zululand acknowledged the injustice of the 'colour line'.[46] Finally, a pastoral letter from the Bishop of St Johns noted that 'on the whole it marks, as we may thankfully believe, a real step forward in the history of our country.'[47]

One clear voice spoke out on Union Day itself. At a special thanksgiving service in Port Elizabeth, the mayoral chaplain, the Rev W Friend, boldly proclaimed the aggrievement of blacks at the terms of Union:

these people are not in Church today thanking God for the Union; indeed it was with reluctance that they abstained from proclaiming this birthday of a nation a Day of Fasting and Humiliation.[48]

Here was a rare recognition indeed of the feelings of those who would now be black South Africans, virtually excluded from decision-making over their own destinies in a region-made-nation at the behest of intruding powers. From another source — the newspaper run by John Dube, a leading African nationalist — came confirmation of the truth implicit in that thanksgiving address delivered in Port Elizabeth:

. . . when there are signs of being handed over to a political oligarchy, men would be dull indeed if they supposed that millions of people were going to be made into mere political chattels to suit the whims and avarice of a privileged few.[49]

Dube was referring specifically to the new Union Constitution and its practical exclusion of the majority of South Africans from a democractic political role in parliament. But, of course, by far the majority of Africans were faced less with the question of a qualified franchise versus none, than with earning their daily bread — or maize as the case might be. Moreover, that a great many blacks found themselves increasingly pushed, even forced, into wage-labour, was itself a new and profound change occasioned by a rapidly industrialising economy. That this happened sooner and faster than ever expected was, as has been said, a consequence of diamond, and more especially gold, discoveries.

Contemporary historians have explored this change more thoroughly and critically than before, especially with respect to the reasons for the high degree of coercion that accompanied the process. Much light has been shed on the dynamics of South African industrialisation, its direction in the hands of a relatively small group whose interests were at best only secondarily concerned with the indigenous population (if at all), and the powerful impact on political development of economic concerns.

Here too it is possible to understand the role of the Church in relation to its wider context as something more than a history of the maintenance and transmission of a religious tradition, for this tradition communicated itself, to those inside and outside the Church, in terms largely drawn from the dominant culture and society of which it was a self-conscious part. The 'more' which the Church transmitted — the additions, omissions and reinterpretations occurring because of cultural and social values — may be referred to as its ideological over-burdening. Here is where we seek to uncover what is concealed in the divine truths which the Church thought it revealed.

From a Privileged Pew

In 1903 Co-Adjutor Bishop Gibson of Cape Town sent to all the Anglican Bishops and to others on the Provincial Board of Mission a letter containing recent resolutions of the Synod of the Diocese of Mashonaland on 'Native Policy' (attaching his own comments). This was to promote a unified policy throughout southern Africa (the Anglican Province went beyond the borders of the four South African territories). The Bishop of Mashonaland had written that 'natives' should be taught to satisfy their wants in 'the most ordered and *nourishing* form of manual labour'. Thus he had called for a conference of all Christian bodies to consider the training of blacks to take their place in the economy. Indeed, 'there should be no *loafers* either in the kingdom of this world or in the kingdom of heaven,' he wrote. The Diocese had resolved, firstly, that two things — polygamy, and the absence of wants — made Africans unambitious to work, secondly, that the desire to satisfy wants should be engendered and, thirdly, that 'the Church and the State should introduce as soon as possible a universal system of industrial training and education.'[50]

These pleas were almost immediately echoed in the proposals of the Lagden Commission which placed a heavy emphasis on industrial training because of its 'particular advantage to the Native of fitting him for his position in life.'[51] Most of the Provincial Board agreed unreservedly. So did heads of religious 'Native Institutions' who later sent a deputation to Colonel Crewe, the Cape Colonial Secretary, petitioning him to assist in the 'very desirable' change of Africans 'from being so largely an indolent people to an industrial people', by which they meant useful workers.[52] Similarly, in a presidential address to the Congregational Union of South Africa Assembly, P Lyon called for the teaching of 'practical industry that each pupil should graduate into a well-prepared worker, enriching his neighbourhood by his toil, and thus becoming a true citizen.'[53] But Dr Wilder of the American Zulu Mission was even more explicit. Addressing the first General Missionary Conference about 'the savage', he said:

> He must be 'denationalised'; which means that he must see that there is dignity in labour, that there is no magic in the printed page, that instead of by deceit, lust and violence, he must now get possession of material things by working for them; . . .[54]

At the second conference two years later, the illustrious Andrew Murray, in a paper on 'Missionary Pioneer Policy', annunciated four principles of mission in the new century; the first three were essentially religious, but the last one was that 'the Native must be taught the dignity of manual labour.'[54]

This sudden interest on the part of the Church to see that Africans learned to appreciate their role as labourers is obviously connected with the first large-scale burst of industrialisation. It is often contrasted with an indigent tribal existence. The new tone contrasts too with what had earlier for long been the predominant theme in the proclamations of the missions — 'Civilisation'. This term, however, rapidly faded out of common parlance among the clerics within the first decade of the twentieth century. The demands and concerns of a modern industrial economy increasingly took over. But above all, the economic processes that lay behind these changes in ideological terms were shaped at this time by the extensive development of the rich gold-mining areas of the Reef.

'Egoli': A Different Way of Life

The mining ventures, the frontier of capital and industry, shifted the economic centre of gravity from the cattle regions where trade had flourished into the midst of the Boer Republics. Gold-mining was the first really large-scale capitalist industry in South Africa, with techniques of management, organisation and ore-extraction derived in large measure from the diamond fields. Both enterprises demanded deep mining in pipes or reefs requiring major capital expenditure, sophisticated processes, and huge amounts of unskilled labour. The combination of these structural requirements and a vast potential of unskilled labour among the colonised people proved fateful.

Firstly, the low-grade quality of the extensive gold veins of the Rand meant that mining would not be viable without very cheap labour. The obvious source was the indigenous population provided that competition for their labour was not allowed to send the cost of labour up. Secondly — equally a factor of the low-grade ore — a high level of output was demanded, implying the need for a predictable, well-controlled labour force among other things. One final structural constraint, the internationally fixed price of gold, helped shape the economic model of gold-mining.[52]

These factors taken together strengthened or gave rise to certain institutions and policies: the Chamber of Mines; a recruiting monopsony; influx control; the compound system; migratory labour; and exploitative (wage) colour bars; Crafts-unions were all-white bodies for the most part ('coloured' artisans were included in some cases), and by virtue of their exclusion of unskilled and semi-skilled workers, influenced the establishment of one further feature designed to receive highly disproportionate prominence: the job colour-bars, which excluded the few qualified blacks from taking 'white' jobs.

The need to organise the recruitment of labour and to take 'active steps for the gradual reduction of native wages to a "reasonable" level', led to the establishment of the Chamber of Mines in the Transvaal in 1887.[57] Though its primary purpose was to deal with matters concerning labour, it also 'served to represent and secure the common interests and policies of the Groups and companies in all areas, and to provide the companies with a wide range of services.'[58] Thus the high costs of capitalisation and of advances in mining technology and organisation could be shared. Not only were key individuals frequently board members of several groups or companies, but operations were often run by the same men who had made the diamond fields a closed monopoly (in order to provide the necessary control over the marketing of diamonds, without which price fluctuations would create havoc).

The methods of the diamond kings were thus available, though less easily maintained, for the lords of the Rand. The organisation of cheap labour especially was an obvious common interest. For this purpose a number of strategies, developed over the years and combined with new inventions suited to fresh demands, were rapidly introduced. The result was a labour structure that shaped the lives of millions of Africans over the next three-quarters of a century and more, one which under the name of apartheid would bring condemnation upon South Africa.

In fact, control over the geographic mobility of labour goes back as far as 1760, when slaves were first required to carry passes in moving between urban and rural areas. Later measures were applied to the rural areas of greatest indigenous population, creating reserves regarded by whites as 'reservoirs of labour'; in the reserves the enormous pressures of 'congestion, landlessness and crop failure were welcomed as stimulants to the labour supply.'[59] Moreover, the official view was that 'the only pressing needs of a savage are those of food and sex, and the conditions of native life in Africa are such that these are as a rule easily supplied.'[60] Thus a combination of factors entered into the creation of a wage-labour force: on the one hand 'population growth, crop failure, stock decimation, soil erosion and the desire to acquire the means of purchasing guns and cattle'; on the other hand, legislation such as individual tenure (particularly sought by the Chamber of Mines), other administrative and corporate measures such as taxation, and the use of traders as recruiting agents (leading frequently to 'debt-enslavement').[61]

The task of labour recruitment was split between two agencies though they were established at different stages. Early on, in 1896, centralisation of recruitment was formalised in the Rand Native Labour Association, which four years later became the Witwatersrand Native Labour Association (WNLA) and focused on Africans residing outside the colonies. Government assistance in the form of legislation to control workers came readily, especially as the mining-houses easily persuaded Kruger of the crucial importance of gold and the need for maximisation of output. Thus in 1895 the Volksraad enacted a special pass law applicable to mining districts which 'provided for a rudimentary form of influx control, and . . . enjoined Africans to wear a metal arm badge (amended later to a requirement that an official pass be carried) numbered as a means of identification.'[62]

This arrangement was disturbed in the crisis initiated by the Robinson Group of mines who in 1906 set in motion strategies designed to give it favoured status for recruitment in Mozambique, a major source area. Mining councils were divided as a result. High level negotiations with the British imperium on both sides complicated matters, and the possible rise in the price of labour seriously threatened many mines. The state had to help, exacting its price for the development of national capital in return. The Robinson Group failed to get what they wanted, but the recruiting monopsony was damaged. The threat of further labour competition driving up the extremely low wages, led to the establishment of the Native Recruiting Corporation in 1912. Its fundamental purpose was to eliminate the cost-maximising competition between the mining companies for African labour.[63]

Difficulties in procuring African labour after the Anglo-Boer War had precipitated the crisis. This also led to another, albeit temporary one as it turned out — the importation of Chinese labour. Begun in 1904 in response to labour shortages, this tactic upset skilled white wokers and their less skilled colleagues. Australian miners by then working in South Africa had faced the threat of cheap Chinese labour in Australia and there had developed strong sensitivities which they brought with them to South Africa. Soon this led to a major white mine-workers strike in 1907, about 4 000 men stopping work. Subsequently importation of Chinese was stopped and repatriation began.[64] The racial attitudes that accompanied the fear of cheap labour were not directed only at the Chinese, but the whole affair reinforced racist tendencies.

It must be noted that recruitment of indigenous labour was not conceived of as bringing a man and his family to the mines. On the contrary, the migratory system assumed that family accommmodation and a supplemental income should not be the responsibility of the mining company but of the reserve susbsistence economy. This system, 'probably the most fantastic labour set-up of any industry in the world', required careful control.[65] On the one hand, 'subsistence earnings needed to be lower than a worker required to meet all his needs so that he would be forced to enter into wage-labour; on the other, rural earnings should not fall below what was required to reproduce labour.' Moreover, the oscillatory migratory pattern provided employers, they believed, with the benefits of 'lower wages, less leave and absenteeism, better control, less risk of the men getting silicosis, and greater output in jobs involving hard physical work.'[66]

The black rural areas thus became the 'sponge that absorbs, and returns when required, the reserve army of African labour' whence healthy and vigorous workers came, whereas 'married quarters for Africans on the mines would be more expensive' than 'hospitals, balanced diets, and even games and cinemas' in the labour compounds.[67] The case for segregated, fixed African reserves rather than a further great reduction in land available to the African, was unabashedly stated by Sir Godfrey Lagden: 'A man cannot go with his wife and children and his goods and chattels on to the labour market. He must have a dumping ground. Every rabbit has a warren where he can live and burrow and breed, and every native must have a warren too.'[68]

In fact, migrancy in a free labour market would not provide the assured, controlled supply of workers needed for the industrialisation leap. On the contrary, many Africans had for long migrated to work, more often than not in earlier times at their own initiative. Wages could supplement the production of a household, make new technologies affordable and allow a purchase of cattle, the main capital base of the African family. In some areas (notably Pondoland) the mines at first tried a system of advances in the form of cattle in return for labour on a contractual basis. This had advantages for the African homestead, for it meant that the migrant labourer's work and income indeed supplemented the rural economy rather than the urban. Moreover, it helped assure the return of the migrant and allowed family control over wages.

But for the mines the system soon showed defects. As the wage was already paid at home, many workers simply deserted before their contract had been completed. Moreover, the mines usually recruited through traders who also took their share, thus increasing the basic cost of labour.[69] It thus became clear that the regulation of migrant labour required control both at source and in the receiving area.

At source, taxation played a role. Conferment of what one historian ingenuously called 'the privilege of being taxed and so contributing to the national revenue — that universal badge of a civilised society' must be seen against the important role of taxation in the system of administration.[70] Taxation was 'designed to achieve the threefold aim of raising revenue, forcing Africans out into the labour market, and effecting social change among them'.[71] In the rural areas the 'Bunga' system of local rule, effective policing, enforcement of magisterial authority and other measures also facilitated control. At the receiving end compounds, pass laws and contracts held total sway over African lives. 'Contract' is in fact a misnomer, as Cresswell, leader of the Labour Party, long ago pointed out:

> If I make a contract to labour for you and I refuse to carry out that contract, your only remedy is to sue me in the courts. If a native enters into a contract to labour for me and does not carry out his contract, it is a crime against the State for which he can be punished with imprisonment. That distinguishes the free system and the quasi-feudal system.[72]

The pass system 'was designed to keep African workers in their labour contracts. It provided . . . a means of enforcing contractual obligations between natives and Europeans and of detecting deserters.'[73] It could of course also be used to check criminality and control resistance. Passes had in this respect two aspects: a 'character column' in which the employers could and did write comments such as 'bad boy'; and the endorsement 'FIRED' for any criminal conviction which, once stamped, left criminal activity the only real option for future work.[74]

These institutions of the work places — passes, recruitment practices, migratory labour, reserves, taxation, contracts — were so central to the lives of a great many black South Africans, even at this early stage, that one would imagine the Church showing considerable interest in them. Africans were after all the bulk of their memberships in almost every case. But do the archival records reveal much interest? Was the Church able to conceive of its task in terms consistent with the daily experiences of the majority of its members? What was its attitude to matters economic? These questions reach to the heart of this book in its intention to search the records in the hope of uncovering a reasonable picture of the Church's sayings and doings at a time crucial to the formation of contemporary South Africa.

The evidence is by and large scanty, in itself already an indication of the low level of interest in these matters, at least in official church quarters. The *Christian Express* drew attention on occasion to the major means of identity control employed in the northern colonies, namely the pass. Clearly the pass was regarded by the colonised people as a major tool of servitude. During the period under consideration, it required monthly renewal at a shilling a time, and unless it was carried on one's person, one was liable to be thrown into prison. Used in part to control deserters, it clearly served a much wider function, and was often used 'for the sole purpose of bullying the Native by police of both colours'.[75] However, this was not much a concern of the churches then, only inconsequential references being found in the records.

On the other hand, labour supply matters received some attention, particularly recruiting practices, though this latter appeared as a concern only towards the end of the first decade. Once again, the *Christian Express* of Lovedale proved its worth and interest, focussing in a 1906 article on a common procedure: rural traders over-extending credit to indigenous people, and subsequently forcing them to seek work in the towns to repay debts.[76] Frequently, handsome fees were paid to traders for recruiting in this manner, a form of control through debt over the worker in the rural areas as well. Thus Robert Callaway of Butterworth wrote in a letter to the editor of *The Church Chronicle* that the recruiting system among the Mfengu, Tembu and Xhosa people of the Transkei was 'the worst form of competition . . . It is a game of grab.'[77] Later that same year the *Christian Express* revealed that

> . . . a vicious system of recruiting by labour agencies has sprung up of such magnitude that in the Transkeian Territories alone it employed last year an army of 112 agents and 2 658 runners. These labour agents receive a premium amounting from 40 shillings to 60 shillings and upwards per head, which of course must come ultimately out of the labourer's wages.[78]

Everywhere in the Transkei one was confronted by 'i-Joyini' (labour recruiting), wrote Godfrey Callaway, compared to which all other matters were ephemeral, he said. 'It means many things this ugly word, it means one thing to the Native, another to the mine-owner, another to the labour agent . . (it is) competition run wild . . . When it is considered that this system is in operation all over the country we may well prepare for a Nemesis,'said he. Yet he thought the inevitable retribution would be a long time coming, for the 'unseen power behind which demanded labour at any price' had great forces on its side, being prepared in the matter of recruiting even on occasion to offer large sums to mission societies for assistance.[79]

The ambiguity of the Church in economic issues comes out most interestingly and clearly in a discussion on taxation recommendations of the Lagden Commission by the same *Christian Express* which so strongly condemned recruiting practices. Concluding that a poll tax was preferable to the hut tax, the journal wrote that 'the direct taxation of the Native, though an evil, is a necessary evil. It is a tax on barbarism.' Arguing on the one hand against the use of taxation to force labour, on the other it nevertheless agreed that from a commercial standpoint 'it would naturally be expected that in a country like South Africa the immense potentialities of the Native as a source of revenue would be patent to the most obtuse mind . . .'[80]

With respect to reserves, migratory labour and the contract system, little is heard. Taken together, all the practices described helped to distribute and control labour. Moreoever, they were at the centre of a labour structure that functioned on the basis of highly exploitative wages, at least for the black South African. But while the Church hardly criticised labour controls, it clearly saw no problem in playing a part in the effective distribution of labour to the best advantage for employers, as we will see in respect of education, training and housing. Members of the Pretoria Board of Missions even felt that nothing should be done to disturb the exploitative wage structure. The Rev WA Goodwin declared that 'for the ordinary rank and file it is not the duty of the Church to civilise the native into an expensive worker for the sake of the labour proletariat . . . Cheap labour has enabled in South Africa many developments which otherwise would have been left untouched.' PW Tracey was convinced that 'the Church should endeavour by all means in its power to bring Our Lord's teaching, and that only, home to the Native . . . the Church has no call to educate the Natives above the white.'[81] The 'universal cry' that blacks must go to work resounded through the pages of the 1908 *Blue Book on Native Affairs*.[82] Finding many responsive murmurs in Church circles, it summed up the dominant view of the decade. Occasionally though, the serious contradictions were painfully noted. As the CPSA newspaper remarked in April of the following year,

> The building of the mining industry on a labour supply that is secured at the cost of such conditions of indentured labour is a horrible mockery of the 'civilising mission' of the white races.[83]

On the Rand, 'housing ran close second for the prize of the most hated single institution governing black urban life' (after the pass laws). Mortality rates were high (eg Klipspruit: 380 in 1 000 in 1914/15; that is 38 per cent), and conditions insufferable, even in the freehold areas of Sophiatown, Martindale and Newclare.[84] But nowhere was control greater than in the 'total institutions' which were the mine compounds.

The introduction of the compound system began with the Kimberley diamond diggings, especially once the consolidation of claims in the hands of a few magnates allowed more effective organisation. Here, blacks were 'obliged to submit to a regime of closed compounds from 1885 onwards thus placing themselves under very close supervision and control.'[85]

When translated to the goldfields, an open compound system was adopted, enabling police control over contract workers. 'The effective control of such large numbers of people by so few authority bearers' required extensive measures, including relative isolation from the wider environment and an assualt upon the self to strip the worker of individuality. Certain practices became normative, among them: (1) utilising a worker's fingerprints and number for identification while his name, his most distinctive personal characteristic, was never used; (2) the invasion of privacy to increase surveillance, even in ablution blocks and lavatories; (3) continuous lighting throughout the night in dormitories to control violence, sodomy and theft; (4) regular detail searches. All these practices 'intended that a conception of self which best serves the needs of the organisation be substituted . . . to create a subservient and contented labour force . . . by means of surveillance and punishment,' and by means of the provision of "recreational activities".'[86]

Day-to-day costs of the reproduction of labour were thereby also minimised by 'direct control over the pattern of consumption . . . to minimum levels required to rejuvenate the worker as a muscular machine.'[87] Even the compound shops, developed as part of the system, allowed the company to make a profit from the food eaten (Rhodes himself guilelessly reported in 1989 'a profit of £24 385 over two years from compound shops, none of which was used for the benefit of African mineworkers').[88]

Within the compounds themselves, a hierarchy of control existed. The *Induna*, a uniformed officer given single quarters (often shared) and appointed by the Compound Manager, received extra beer and meat rations and a relatively high salary, and was 'seen by management as a tribal leader of tribal people' and an intermediary. Below them were Policemen, also uniformed but living with other workers. Management called them 'Tribal Representatives', but 'in fact they are neither representative nor tribal; they are minor bureaucrats in the administration system.' Finally, the *Sibonda,* an elected leader of the compound room, was expected to refer serious offences to the compound authorities as well as generally act as spokesman, though mostly *Sibondas* were reluctant to support management and even sided with workers in confrontations.[89] Overall the system functioned effectively to maintain order and control at minimum cost in what amounted to a captive situation.

A solid history of the compounds awaits an author, but enough is known to make seriously deficient Wilson's judgement that compounds were devised primarily to house the large numbers of men required for labour who would otherwise be unwilling to come or who would not be allowed by their respective neighbouring governments to leave permanently, thus draining their home country of able-bodied men.[90] Rather, Johnstone's analysis of the role of the compound system in the economic structure offers a much more satisfactory description, and a good summary of the data:

It constituted an important form of labour control, from which the mining companies derived economic and political benefits.

Economically, the system helped to reduce costs and to stabilise the African labour supply. The standardised mass feeding and housing of African workers permitted economies of scale, and established living standards at a level of subsistence and cost chosen by the mining companies. And the compounding of workers served to inhibit absenteeism and desertion.

But the most important advantages were of a more political nature. The system served both to maximise the control of the companies over the behaviour of African workers, and to isolate these workers from the society around them. The fragmentation, isolation and concentration of the African labour force in separate, dependent and prison-like compounds was of great advantage to the companies in the management of unrest and insubordination among African workers. The compound system also served the political interests of the companies by isolating African mine workers from other workers and Africans and life generally on the Rand. This isolation was not total; African workers could and did leave the compound — for which they had to obtain a pass. But their general life and work situation in the mine compounds was artificially removed from the society around them.[91]

The South African Compounds and Interior Mission, established in 1896 on an interdenominational basis, sent church workers into these compounds preaching repentence and restitution. Four afternoons a week visits were made to compound rooms and classes were held each day.[92] As the Wesleyan, the Rev JS Morris, later said, 'mine compounds are a unique field for Christian work and ought to be cultivated.'[93] Those who worked in the compounds clearly recognised the oppressive conditions but their response appears to have been largely sentimental. Thus a representative of the Diamond Fields Compounds Mission, commenting on the harsh and difficult compound life with no apparent understanding of the material conditions he encountered, could say of the workers:

> Sometimes their hands hang down and their knees become feeble in the stress of the hot and weary days; but there is joy in the eventide as memory recalls souls that have passed from darkness to light and from the power of Satan unto God, and that in many cases these new born babes will become heralds of the Cross in the 'Regions Beyond'.[94]

Some people did advocate that compounds be run along healthy lines, with good food, entertainment and health care — such as those, it was felt, at Kimberley — because this had distinct advantages in recruiting and holding labour.[95]

The alternative to the compounds for many was the 'location', isolated land separately set aside for the residence of Africans coming to work in the towns. 'It is a special kind of living arrangement that cannot be compared with anything outside this country,' wrote Harry Bloom. The term location 'is itself a significantly unique use of the word, for it denotes not a place where people live, but one where something is found.'[96]

Locations policies go back to the middle of the 1800s, as utilised by Sir George Grey, Theophilus Shepstone, and later as part of the Glen Grey Act scheme sponsored by Rhodes. But the controls over labour envisaged in various locations policies were first fully formulated by the Lagden Commission. These have been more or less the basis of policy ever since. The growing industrialisation of the core economy led to greater demands for labour, and with the consequent escalating presence of workers in the towns, locations and their associated controls seemed the obvious solution to the problem of accommodating black workers.[97]

As an influential Methodist, the Rev F Mason, put it, 'the system has its disadvantages, and they are serious enough, but less than those from which we now suffer' (by which he meant the presently insufficient control over tribes). Recommending locations, he believed that 'these, when introduced, must be under the control of competent superintendents and strong bodies of police'. At the same time, seemingly unaware of the contradictions involved, he blithely declared that 'on the subject of sympathy with the natives and their needs, too much can hardly be said'.[98]

The place of both locations and compounds — their integral incorporation into the economic and political structures of control and exploitation — was not only well perceived by at least one highly placed clergyman, but also crudely regarded as necessary and even helpful to the inhabitants, and the Church:

> A location, well managed and efficiently superintended, would give (to the Kafirs) within its own limits, far more of the freedom . . . than they can possibly have in lodgings scattered about in town . . . and would minimise the differences of Christian ministrations and instruction, by concentrating the people into certain defined areas. For that is the real meaning of a native location: concentration, supervision and discipline.
>   This implies, of course, class legislation: and, as such, may fall hardly upon some . . . and be objected to by others. But class legislation is often absolutely necessary . . . as a temporary, educative and protective measure, designed for the good of those on whom the legislation is imposed.[99]

In general, however, the evidence of the archives reveals extraordinarily little concern for material conditions in the compounds and locations, though relevant records of missionary societies and denominations contain yearly reports on the religious needs and progress of their 'flock'.

Our picture of African mine-workers is incomplete without reference to the specific wage-minimisation system applied at the mines themselves. The chief measures adopted were (1) wage fixation, whereby companies agreed on the price of labour at the lowest possible levels (an average of two shillings per shift); (2) the maximum average system, whereby piece work employees could not exceed an average earning per shift in any one company (2s 3d); and (3) the loafer ticket system, whereby unfulfilled piece work rates — ie less than the contracted minimum number of inches per shift drilled — as well as extra-contractual work (such as 'lashing'), went unpaid, and the time actually worked was ignored in measuring the worker's contracted number of shifts.[100]

Thus the total picture is one of African mine workers 'constrained by a more extensive system of exploitative labour and wage controls than were the rest of the African workers' through the recruiting, compound, contract and wage-minimisation systems.[101] Benefits to the mining companies of this system-complex included prevention of effective class mobilisation (through oscillating migration) and the provision of an 'ideal technique for the control of labour' in the quasi-military institution of the compound.[102] The justification for paying subsistence wages lay in the reserves policy, whereby no responsibility was taken for the support of a worker's family who were meant to care for themselves. Once again, however, these issues do not receive any notice in the records of the churches though it must be recognised that the prevailing settler ideology saw in traditional African life nothing of worth compared to the 'dignity of wage labour', however low the wages paid for such labour.

In fact de Kiewiet regards the universal dependence on black labour as 'the greatest social economic fact in the history of the century'.[103] At the same time South Africa has never provided a good living for the ordinary labourer, and Wilson has pointed out that with the exception of a short period in the mid-1940s, dividends paid out by gold mines to shareholders between 1911 and 1969 have alone consistently totalled more than the gross earnings of black mine-workers.[104]

The combined effort of all these policies helped create a 'new' South Africa of untold riches, but riches rather tightly confined to a small group, as may be seen in the following figures from 1936.

Table 1: Distribution of South African National Income,
Composition of Population and Ratio in Per Capita
Earnings (Africans = 1,0) in 1936

	Whites	Africans	Asians & Coloureds	Total
% of Nat Income received by	74,5	19,6	5,8	99,9*
% of Total Population	20,9	68,8	10,3	100,0
Ratio in Per Capita Earnings (Africans = 1,0)	12,5	1,0	2,0	—

* Percentages do not add up to 100 because of rounding errors.

(Sources: *Investment in the Union of South Africa*, p8; FP Spooner, *South African Predicament*, p173; Report of the Special Committee on the Policies of Apartheid of the Government of the Republic of South Africa, p101.) Figures taken from P van den Berghe (1967), p303.

The Liquor Complex

Prior to the 1899—1902 War both farmers and miners had certain common interests: 'their coincident needs and perceived solutions provided the basic
terms of settlement between the partners-to-be, gold and maize; political con-
summation was effectively celebrated in the first three years of Union government'.[105] The Transvaal in particular was dominated by the great interests of
mining and agricultural capitalism, but these were not without their contradictions. Alcohol, interestingly enough, became a pivotal source of conflict, and
a focal point of Church moralism.

The development of the liquor industry in the Transvaal is of particular interest to us, for it was here that the prohibition campaign took place near the
turn of the century, and it was as a result of this campaign that church
spokesmen took up the matter. The great many references to liquor abuse in
ecclesiastical documents of the time indicate a particular concern. The way in
which this concern found expression, however, allows us to observe once more
the limits to the ethical and moral vision of the Church. In this respect van
Onselen's lively analysis of the development of the liquor industry is
helpful.[106]

In 1883, the year of Paul Kruger's installation as President of the South
African Republic, he opened De Eerste Fabrieken in de Zuid-Afrikaansche
Republiek Ltd, a new distillery and the first major capital project of the young
state; here liquor was brewed from maize, potatoes and other suitable crops.

Prior to 1896 the retail liquor trade boomed, but the products which found
their way onto the market were by no means healthy. They 'killed hundreds of
workers — black and white — who consumed the working class poison that
passed commercially as liquor'. The consumption of liquor created significant
social and human costs in the heady, wild atmosphere of the raw gold-mining
town. However, a weak state, ambivalent mining magnates, the 'studied indifference' of Afrikaner rulers whose grain was sold in large quantities, and the
sympathy of the Licensing Boards to the trade, meant that little was done to
control the situation.

For their part, mine owners had a double interest in the 'Hatherley'
distillery (as the original factory became known from 1892 on). Firstly, many
had direct connections to the liquor business; secondly, alcohol sold on the
mines was an incentive to workers and helped recruitment without direct cash
cost to the company. But one problem remained: workers needed to be alive,
productive and efficient, but alcoholism and drunkenness began to take their
toll. By 1895—6 this contradiction became sufficiently serious that 'any further expansion in the large and profitable liquor industry would be at the expense of the very motor of capitalist development — the gold mines'. The
Chamber of Mines therefore sought to control the sale of alcohol, in particular

among illegal outlets. Thus, whereas previously they had tried to mute public opinion on total prohibition for Africans, they now took bitter complaints about the illicit liquor trade to the Industrial Commission of Inquiry in 1897, favouring strict control. But this also meant a loss of sales to the liquor producers. Moreover, the earlier Transvaal Prohibition Law, effective from Janaury 1897, had had a dual effect. At least half of the independent canteens in the mining areas had been forced to close, drastically reducing competition for the privileged mine canteens and allowing the mines to control supply to their workers. Nevertheless, demand generally remained high even as supply was effectively reduced. Profits therefore rose markedly. Consequently the illicit liquor market also blossomed.

Thus the mines, fighting on two fronts, were forced to develop a strategy of public opinion-making, their main 'cudgel' being the *Transvaal Leader* which set out on a crusading campaign to expose the illicit liquor runners. Most significantly, amongst many other revelations 'not once . . . did the *Leader* devote so much as a single line to the activities of the liquor producers — the capitalists'.

Meanwhile local congregations supported the campaign and helped organise a 'great public meeting' in Johannesburg to attack the illicit liquor trade. Here, as van Onselen remarks, 'ministers of religion sat astride their highest moral horses, striking out blindly at the enemy' African leaders concerned for the health of their kinsmen also mobilised, often in churches. During May 1899, the Wesleyan Rev Scholefield 'led his congregation on an attack on a neighbouring shebeen; and in the same month the Dutch Reformed Church led a delegation to petition President Kruger'.

However it was the Anglo-Boer War which altered the situation somewhat, the victorious British military commander having closed the Hatherley Distillery and crushed the independent retail syndicate. Then Milner set up a Liquor Licensing Commission in 1901 to control illicit deals and to establish a regulated state-controlled retail liquor trade. Much to the taste of mineowners, these measures reduced absenteeisms from an earlier 10—15 per cent average down to one per cent. Thus 'within 36 months the British Administration had closed the Distillery and compensated its owners, passed legislation to prevent any further distilling, smashed the illicit liquor syndicates, and rendered the entire black work-force on the Rand more efficient and productive on their newly reduced wages'.

This happy solution to the problems facing the mines as a result of a liquor industry that had threatened to run out of control was not coincidental. In fact it was the Chamber of Mines that had thrown its weight behind a new post-war organisation, the South African Alliance for the Reform of the Liquor Traffic, which 'united men keenly interested in the moral and material welfare of South Africa, mine owners, mine managers, merchants, ministers of religion and private citizens'. Van Onselen indicates that ministers of religion 'undertook most of the agitation and public relations for the Alliance'. The general desire was for restricted liquor supply under state control rather than total prohibition, a position giving the captains of industry all the advantages of both controlled consumption (and thus relatively more efficient labour) and a lure to labour. But churchmen were left to explain why the mines should be allowed to continue supplying alcohol to their workers: 'It seems unfair,' said the Rev J Darragh of the Alliance, 'to deprive them altogether of what they regard as solace.' Why they should need solace in the first place does not appear to have been an issue of much note.

Among church folk the debate awakened during the earlier period continued later. This debate was fuelled from two sides: some wanted total prohibition,[107] others only well-policed restrictions.[108] To be sure, Bishop Carter (later Archbishop) recognised that 'the whole purpose of the Liquor Bill (1907) is to attract natives to the mines'.[109] But all in all, concerned Christians did not see through what was happening, nor understand the key issue behind the whole affair. As van Onselen notes, 'alcohol has more to do with profits than with priests and is concerned with money rather than morality'.[110]

Since then the policy of controlled liquor supplies to black workers, a fixed feature of South African labour controls, has been applied in African 'locations' as well, but usually under the control of local authorities who have used beer profits in particular to subsidise their work. (In 1945, for example, beer profits were estimated to provide about one-fifth of the cost of services and amenities for locations, a practice condemned as a 'highly regressive concealed tax' by Welsh.)[111]

For the purposes of this study, the whole question of liquor supply and control boils down to the exploitative mechanisms involved which influenced decision-making and propaganda either for or against alcohol consumption far more than any moral considerations, though moral considerations proved to be an important ideological weapon in the hands of mine owners.

A Proper Education

Finally, we turn to the issue of education. Here the record of the churches is strongest. The educational efforts of the missions and churches in South Africa are the most potent argument in their favour brought forward by their defenders. Unquestionably much positive work was done, and it is futile in the modern international political economy to speculate on the possible outcome for the indigenous population had the Church schools not existed. In fact, during the time with which we are concerned, at least 1 265 mission schools were providing for some level of black education.[112] Commentators frequently gave credit to the churches for their educational efforts, regarding these as of crucial value notwithstanding other failings of the missionary endeavour. While the work of education undoubtedly enabled many people to cope in a rapidly changing and unfamiliar world, one may legitimately ask how the educational process meshed with developments in the political economy.

As already indicated, the demands of industrialisation, coupled with colonial settler rule over the territories of South Africa, had already created a situation increasingly constraining the colonised Africans to seek their livelihood in wage labour. Moreover the highly exploitative nature of the emerging wage structure is also clear. In this context the Lagden Commission recommendations were suitably rational. Only when these factors are seen together is one able to appreciate the ideological significance of the call from the churches to their black membership, to honour and respect the 'dignity of manual labour'. For many this became a self-understood, natural 'fact' of the Church's educational role. To be sure, a select number of Africans found their way into higher education, but for the great majority manual labour was their destiny, and for this they were prepared. It was for the churches an extension of the 'civilising mission' of the previous century.

Many Africans recognised the place they occupied in this civilising mission and therefore sent their children in considerable numbers to North America for higher education, a factor regarded by religious educational institutions and colonial authorities likewise as undesirable because of the 'notions with which they come back to this country'.[113] This exodus, accompanied as it was by an increasing ability to understand and resist local patterns of education and training, was not to be tolerated: 'The Natives are educating themselves: it is our wisdom to control that education, and see that it is on the right lines,' stressed an Anglican tabloid.[114]

The 'right lines' manifestly did not normally imply an education of the type that white children were offered. On the contrary, the churches had a separate set of schools, usually modelled on the British public schools, for whites. These were consciously geared towards an education for the 'upper' social strata. Even where whites attended schools meant primarily for blacks, the fundamental pattern was different. For example, Lovedale took about 30 to 40 white boarders in the 1890s, but they were certainly not treated equally. 'They filled the front benches in class, ate at the High Table, were not expected to do manual work', whereas 'the Native boys were marshalled, military fashion into work companies . . . detailed to keep the grounds in order'.[117]

Education of blacks for 'their place' in the South African scenario did not involve only the schools. Besides developments in mining, farming and local manufacture, the political economy of South Africa is marked by the extensive use of unskilled black labour in various service industries, among the most significant being domestic work. Jacklyn Cock has traced the pattern of domesticity in *Maids and Madams* and shown the close link of 'the ideology of domesticity' to missionary teaching.[116]

The prevailing attitudes towards the training of blacks for labour thus extended beyond industry and agriculture into the home. In this case women were the most suitable subjects to be trained, in accordance with European gender role ideas, for domestic work. In Johannesburg the 'Native Mission' began suitable programmes, though most domestic workers on the Reef at this stage were 'houseboys'.[117] These could however be better used elsewhere, according to a Mr Hands of the Board of Missions, who recommended to the Board that they should be replaced by 'girls' (about 20 000 needed). One good reason for this was that a 'number of them would in all probability be driven to work on the farms'.[118]

Lovedale Institution was a model for the 'right' kind of education. Here skilled male workers were trained for the labour market. But education for women 'focused on the elaboration of domestic skills' with the two-fold aim of 'preparing Black girls for domestic life in their own homes' and of course for the homes of white employers. The same pattern was followed by St Matthews Training Institution (Anglican) in the Ciskei, and also at Healdtown, Lessington, Peddie, Blythswood, Butterworth and Salem. Education for women was down-graded proportionately, and employment opportunities were obviously thereby seriously limited.[119]

European definitions and appropriate gender roles were imported and applied to black women to produce a particular category of wage-labourers incorporated into the general political economy of colonial privilege. Thus besides wives and daughters of black families legally able to settle in the urban areas, many of whom were absorbed into the domestic market, there was also 'those coming unattached or fleeing from their homes, who became domestic servants, washer women or prostitutes, or took up illicit liquor selling to earn an income'.[120]

One cannot avoid the conclusion that the Church's role in the education of the indigenous population was a double-edged sword: it provided access to a world of global dimensions, but it also ensured that by and large they would fit into the appropriate niche determined by and for the dominating class of settler colonists. Was the Church critically and self-critically aware of this? Such a question may be answered by pointing to a person here, a resolution there. where some critical grasp of the situation is evidenced. But it is more significant to consider the attitudes and actions of the Church precisely in relation to that which they were helping to create — a controlled, adequately trained class of indentured labour. The question then becomes: to what extent was the Church aware of and concerned with its role in what it assisted willy-nilly in creating? By way of summing up the picture to this point, we will attempt to respond to this question.

Summary

In general it may be seen that the Church paid little attention to the most fundamental structures of exploitation and control, usually indicating if anything an uncritical, favourable attitude to contemporary practices.

Contracts are not commented on at all and nowhere could I find direct reference to exploitation wage structures or wage minimisation policies (such as the maximum average and loafer ticket systems on the mines). Recruiting practices are an exception, but even there the criticism tends to land upon the traders and agents rather than the system itself. Migrant labour with all its destructive effects in the South African social formation is mentioned only in the form of a comment on the difficulty of 'Christian work' among the rapidly changing population of the locations, though an advantage was seen in the resultant transmission of the Church's message to 'their distant kraals'.[121] Liquor traffic, frequently of concern, is viewed only as a moral problem, and even then the legal liquor manufacturing syndicates who benefit from it are not analysed as part of the problem, even among those calling for total prohibition.

In general the Church's concern for labour qua labour appears to have been minimal. This viewpoint was powerfully expressed in a letter from LM Sanderson to *The Anglican*: 'The Church is not in touch with the working man,' he declared, 'it does not grasp or understand the working man's aims and ambitions, and his surroundings are beyond the ken of the greater portion of her clergy.' He continued:

> The working man, though presumably able to manage his own affairs fairly satisfactorily, is not allowed to have a vote in Church matters because he is not in a position to contribute largely individually to Church funds . . . (Moreoever) much of the more useful and important work is transacted in synods and other meetings held in the working hours . . . It is not sufficient that the Church should throw open its doors, it must go out into the world, mix with the people, learn of the bitterness and cruelty and oppression and wrongs that exist, . . . extract knowledge of the results of the iniquity and uncharitableness it now preaches so guardedly against, and then it will be in a position, if courageous and fearless, to fight the good fight . . .[122]

The response to this letter came from Bishop Hutton of Kimberley. He resisted strongly the idea that clergy should concern themselves with matters of labour, 'in regard to questions of which they have only a lay opinion'. For him spiritual creation and redemption were the real issues and ordained men should not estrange anyone no matter what convictions they had.[123]

In essence here is the real Church of the time, a community theologically formed by the parent bodies in Britain and Europe who had succumbed to the separation of religion from public life as regards any pervasive ethical (or practical) existence. That is, religion, and Christianity in particular, had already been relegated to the private sphere, committed to the realm of personal convictions, to an internal spiritual life, to a set of moral precepts governing behaviour and attitudes at the micro-level.

Thus despite the public rituals connected with Church-going, the predominant tendency among English-speaking churchmen and women in South Africa was to exorcise the full complexity of public life from the body of Christ. This contrasted markedly with the thrust of Afrikaner Calvinism which was beginning to move in exactly the opposite direction, though with its own exclusive agenda. The marked absence of insightful critique of the dominant powers at work in South Africa, the inability to grasp what Africans who had been conquered, colonised and increasingly coercively governed were feeling or saying — these were the direct consequences of an impoverished theology.

Thus voices critical of the prevailing economic system and its trends were rare. The most highly placed was the Bishop of Lebombo (Mozambique), the only member of the Provincial Board of Missions to react strongly against the resolutions on 'Native Policy' proposed by the Diocese of Mashonaland and supported by Co-Adjutor Bishop Gibson. From a laissez-faire liberal point of view, he wrote that Africans should not be forced by various pieces of legislation and practice into labour for 'by God's law no man is bound to do more than is necessary to keep himself and those dependent on him', and 'no man has the right to throw away his chance of leisure time'.[124]

Church synods, conferences, documents, papers and journals in the first decade reveal minimal understanding of, or immediate concern with, the issues described above, the single exception being the *Christian Express* later to be renamed *South African Outlook*. In short, the initial response to the question with which we began — was the Church crtically and self-critically aware of the political economy within which it had to work? — is in the negative.

Resistance

If the previous analysis of the Church's relationship to the political economy points in the right direction, one should expect to find a negative reaction to any black resistance against the economic and political dominance of the whites.

General

The years leading up to Union had already seen resistance changing its nature in an industrial context. The Bambata (Poll Tax) Rebellion was perhaps the turning point, the last major military campaign of resistance of the old era.[125] In Natal the introduction in 1906 of a £1 per head Poll Tax on Africans, aggravated by the release of 2,6 million acres out of 6,5 million acres of Zulu land for what amounted to white purchase, led to the rebellion. Numerous small incidents connected to refusals to pay the poll tax finally resulted in two white policemen being killed. Martial law was imposed, several people executed in the face of contrary advice from Britain, and at last Chief Bambata took a number of people into open rebellion.

The conflict flared into a large unco-ordinated campaign ending in a massive slaughter of the rebels and the crushing of resistance. Roughly 3 000 Africans were killed, as well as 30 white militia.[126] Natal authorities blamed the unrest on 'Ethiopianism' and criticised missionary education and influence on Africans, especially that of the American Board Mission. But the attack on Mission 'Amakolwa' (Christianised Africans) was strongly refuted by the churches, and the Commissioner of Natives absolved them of general blame. In any case, it seems the 'Amakolwa' were as divided over the rebellion as other tribesmen.[127]

The crushing of the rebellion was inevitable. The prevailing attitude of the churches to the Bambata affair appears to consist, on the one hand, of support for the firm and vigorous suppression of rebellion whether open or covert (to be undertaken with only the necessary amount of force, it was said), and on the other, of an affirmation (in itself revealing) of the 'continued and undoubted loyalty' of Church members to the British throne.[129] The Rev F Mason subsequently proposed that controls over chiefs should be established, in the form of making them stipendiaries of the government and forcing them to act only with the concurrence of European magistrates.[129]

To digress for a moment, another interesting aspect of the Bambata Rebellion is revealed in Sir Godfrey Lagden's papers. Whereas Davenport doubts that the rising could have been co-ordinated in the Johannesburg mine compounds,[130] a private letter from Lagden to Lord Selborne indicates that migrant workers were regularly acting as messengers between Johannesburg and Natal.[131] But whatever the dynamics of resistance, the churches clearly saw only one possible response — loyalty to colonial authorities.

This kind of attitude was well-expressed by the Rev N Robson of the Wesleyan Church, this time in response to riots among 'coloureds' in Cape Town which centred around exploitative and oppressive housing conditions. Though Robson sympathised with their legitimate grievances, he spoke strongly against 'agitators — socialistic, political and religious' who were urging organisation of the aggrieved. He demanded that those aggrieved should nevertheless 'so conduct themselves that both master and mistress would desire above all things to keep them.'[132]

However, if any confirmation of the role of the churches in resistance was needed, it is contained in Lagden's own summary towards the end of the decade of his experience with the churches and their mission:

> . . . of one thing we are quite certain, which I want to emphasise, and that is, that in terms of anxiety, trouble and disturbance, the loyalty of the Native Christians has been proved to the hilt. Therefore, I am convinced that our best safeguard against rebellion and seditious agitation in the danger zones of Africa or India is to be found in the spread of Christianity. As Christianity extends it ensures our government the faithful adherence of a strong section of orderly, well-disposed people.[133]

There is one interesting exception to the rule: the reaction of the Diocese of Pretoria to the white miners' strike of 1907. Though Bishop Carter thought the strike inopportune and foolish, he sought arbitration from the Chief Justice.[134] The Diocesan journal pronounced 'nothing sinful or wrong in the principles of the strike'. In a quite remarkable piece of theology, the editor declared that it was

> . . . not altogether fanciful to describe the exodus of Israel from Egypt as at least a great political deliverance if not the emancipation from tyranny and oppression of a horde of slaves who went out on strike against their masters. Moses would thus aptly be described as a strike-leader appointed by Almighty God to rescue the oppressed, and to place them in surroundings in which they might be able to live a free, healthy life, and be slowly and surely educated for their great future as the chosen nation of God.[135]

Why the first major strike in South Africa should occasion such insight is not easy to determine. The issues involved — white worker resistance to the importation and use of cheap Chinese labour, the encroachment of both African and Chinese into white-controlled skilled labour categories, and the replacement of British immigrant miners by Afrikaners in breaking the strike (which Bishop Carter foresaw)[136] — would suggest a close identification with the British settler labour aristocracy.[137]

It is worth making a comment here on the lack of organisation of black workers at the time. In fact the lack of such organisation probably made it easier to ignore or overlook their concerns. No developed class consciousness was displayed by black workers at this early stage, and groups formed in the compounds were largely concerned 'to protect themselves from the compound police, possibly other groups, and most of all, from the coercive measures of management'.[138]

But there was some early organised industrial action and other strategies of defence and protest. Among the latter, following van Onselen's contention that evidence of worker consciousness must be sought in the nooks and crannies of the day to day situation, we may include desertion (a major problem in the period under review which led to increasingly sophisticated identification and detection systems), as well as absenteeism, theft and sabotage.[139] In respect of industrial action one can trace back to the turn of the century organised strikes and mass desertions at the Consolidated Main Reef, Geldenhuys, Langlaagte and Durban Roodepoort gold mines, as well as at the Vereeniging Coal Mine and the Brakpan Electrical Works, actions not generally confined to any one 'ethnic' group.[140]

Given the times, one would therefore not really expect the churches to be faced with workers' issues in the form of demands or requests from the workers among its black membership. On the other hand, the political position of blacks was not concealed from public awareness, for many voices had cried out.

Quite evidently the solicitude of the churches, grievously limited by their essentially British perspective, vanished in the face of any real threat to the political economy upon which they fed. Herein lies the solution to the apparent contradiction between a church championing the oppressed while expressing deep antipathy towards any immediate resistance on their part.

African Independent Churches

An investigation of the relationship between the mission churches and the African Independent churches should reveal the ambiguity at another level. The incorporation of traditional Christianity into the various and rapidly multiplying independent churches was uneven, ranging from almost nil to a virtually western structure of liturgy and organisation. But one factor united all in the 'compound of the religious, social and political aspirations which the independent movement represented: . . . it is the reply of the Native to the unfriendly, almost hostile attitude of the colonist'.[141]

For this reason, the generalised term 'Ethiopianism' was often applied to the phenomenon of the independent churches (though it has more recently been used by Sundkler technically in contrast to 'Zionism').[142] The original usage showed that black Christians took into account the situation of their oppression. It was exactly this element that so disquieted whites by virtue of its implied threat to their dominance. As Kamphausen points out, the Ethiopian movement understood precisely their oppression 'as the starting point for their questions about the meaning of the gospel'.[143] But this characteristic was found among both the Zionist and Ethiopian groups as defined by Sundkler.

Ethiopianism will therefore be taken to mean a particular movement as defined by Kamphausen, that is, one which was a direct religious response to oppression and conquest. This fits better in any case with the picture found in the church records of the time.

In an address to the General Missionary Conference of 1904, the Rev M Bridgman probably correctly characterised the movement as one motivated by a 'National Spirit', and its adherents as 'anti-white, hostile to the colonists, and. . . very apt in politics'.[144] That this should be so may be understood in terms of the beginnings of industrialisation: 'Africans of many different tribes were meeting one another as labourers on the railways or in the mines . . . The conception of a common church from which the whites would be excluded had a wide appeal.[145] This interpretation is supported by Kamphausen's important study where he comments that perhaps the most important function of the Ethiopian movement in industrial conditions was 'the raising up of black identity and the creation of an inter-tribal church-based communications system'.[146]

The forces producing forms of religiously conceived resistance can already be seen in the early parts of the nineteenth century in the person of the prophet Nxele (or Makana or Makanda) who acted as war doctor in Chief Ndlambi's defeat of the colonist-supported Ngqika in 1818, and in his subsequent attack on Grahamstown. Nxele/Makana's song, explicitly anti-colonist, expressed Xhosa resistance in no uncertain terms:

> To chase the white men from the earth
> and drive them to the sea.
> The sea that cast them up at first
> For AmaXhosa's curse and bane
> Howls for the progeny she nursed
> To swallow them again.[147]

But Makana's purely African millenialism found a counterpart in the Christian-inspired Ntsikana who was councillor to Ngqika. The latter selectively accepted the incoming culture and its religion, produced an indigenous Christian theology and opted for evolutionary change within the dominant system.[148] Both men attempted a religious synthesis, in different ways, of traditional African religion with new elements — a necessary task of 'explaining the presence of these strange people' (the missionaries) and 'suggesting a means of controlling them'.[149] At the same time, certain elements of Christianity appealed to many, for example, the talk of resurrection, which may well have been understood to mean the return of the dead and especially of one's ancestors. But the differences between Nxele and Ntsikana were significant. As Peires describes it:

> They are giants because they transcend specifics to symbolise the opposite poles of
> Xhosa response to Christianity and the West: Nxele representing struggle and
> Ntsikana submission. Nxele died defiant to the end: Ntsikana dug his own grave.
> So exactly does their rivalry foreshadow the struggle for the Xhosa mind that the
> contest between the two would surely be taken for a myth if it were not known to
> be reality.[150]

Within the parameters of these two early options — that of Nxele and that of
Ntsikana — the independent church movement adapted to or resisted colonisation with varying degrees of ambivalnce in relation to the doctrines of the
settler churches. But wherever criticisms of the colonial authority or white
control arose, there too arose a negative reaction from white Christians on the
whole. Thus it is not surprising to find widespread white antagonism to the independent movement around the turn of the century, Ethiopianism frequently
being blamed for political hostility to the settlers even when little evidence of
any leading role on its part was present.[151]

The characteristics of this resistance-in-religious-form were indirectly
manifest in reaction to many independent church groups. JW Houston, in an
article tracing the origins of the Ethiopian churches back to the ex-Wesleyan
Rev Nehemiah Tile (at Qokolweni, 1884) notes that 'as to the political
significance of the movement there was never the slightest doubt'.[152] The black
American influence on some groups must be regarded with particular suspicion, another clergyman pointed out, for here is found 'a political movement
disguised as a religious one' whose aim is 'to teach the native the country
belongs to him and stir him up to assert his right'.[153] Similarly, the Lieutenant-
Governor of the Orange River Colony specifically warned students at the
Thaba'Nchu Native Training Institution against American-influenced independent churches: 'I earnestly implore both you and other natives of this
colony,' he said, 'to think twice before separating yourselves from the churches over which white missions have control.'[154]

The radical missionary Joseph Booth, who helped form an independent
movement under the slogan 'Africa for the African', was probably the target
of another Wesleyan church attack made by the Rev W Smith-Foggit. The latter declared that the movement, influenced as it was by American ideas, would
'undermine the loyalty of the Native' and be able 'to gather up the scattered
threads of disaffection among our Native tribes and bond them into the cable
of rebellion.' It should therefore be made clear to them that these attempts
would 'bring them into conflict with the only Empire which has declared for
the freedom and just treatment of the subject races of the world'.[155]

The repeated references to American influence indicate the strong connections that did in fact exist between American and South African blacks, connections in turn shaped by renewed attempts of blacks in the USA to secure rights often absent.[156] The feeling that such links to concerned foreign groups were somehow subversive thus has a long history in South Africa. This no doubt also accounted for the negative attitudes often displayed by the South African mission churches to American education for blacks at this time.

The one clear case in which settler fears were fully realised was that of the Bambata Rebellion. Though there is no evidence that the independent churches fomented the militant response, it is true that Moses Mbhele of the Inbandhla Li Ka Mosi church, born of the Dutch Reformed Mission, acted as military chaplain to Bambata's forces.[157] Accusations against 'Ethiopianism' also appear to have been made in respect of the Herero Uprising in then German West Africa (Namibia), but again no confirmation was obtained.[158]

Interestingly, some testimony to the positive role of the independent churches among workers, particularly in respect of providing meaningful material benefits within a highly exploitative industrial environment, is available, and a clear connection between church affiliation and class may be detected.[159] But the major concern of critics remained the potential threat implicit within the movement, and only when independent groups could unquestioningly be ascertained as being non-political, or when they came within the orbit of a settler church's control, did the criticism abate. Perhaps the only place where the Ethiopian movement was reasonably responded to was in the pages of the *Christian Express*. Once again it showed its exceptional position in contrast to the churches at large.

In conclusion, despite the threat to missionary work, a common consensus among the missions was that 'Thiopianism (sic) needs careful guidance — not repression'.[160] (Pre-eminent among groups regarded as worth guiding was the Order of Ethiopia, officially attached to and supported by the CPSA.)[161] On the other hand, only in the latter part of the 1920s did fears of the movement finally subside.[162] Even then, American-oriented movements such as that of 'Dr Wellington' Buthelezi, heavily influenced by Marcus Garvey, were strongly opposed by churchmen without much consideration for the grievances being articulated.[163]

Though not conclusive, the summary impression remains strong that the churches displayed in their response to the independent movement those same ambiguous, contradictory characteristics and ideologically limited tolerances which we have observed in other respects. Their worries subsided only once the Ethiopian movement itself crumbled in the face of their political failure, that is, their inability to successfully confront white dominance in all spheres of black life. The religious sphere they could hold onto but, in their powerlessness, only by restricting their own domain, and thus in effect betraying their own origins. This the mission churches appear to have tolerated much more easily. Into the bargain they did not really see any reason thereafter to take much interest in the large and growing number of African Christians who found their home in the independent church family.

Notes

1 Rev H Calderwood, *Caffres and Caffre Missions,* p137.
2 Twenty-four societies were present, including all the major denominations except the Roman Catholics. See GMCSA, 1904—1932, Summary p5. See table 16, Appendix C.
3 'Select Committee on the Labour Question, 1890', p51, cited in F Wilson, 'Farming', in OX: p125.
4 L Thompson, 'Compromise of Union', OX: p331.
5 GB Pyrah (1955), p83.
6 C Bundy (1979), pp29—32 *passim*. The move into wage labour was not always a matter of coercion, as is apparent in the significant number of people who were under no pressure to enter the labour market, but who did so to supplement income and thereby exploit new opportunities they saw for themselves. Despite this, coercion remains a highly prominent feature of the South African labour market in the last hundred years or so.
7 CW de Kiewiet (1937), p159.
8 J Stone (1973), p113. See also CW de Kiewiet (1937), p59.
9 S Marks and S Trapido, 'Lord Milner and the South African State', in P Bonner (1981), p59.
10 J Gallagher and R Robinson (1968), pp434 & 432 respectively.
11 L Thompson, 'Great Britain and the Afrikaner Republics', in OX: p231.
12 C Headlam (ed), *The Milner Papers (SA) 1897—1899,* vol II, p35 (Cassell & Co, London, 1933); the emphases are Milner's.
13 TRH Davenport (1977), p160.
14 *Ibid,* p152.
15 TRH Davenport (1977), p152, describes the broad results of the Commission; see also p332.
16 Cited in D Welsh, 'English-speaking Whites and the Racial Problem', in A de Villiers (1976), p226.
17 See F Cooper (1981), pp300—5.
18 B Bozzoli (1973/4), p60.
19 Sir Godfrey Lagden Papers, May 1905, p765, CPSA Archives.
20 H Houghton (1967), p15.
21 L Thompson, 'Compromise on Union', in OX: p347.
22 TRH Davenport (1977), p176.
23 E Roux (1964), p59.
24 L Thompson, in OX: p355.
25 Parliamentary Debates, 5th Series, Commons, ix column 1010, 1909: cited in L Thompson, *op cit,* pp357—8.
26 AB Webb, 'Colonial Church Expansion', Pamphlet, 1894/5.
27 AGS Gibson, October 24, 1897, Cape Town.

28 Sir G Lagden, Papers, 25 July 1907, para 272, p52. The terms of the Commission were stated at the Inter-colonial Conference, Bloemfontein, 1903; see 'The 19th Century', May 1905, Sir G Lagden Papers.

29 SAMSR, (23rd), 1904, p21.

30 CE, March 1, 1905, pp33—4.

31 Bishop WT Gaul, 'Charge to Diocesan Synod', Mashonaland, July 1906.

32 March 1905, Diocese of Pretoria.

33 *Cape Times Weekly Edition,* November 1, 1905.

34 CE, July 1, 1906, pp153—4.

35 Provincial Board of Missions, 'Native Policy Proposals', Ts 1903.

36 'The 19th Century', p765, May 1905; Sir G Lagden Papers.

37 TMC, June 13, 1906.

38 GMCSA: Summary, p22; on Schreiner, see GB Pyrah (1955), p117.

39 Bishop WT Gaul, Papers, 1908.

40 TMC, April 6, 1909.

41 TCC, March 31 & May 13, 1909. See also L Thompson, 'The Compromise of Union', in OX: p356.

42 Archbishop W Carter, ALS, August 11, 1909.

43 TCC, February 17, 1909.

44 'Minutes of Conference', 1909, pp149 & 152.

45 *Ibid,* 1910, pp158 & 163.

46 Bishop's Charge, 1909.

47 Bishop JW Williams, Diocese of St John's, April 10.

48 *Eastern Province Herald,* June 1, 1910.

49 CE, April 1, 1909, p68.

50 Provincial Board of Missions, Ts, 1903, emphasis in original; the Diocesan resolutions refer to Synod August 21, 1902.

51 M Ashley, 'The British Influence on Education in South Africa', in A de Villiers (1976), p256.

52 TMC, March 1, 1905.

53 *Cape Times Weekly Edition,* November, 1905.

54 GMCSA: Summary, p14.

55 *Ibid,* p40.

56 F Johnstone (1976), pp2, 48 & 17.

57 F Wilson, 'An Assessment of the English-speaking South African's Contribution to the Economy', in A de Villiers (1976), p163.

58 F Johnstone (1976), p16.

59 D Welsh, 'The Growth of Towns', in OX: p182.

60 Report of the Transvaal Labour Commission, 1894 (London, 1904), para 70, cited in D Welsh, *op cit,* p177.

61 F Johnstone (1976), pp27—8.

62 AH Jeeves, 'The Administration and Control of Migratory Labour on the South African Gold Mines', in P Bonner (1979), p135ff.

63 F Johnstone (1976), p30.

64 See E Katz (1976).

65 H Houghton (1967), p85.

66 F Wilson (1972), pp74 & 135.

67 G Findlay, review of A Hoernlé's 'South African Native Policy and the Liberal Spirit', 1940, cited in C Bundy (1979), p242.

68 C Bundy, *loc cit.*
69 W Beinart (1982), p60ff.
70 JH du Plessis (1911), p404.
71 D Welsh (1971), p23.
72 Cited in F Johnstone (1976), p36.
73 F Johnstone (1976), p37. D Welsh, 'The Growth of Towns', in OX: pp196—202, supplies good detail on the history of labour by identity legislation.
74 P Bonner (1980), p13.
75 CE, November 1, 1907, pp167—8.
76 *Ibid,* October 1, 1906, p212.
77 TCC, February 3, 1909.
78 CE, August 2, 1909, p127.
79 'At the Gold Mines', CPSA Pamphlet, December 1910.
80 CE, September 1, 1906, pp190 & 192.
81 Diocese of Pretoria, Board of Missions, Minutes, 1909, 'Native Education' & 'The Native as a Skilled Workman'.
82 CE, August 2, 1909, p127.
83 TCC, April 28, 1909.
84 P Bonner (1980), p16.
85 TRH Davenport (1977), p355.
86 P Pearson (197?), p9—11.
87 R Davies (1979), p57.
88 D Welsh, 'The Growth of Towns', in OX: p180.
89 P Pearson (197?), pp3—5, 14—16.
90 F Wilson (1972), p7.
91 F Johnstone (1976), p38.
92 JH du Plessis (1911), p398.
93 GCSA: Summary, p11.
94 SAMSR, (26th), 1907, p21.
95 CE, August 1, 1906, pp175—7.
96 H Bloom (1982, originally publ 1956), p10.
97 The Methodist Church Committee of Privileges sought to investigate the effect of the Lagden Proposals on the rights and privileges of Africans, but nothing much ensued; see Minutes of Conference, 1905, p90.
98 Rev F Mason, 'Native Policy in Natal', 1906, pp30—2.
99 Co-Adjutor Bishop Gibson, Cape Town, citred in P Hincliff (1963), p195.
100 F Johnstone (1976), pp40—1.
101 *Ibid,* p192.
102 E Webster (1978), p12.
103 CW de Kiewiet (1937), p2.
104 F Wilson (1972), p35.
105 C Bundy (1979), p115.
106 C van Onselen (1974/5): the following narrative is a summary of his essay frpm p53—90.
107 See Johannesburg Evangelical Church Council statement on Native Policy, and the Lagden Commission, TMC, June 13, 1906.
108 CE, August 2, 1909, commenting on the Blue Book of Native Affairs, 1908.
109 Bishop WM Carter, Pretoria, ALS, August 2, 1907.
110 C van Onselen (1974/5), p89.

111 D Welsh, 'The Growth of Towns', in OX: p233.

112 GBA Gerdener (1958), p242.

113 TMC, March 1, 1905.

114 'The Kingdom', Diocese of Pretoria, June 1906.

115 P Randall (1982), p60.

116 J Cock (1980), especially pp197—228.

117 'The Kingdom', Diocese of Pretoria, August 1908.

118 Diocese of Pretoria, Board of Missions, Minutes, 1909.

119 J Cock, 'Domesticity amd Domestication', *African Perspective*, no13, Spring 1979, pp17—21.

120 P Bonner (1980), p9.

121 SAMSR (23rd), 1904, p28.

122 'The Anglican', Pretoria Diocese, February 1904.

123 *Ibid,* March 1904.

124 Provincial Board of Missions, Ts, 1903.

125 See S Marks, *The Reluctant Rebellion,* (Clarendon Press, Oxford, 1970).

126 See E Roux (1964), pp87—100.

127 D Welsh (1971), pp309—311.

128 Wesleyan Methodist Church, Minutes of Conference, 1906, p121; see also SAMSR (25th), 1906, p7.

129 Rev F Mason, 'Native Policy in Natal', Pamphlet, 1906.

130 TRH Davenport (1977), pp152—3.

131 Sir G Lagden, Papers, ALS, March 1, 1906.

132 TMC, August 21, 1906.

133 'The Mission Field', December 1909, p364.

134 Bishop W Carter, ALS, 1907, May 26 & June 2.

135 'The Kingdom', June 1907.

136 Bishop W Carter, ALS, 1907, June 10.

137 E Katz (1976), p77.

138 S Moroney, in E Webster (1978), p40.

139 *Ibid,* p37 also P Pearson (197?), p17.

140 P Warwick, in E Webster (1978), p20.

141 Rev FB Bridgman, American Board Mission, 1903, cited in D Welsh (1971), p254.

142 B Sundkler (1961), p38ff & p47ff.

143 E Kamphausen (1976), p22 (German original, my translation).

144 Rev F Bridgman, GMCSA: Summary, pp20—1.

145 E Roux (1964), p78.

146 E Kamphausen (1976), p485.

147 E Roux (1964), pp13—14.

148 J Hodgson, 'Ntsikana's Great Hymn: an African Expression of Christianity, 1815—1821', monograph, University of Cape Town, 1980, p2. See also discussion on Nxele and Ntsikana in JB Peires (1981), pp69—74.

149 JB Peires (1981), p68. E Kamphausen (1976), pp53—4, also notes that 'in accepting Christianity, the colonised peoples sought to usurp the secret of the whites in order thereby to possess the instruments which guaranteed the superior power and mastery of the whites. The absorption of the religion of the whites nevertheless also led to a break with their own traditions . . .' (German original, my translation.)

150 JB Peires (1981), p74.

151 L Kuper, 'African Nationalism', in OX: pp442 & 436.

152 TMC, July 24, 1906.

153 *Ibid,* September 26, 1905.

154 Sir G Lagden, Papers, May 1905.

155 TMC, October 16, 1906.

156 On USA influences on the Ethiopian Movement, see E Kamphausen (1976), pp17 & 367ff, as well as his treatment throughout of specific groupings. The strongest links were probably with the American Methodist Episcopal Church — the AME.

157 GMCSA: Summary, p33.

158 TMC, March 20, 1906.

159 S Moroney, 'Mine Worker Interest on the Witwatersrand, 1901—1912', in E Webster (1978), p42 and M Wilson, 'Growth of Peasant Communities', in OX: p82.

160 GMCSA: Summary, p11 & pp20—21.

161 Discussion on the Order of Ethiopia in its origins and development can be found in *Pan-Anglican Papers,* Rt Rev WM Cameron, Pan-Anglican Congress, 1908; also C Lewis and GE Edwards, *Historical Records of the PCSA,* 1934, pp217—226; and B Sundkler (1961), p41. A detailed and more recent analysis of the Order and its growth is to be found in E Kamphausen (1976), Chapter IV.

162 See 'Forward', November 1, 1925; also of July 1927, p16; and TMC, June 20, 1927.

163 See B Edgar (1974/5), pp100—9.

CHAPTER FOUR

Land and Labour: 1911—1919

Who are those hooded hordes swarming
Over endless plains, stumbling in cracked earth
Ringed by the flat horizon only
What is the city over the mountains
Cracks and reforms and bursts in the violet air
Falling towers

. . .

In this decayed hole among the mountains
In the faint moonlight, the grass is singing

TS Eliot, *The Waste Land*

The decade marked by the First World War and the psychological destruction of the dream of inevitable human progress also unleashed forces that would change the face of the earth. One discerns on the one hand a widespread upsurge in an instrumentalist view of technology; on the other, the first successful socialist revolution. These two things symbolised, respectively, the powerful hand of a rapidly adapting entrepreneurship, and the marching feet of a determined body of labouring people. Both sets of changes affected the colonies, in the first instance via the nature of their political and economic developments and in the second via the character of resistance. Nevertheless in South Africa global currents were constrained by local conditions. The continued working out of earlier trends is the primary trait of the post-Union period, punctuated only by the abnormal years of World War One.

Among the most relevant political developments were the Mines and Works Act of 1911, which formalised the job colour bar in mining and prohibited strikes by African contract workers; the establishment of the Land Bank (1912) designed to aid settler agriculture, though not African; the hated 1913 Land Act, a culmination of territorial separation and a death knoll to stable and extensive African farming: and the end of recruiting competition between the mines with the establishment of the Native Recruiting Corporation in 1912 following on the Native Labour Regulation Act of 1911. World War One may have dominated the public mind for the latter half of this period, but land and labour issues define most clearly the primary poles upon which policy and practice turned.

On Field and Farm

The unique structure of labour supply and control developed by the gold mines was not a phenomenon isolated from other aspects of the political economy. The black mine-worker did not arrive as a gift of the gods but primarily as a result of colonial penetration and economic dispossession which forced him to seek wage labour. Yet the mines were not the only bidders for such labour. Farmers too demanded their share, often in bitter competition with industrialists.

One positive result of the Anglo-Boer War for the 'Boers' ('farmers') was the willingness of the British to make concessions to the agricultural sector. This factor, together with the assumption of power by Louis Botha, and later by Smuts and Hertzog, while nicely fitting in with dominion policy, enabled farmers to gain a significant measure of political power as manifested in favourable labour and protection policies. In fact, the necessary mechanisms were already in operation by the end of the nineteenth century, encapsulated most clearly in various pass laws, the Glen Grey Act, and labour tenancy practices.

Bundy has demonstrated the original highly rational deployment of prevailing techniques of the indigenous farmers in a relatively inclement climate and soil. This took the form of shifting cultivation finely adapted to the limits of water, weather, disease, transport and available technology. With colonisation came new technologies and new ends in farming: diversification of crops, raising crops for sale rather than for the consumption of the producer, the ox-drawn plough, and the transport wagon. All made an impact at least equal to legislation such as individual tenure.[1] In this situation, taxation, land-pressures, water shortages, climatic setbacks and the demand for wage-labour squeezed African homesteads, though some were able to utilise the situation to their benefit as long as they could remain relatively independent.

The many Africans who managed to make a reasonable living as peasants were in turn faced with new constraints, among them the contractually unfavourable exchange with traders. Bundy notes that

> . . . in exchanges between peasant and trader, the terms of trade were against the contractually inferior peasant producer-consumer. In the trader's hands were concentrated the several economic functions of purchaser of agricultural produce, purveyor of manufactured goods, and supplier of credit. The trader's control of these functions meant that agricultural surpluses tended to be absorbed in the form of his profits rather than made available for re-investment by the peasantry. Trader and peasant enacted in microcosm the adverse terms of trade of a colonial relationship.[2]

Bundy further locates several specific features central to the assault upon peasant farmers by capital during the period 1890—1913, including the commercialisation of agriculture and a changed demand for African labour. Though some peasants were able to consolidate and others to achieve first successes, still more bowed down under the weight of low market prices, transport costs, debt, recruiting practices, legislation, demography and adverse natural causes.[3] Most Africans were rapidly separated from the means of production, though a small but relatively stable peasantry has remained. By 1914 the underdevelopment of many reserve areas was severe, and proletarianisation of Africans had become the order of the day. On the other hand those peasants who succeeded frequently proved more effective farmers than European settlers with whom they competed.

Meanwhile the mineral discoveries not only shifted the centre of gravity of the South African economy but also isolated the reserve areas whose access to markets, already relatively disadvantaged geographically, was made more difficult by the routes that railway lines took. Colonist farmers were by and large the beneficiaries.[4]

In 1894 the Glen Grey Act, often favourably commented on by many churchmen, added a legislative cross. Based on segregationist principles, the Act laid the foundation for much subsequent 'Native Policy', establishing the Bunga system of local governing councils in the reserves, enforcing labour taxation, and institutionalising individual tenure on a quit-rent basis. The Glen Grey territory was to be split up into locations, in turn divided into lots 'indivisible and inalienable without the consent of the Governor'; and the franchise was not given.[5] The express aim of the Act, a system of land administration and magisterial control, was to produce a landless class available as a labour reserve or forced to enter the wage labour market. Taxation added to the pressure.

These elements presage the later mass resettlement of African in the reserves as a cheap labour pool. The resultant decline of the African rural economies is widely attested: they ceased to export grain or even grow sufficient to feed themselves, and the value per capita of sales of peasant produce and purchases of traders' goods in some areas decreased well below half what they had been.[6] Wage labour, often at remarkably low levels of pay, became the norm for the great majority. Thus land expropriation and control measures were effectively also labour laws ratifying conquests, displacing traditional societies, and creating an exploitable proletariat.

At the same time the conditions of conflict within traditional societies meshed with the varying and sometimes contradictory interests of settlers and colonists in such a way as to encourage the directions in 'Native Policy' laid down by the Lagden Commission. The Commission recognised the collaborative role 'traditional' African political systems, suitably modified, might play in the demarcated areas. For many traditional African leaders in the rural areas, one might say such a role at least guaranteed their survival within limits.[7] Dues from migrants also returned something to the rural economy.

All in all, from the viewpoint of the dominant whites, the emerging political solutions thus offered many advantages, at least for the foreseeable future. The emerging social structure met needs of ideology and prejudice, it enabled better supply and control of labour at low cost, it kept the rural reserves in reasonable order and it 'solved' some of the pressing political questions about the future place and role of Africans. In short, the Lagden Commission proposals 'took a lengthy and portentious step towards the selective preservation of traditional (African) institutions and structures and their manipulation instead of their abolition'.[8]

The Commission recommended policies not much different from those already foreshadowed in the Glen Grey Act. It indicated into the bargain that the establishment of African reserves should not deny the Crown the rights to all minerals and precious stones, the right to removal and re-entry in the case of rebellion, and the power to apply regulations.[9] Thus by the second decade of this century the structures of land use and control more or less fitted these parameters. Accepting this as given, the General Missionary Conference of 1912 resolved that the deteriorating conditions of the reserves and their inhabitants demanded strong efforts to improve methods of cultivation and distribution of products, including 'the spread of Native Farmers' Associations, and the training and the employment of agricultural demonstrators in Native areas.'[10]

Stratification among Africans was also increased by the new legislative controls, to the extent that some Africans who had the means of purchasing what land was available, began to regard their fellows in terms borrowed from the colonisers: blacks generally are 'a class of people who are still lost in heathenism and darkness', said the Rev Mr Mpele and six other more advantaged Africans to the Lagden Commission, this in contrast to themselves who 'represent what we call the enlightened people . . . governed by the Church laws'.[11]

As more and more Africans went to work for wages in the towns and cities, another worry began: the danger of a large, organised proletariat. As early as 1907, commenting negatively on the powerful, direct pressure brought to bear in the rural areas to drive them into seeking wage labour, the *Christian Express* pointed out the serious danger of the blacks in the towns becoming numerically too many to control. What was needed, in its view, was effective administration of the Location Act, better agricultural education and, on the part of the farmers, 'a little interest in the moral and intellectual welfare of their tenants'.

Earlier the same journal had published a letter from a African correspondent protesting against the restricted access to land resulting from such things as private ownership of land, quit-rent tenancy — called *boroko*, meaning 'a place to sleep' — locations, and appointed Crown lands.

In contrast, the *Christian Express* defended point by point the 'brilliant product of the genius of the late Mr Rhodes', the Glen Grey Act which so clearly helped create mechanisms of land control unfavourable to blacks as a whole.[12] Thus even the journal most favourable towards, and insightful about, black opinion, finally failed to free itself from the view of the dominant.

It is not surprising therefore that despite the substantial alterations to the economy of the agricultural areas and resultant impact on African life — much of it rather negative — the years up until 1912 show little evidence of any critical analysis by the Church of the structures of expropriation and exploitation on the land. The 1913 Land Act was to change this somewhat.

The Land Act was a sweeping measure designed to demarcate the 'Native Reserves', and to reduce rent-paying squatters and share-croppers 'to the level of labour tenants'.[13] The partnership principle in the system of farming-on-the-half was intended to be done away with, further eroding the basis of black wealth and correspondingly increasing poverty.[14] Many Africans regarded this 'most iniquitous measure' as 'simply and solely in the interests of the farmers and miners', and one which would affect hundreds of thousands of people adversely, driving the majority into wage-labour in the mines or on the farms under severe disadvantages.[15] By banning African purchase of land outside the reserves, the Act also 'prevented the most obvious form of accumulation open to successful black peasants'. It also set out to 'freeze social relations in the Reserves', both to avoid the situation where subsistence agriculture would no longer help reproduce migrant labour at no cost to capitalists, and to reduce the possibility of a threatening mass urban influx of unemployed wage-seekers.[16]

Some Africans, most frequently chiefs and headmen, used their connection to the colonial administrative and magisterial system to guarantee their holdings and position, thereby often increasing the gap between them and commoners. The Land Act had something for them in fixing their rights within the reserve areas. Thus, Cingo, advisor to the Pondo chief, Marelane, attacked the newly formed South African Native National Congress position against the Act in a series of letters, mainly because very few Pondos had land outside the reserve and what they had could thereafter not be bought up by colonists.[17]

The total effect of the Land Act and its precedents manifests itself most clearly in the vast and depressing body of evidence as to the nature and extent of underdevelopment in the reserves in the next forty years;[18] in the debilitating results of cheap migratory labour practices; and in the structures of exploitation and neo-colonial domination reproduced in the euphemistically termed 'homelands'. Yet ninety-nine per cent of the House of Parliament accepted the Bill, 'even friends of the natives' who were often influential opinion-makers among leading churchmen and women. Many held the view that the extension and protection of separate African areas would allow them to develop without excessive interference, a view which coincided with Cingo's, among others. Also among those who found the Bill acceptable was an increasingly discredited Tengo Jabavu and his South African Races Congress, an opposition organisation to the newly founded South African Native National Congress (SANNC).[19]

Prior to the official enactment of the Land Act, missionary societies called for a commission of enquiry into the proposed legislation, while pointing out that black opinion was not uniform.[20] Both the *Christian Express* and Tengo Jabavu had expressed qualified approval, the former being taken to task in its own pages by the Rev Amos Burnett and Sol Plaatje (who called the Act 'a carefully prepared, deliberate and premeditated scheme to compass the partial enslavement of the native').[21] The *Methodist Churchman* took Jabavu to task for his 'mistaken view' though it also admitted in a revealing comment that 'our missionaries; and those whom we regard as Native experts have, for the most part, been silent'. The *Churchman* carried an address by Dube, then president of the SANNC, in which he launched a powerful attack on the complicity of the Church:

> And yet you tell us that with you might is not right, that your rule of life is to live and let live; to do unto others as you would be done by; that you are children of Christ and heirs to His Kingdom, guided solely by the eternal principles of blind justice, regardless of colour and creed. What contemptible cant! What a BLASPHEMOUS FRAUD![22]

The South African Missionary Society (Wesleyan) acknowledged that the Church had suffered as a result of the Act,[23] while the Anglican Provincial Missionary Conference, responding to a call by the Rev H Mtobi to 'condemn the Act as a piece of class legislation', even directed an appropriate and lengthy resolution to the government.[24]

Confusion and ambiguity, however, continued to mark the response of various church bodies and publications. The Methodists proved most consistent in their opposition to the Act, perhaps reflecting their strong rural base in the reserves.[25] But even then the official Methodist newspaper regarded as extremely important the response of Prime Minister Louis Botha to an SANNC delegation led by Dube and Rubisana. Referring to Botha's affirmation of the principle of territorial separation, and his promise of a better deal for blacks later, the delegation felt that Botha 'gave them sound advice, and was certainly not harsh, or even unsympathetic'.[26] The Anglican paper, commenting on the approval of the principle of the Act by 'many of those who are most deeply interested in the natives and their uplifting,' went even further: 'We are encouraged to believe,' it avowed, 'that we are on the track of a right solution of the Native Problem'.[27] Later, the London-based *Church Missionary Society's Review* generally agreed with this, though it thought a better solution would be to offer Africans ownership or leaseholds 'in those parts of Africa where the white man cannot settle and rear children'.[28] Part of the equivocation of the churches lay in the fact that some chiefs and headmen, as indicated, supported the Act, preferring the demarcation of some areas as reserves to the possible loss of all land. In this respect, merely listening to the supposed African voice was clearly unhelpful in assessing the changes to be introduced. One needed some analytical insight too.

Interestingly, the *Christian Express* changed its favourable attitude quickly once the Act's provision began to bite. Two years after the Act, in an article discussing a controversy between Africans and white farmers over plans to allocate a piece of land to the former at Stutterheim, it analysed the issue in a remarkably contemporary manner as a 'manifestation of the world-wide struggle between the conflicting interests of the rich and the poor, the haves and have-nots', adding the insight that the whole conflict was embittered rather than caused by racial feeling.[29] Similarly this journal carried a later article on the deleterious effect of the Land Act (and supplementary legislation) on the reserves. It also speculated on the colonial form of class division, and projected a rather intriguing view of the future hierarchy of wealth and privilege:

> Looking ahead we foresee South Africa peopled thus:
>   I A few wealthy farmers and employers of large bodies of cheap Native Labour (. . . British and Dutch), large merchants and professional men.
> II A body of mixed European aliens living only as they can do.
> III A large mass of most miserable Coloureds sinking steadily to the level of the Natives.
> IV A much larger mass of Natives . . .
> . . . This is the inevitable consequence of unlimited cheap Native Labour.[30]

The actual situation among Africans on many farms and in parts of the reserves at the time of the Act is most poignantly captured in the story of the farm labourer who asked a missionary if becoming a Christian would secure him larger rations from the farmer. This 'strange request' emerged from a conflict of values: 'Missionary,' said the man, 'the words of Christ teach us not to steal. If I become a Christian I would stop stealing. But if I did not steal my family would starve.'[31] His point was clear. Poverty meant that stealing was necessary to continued survival under the prevailing economic conditions and coercive legislation. Such realities were intensified by the Land Act.

Generally speaking, the Land Act produced the second major conflict between the churches and the state, though protests never amounted to more than requests for reconsideration or delay in the implementation of the Act. After an initial flirtation with the Act, the *Christian Express* again proved to be the most penetrating in its critique. However, no concerted policy or action emerged from the churches. In any event, opposition to the Act on the part of the churches appears to have been focused more on its intentions to exclude blacks from reasonable access to land and agricultural facilities (where they could afford them) and less on the overall place of the legislation in the national system of exploitation and control. In this respect, earlier tendencies to limit any support for black aspirations continue. A proper investigation of this point requires us to turn our attention to what one may term the other end of the labour supply chain — workers in industry.

Church and Proletarians

One often supposes that the interests of workers and the churches are largely incongruous, perhaps even incompatible. They are concerned with different 'aspects' of human life some might say: others more Platonically believe them to be on different 'levels' (the material and spiritual). Of course, many Christians are workers, and vice versa, so here the assumed duality may be reflected in one individual. But whether or not churches and workers' organisations have had much interaction (in South Africa there has been remarkably little), comments about workers have certainly not been missing from ecclesiastical discourse. It is these we wish to situate here within the years under question.

Intensifying Conflict

As in other fields, after the South African War the rapid acceptance of segregationist policies as the legislative base for the new industrial era made itself evident in the field of labour relations. In 1904 the Transvaal Ordinance 17 established control of the access by 'unskilled non-European labourers' to the lucrative Witwatersrand, and also reserved skilled and semi-skilled jobs for colonials.[32] Though the massive wage gap between Africans and colonials was threatened at this time by labour shortages (which tended to drive the price of labour up beyond levels acceptable to the mining industry), this led not to a re-evaluation of the viability of the mines, but to an extension of exploitation through the importation of Chinese labour, from 1904 to 1907.[33]

Many Africans gained some degree of semi-skilled experience as they work-ed, and were available for upgrading at much lower levels of pay than colonial (white) workers could accept. This resulted in strong white labour resistance. It was the award of the Blasting Certificate rather than the increasingly blurred distinction between unskilled, semi-skilled and skilled mine work that struc-tured the labour pattern on the mines. Eligibility for the Certificate was jealously guarded by the 'skilled' white miners from whom Africans were learning by observation and practice. This protected the former's senior posi-tion. As a result what had existed as a co-incidental racial bias hardened into an ideology of prejudice which found expression in the white supremacy plat-form of the South African Labour Party established in 1909.[34]

Here one recognises the simultaneous structural privilege and insecurity of skilled white workers. Of necessity, they were drawn from Europe and other European-settler areas by attractive offers. Because the scarcity of skilled labour gave them considerable economic and political power they were not 'ultra-exploitable'. They were also politically free to organise — in the sense of 'not being subject to the system of forced labour, of being free from extra-economic restrictions of mobility in the labour market'. This freedom they used to control through craft-unions the distribution of skills, and to form political parties capable of fighting effectively for the exclusion of those who threatened their privileges the most: the ultra-exploitable, colonised (black) work-seekers.[35] Thus Riley, the President of the WLTC, could say in 1907 that 'it is a case of who can survive best under the present conditions . . . I think the whole question lies under the heading of self-preservation'. He therefore advocated that 'certain territories are set apart for the natives of this country; and with repsect to the Indian coolie and the Chinese I would absolutely ex-clude them altogether'.[36]

The elite position of white labour on the gold mines had a precedent at Kimberley in 1891. Here the 'Knights of Labour' were formed, pledged to a 'war on two fronts'. These white workers set out to 'champion the labouring classes everywhere against monopoly capital and the insidious attack of cheap labour competition'. Clearly for them the labouring classes did not include blacks.[34]

But it was during the first decade of the new century that the specific struc-ture of the industrial labour force was formalised and colour bars 'became vital subjects for debate and legislative action'. The outcome was that 'the in-dentured labour system, racial prejudice and the restricted franchise assured that organised white labour moved away from, rather than towards working class solidarity.'[38] The first major sign of this process came when 4 000 white mine-workers struck in 1907 against a proposal by mine-owners to permit African and Chinese workers to perform more skilled work at much lower wages.[39]

The crucial point for the purposes of this study concerns the structural basis in the political economy for the division of the forces of labour and the growth of an attendant racist ideology. At the core were massive wage differentials — best described for colonised Africans as a system of exploitative (wage) colour bars. This term is distinguished from job colour bars by Johnstone. It indicates the ultra-low wage structure applied to African mine-workers, a structure arising out of the mine-owners' need to keep wages as low as possible in order to make sufficiently profitable the extraction of low-grade gold ore from deep-lying reefs. The job colour bars on the other hand protected white workers, whose wages were relatively higher, from black competition. The higher unit cost of white labour was accepted by the mines as the price of the division of labour and bacause the total cost could be borne given the much smaller white working force. Moreover, the organising experience and political clout of white workers could not entirely be discounted.

In these first years of the twentieth century, the job colour bar received very little attention from Church circles. This was a far cry from the prominence it was to attain somewhat later when the more articulate, usually church educated and more advantaged blacks cried out against restrictions on their economic and political mobility. However, the more fundamental controls remained intact, becoming something of a permanent way of life for the majority. Among these controls were the mechanisms incorporated in the compounds, in contracts and passes, in taxation and recruiting practices, in wage minimisation policies and, at the root, in the exploitative wage structures applied to the colonised.

The implication of these practices was clearly seen even as they emerged. A prescient statement, contained in a letter to Joseph Chamberlain from the executive of the South African Native Congress, made it quite clear. South Africa's labour troubles, just commencing (the executive noted), were not simply a question of race despite the high feeling on this issue. They were a consequence of 'the attempts to reconcile low wages with high living', a situation which 'will continue to agitate the country long after the present generation has departed'.[41]

Developments in labour creation and capital accumulation such as those described were accompanied by attempts on the part of workers to organise themselves. The association of skilled workers which was the British 'craft-union' became the early model for worker organisation in South Africa. But not surprisingly, this was confined almost exclusively to whites. Houghton points out that:

The craft-union pattern fitted naturally into the South African setting, and its objectives of furthering the interests of skilled workers soon became associated with a policy of preventing the position of the white workers from being undermined by the use of black or coloured workers in any but unskilled jobs. British trade unionism of the 1880s thus reinforced South African convention in these matters.[42]

Australian unionists out of the same tradition further influenced the issue. In particular 'the resentment of artisans towards those Africans who performed skilled tasks . . . stemmed from the fact that Africans who came to the towns, particularly the country towns, were often employed at half the rates paid to white skilled artisans'.[43]

White mine workers, increasingly conditioned to regard themselves as superior (an 'aristocracy of colour'), were vulnerable to racist ideology because of their unique position in relation to the wage-structure. While their bargaining position was undermined as others acquired some skills, they were nevertheless profitably employable for their skills because of the cheapness of, and heavy reliance upon, unskilled labour. Moreover they had a skills advantage gained in the initial process of colonial industrialisation. This they now strongly defended.[44] The competition between national and foreign capital also intruded, the former finding some political base in Hertzog's National Party (established in 1913) which was able to appeal to workers with some success for support against the mine-owners.[45]

But other factors also contributed to the growing distinction between the white and black working class, among them that the white worker had access to political power, relatively easy entrance into the bourgeoisie (especially for the artisan), supervisory control in the case of miners over Africans contracted to work with them, an 'open' work situation (no compounds, contracts or passes as with Africans), and a stable living environment (migrant labour, besides affecting Africans individually, also prevented them effectively mobilising as a class). On the other hand, for many Africans the evolution of the job colour bar, increased resistance to their economic demands, the division of the labour struggle, and the reinforcement of a racist hierarchical structure in the social division of labour meant an intensification of their exploitation.[46]

In fact until 1918 African workers, in Roux's startling image, were largely 'but spectators whose fate was being decided, incidentally, by the battles they witnessed'; more like 'cattle in a wild west film which to be sure are stolen and recovered at intervals as the drama proceeds, but which, nevertheless, are merely incidental background from the point of view of the story'.[47] Though present research is likely to alter this view of a passive black labour force prior to 1918, major strike actions reflected the struggle of the white, relatively privileged labour aristocracy. Thus the South African Labour Party established by Creswell and others in 1909 was avowedly colonist. It took public responsibility for white workers, but did not include blacks. It was led by people who were neither workers nor socialists. Thus, in complete contradiction to its name, it officially incorporated segregationist policies into its 1912 constitution, and later called for the repatriation of Indian workers.[48]

In the realm of legislation, the 1909 Transvaal Industrial Disputes Act embodied the fundamental principles which formed the basis of South African industrial conciliation legislation. At the same time, it maintained the division 'between the unskilled coloured labourer and the white labourer'.[49] Nevertheless African workers did attempt to join together with others, though each wave of unionisation was followed by repressive legislation. In the end, the non-racial trade union movement was severely hampered by the nexus of economic, political and ideological factors which made combination and organisation difficult.[50] The advantaged position of white workers was not only in their favour but as often as not in the favour of their bosses too. Many of these issues came to a head in the strike by 18 000 mine-workers in 1913.[51]

The strike issue overtly concerned Saturday afternoon work, but turned into a major challenge to capital and the state. The state, unprepared for the problem and with a defence force still in its birth pangs, had to concede a protected place for white workers in the form of exclusive collective bargaining rights. This further separated white from black workers, the former feared more by the government, because they had the means and the experience to organise worker action which might later include blacks en masse.[52] In the aftermath of the strike action, the government realised the need for legislation to secure the welfare of the white mine-workers while the Chamber of Mines conceded the necessity of trade unions and machinery for negotiations. But the state took the line of increasing white employment possibilities on the mines, contrary to the policy of the Chamber.[53] The result in political terms was the beginning of a potentially powerful alliance between major sections of national capital (and especially Afrikaner voters) and the South African Labour Party, an alliance which gained added significance as Afrikaners formed up to 75 per cent of the white labour force on the gold mines by 1918.[54] The striking workers themselves made their position clear in the post-strike 'Workers' Charter' which in many respects reveals 'the major unstated aim of preventing non-white encroachment in skilled, semi-skilled and even unskilled occupations.'[55]

A further test of power followed in strikes and disturbances on the Rand at the beginning of 1914, but this time they were met by force. Martial law was declared on 14 January, many strikers were arrested, and nine strike leaders were deported.[56] However, the position of white workers, far from being undermined, was consolidated in the Status Quo Agreement of 1918 which extended the job colour bar of the Mining Regulations to less skilled white workers. Coinciding with a rapidly growing profitability crisis on the mines, the new job colour bars were soon to produce considerable drama on the industrial stage and not a little tragedy.

By 1921 as much as two thirds of the mining industry operated at a loss with the premium price steadily falling. To add to the difficulties, demand for African labour from other employers such as farmers, manufacturing concerns and collieries led to a labour shortage on the gold mines, never the most attractive of workplaces.[57]

Employment of white work-seekers in unskilled labour could only undermine profitabiliity, so that the mines had in fact to opt for reducing white labour costs and increasing the work and responsibilities of white and African workers.[58] Both imperatives necessitated an attack on the job colour bar through wage reductions, retrenchments without replacement, and 'the substitution of ultra-cheap forced labour for expensive white labour in certain occupations'. Moreover, the job colour bar constituted a significant source of grievance to African workers. A reduction of grievances was in the interest of the mining companies.[59]

But the attack on the job colour bar had to deal with the power of the white mine-workers. In any case the function of the colour bar in maintaining and reinforcing the prevailing division of labour in the industry remained of considerable advantage to capital. Thus by 1919, 'a wide range of apparatuses and institutions functioning on a racially discriminatory basis to regulate and institutionalise the struggles of white wage-earning employees' had emerged.[60] In the process the fuse for major conflict over the contradictions of the colour bar had been set, though the detonation came only some years later in the 1922 Rand upheaval.

Whereas the conflicts surrounding the white labour policy had considerable political and economic significance, no less important was the development of worker consciousness among Africans. The Johannesburg tramwaymen's strike of 1911 (exceptional for the solidarity between all elements of labour), and the 1913 strike to a much lesser extent, still held the possibility of an effective, and indeed enormously powerful combination between white and black workers. But the exploitation wages and forced labour conditions of Africans made such combination increasingly difficult in a colonial climate in which a racial ideology so readily served contradictory interests.

Thus after white mine-workers had secured a protected position for themselves, African strike action tended to emerge as a separate phenomenon. The spur to such action was given by the worsening conditions and terms of employment occasioned by contradiction and crisis in the mining industry, post-war inflation, and pressure from the labour reserve created by the Land Act and related policies. The first post-war manifestation of trouble came with the 'Bucket Strike' of African sanitary workers on the Reef in 1918. This was followed by food boycotts in the compounds. Forty-seven strikes during the following years demonstrated the rising tension, a tension also reflected in the widespread pass campaigns during which thousands were arrested.[61] That same year Clements Kadalie established the Industrial and Commercial Workers Union (ICU), which was later to receive renown.

A meeting between the State and Rand Africans in an attempt to resolve the deteriorating situation made clear the issues of greatest moment:

> . . . the Africans attacked the system of coercive labour controls, which they blamed for their failure to secure wage increases and for keeping Africans 'in a state of economic bondage', and for preventing the African worker 'from selling his labour to the best advantage'.[62]

The Transvaal Native Congress similarly defined the problem as one directly connected to an exploitative economic system, declaring that 'civilisation' was, in their view,

> a system that (1) causes artifical ways of living, (2) manufactures suffering, (3) perpetuates slumdom, (4) creates a chronic state of poverty and want, (5) brings about cheap and sweated labour, (6) exploits the masses.[63]

Given all the disturbances of the period, one may wonder to what extent socialist ideas had gained hold, particularly in the light of the successful Russian Revolution. A Socialist Party established in 1910 was short-lived.[64] Though many trade-unionists during the 1913 strike advocated socialism, the workers themselves were concerned with the improvement of working conditions (and work security) rather than with a challenge to the dominant system. In all cases, little or no black presence was evident. Even leading radical socialists largely ignored black workers until the International Socialist League (ISL) came into being in 1915 as a breakaway group from the South African Labour Party.[65] From 1916 the ISL 'called for the abolition of indentured labour, compounds and pass laws in the interests of working class emancipation; and urged the lifting of the Native workers to the political and industrial status of the white'.[66]

The period reflects on the one hand the consolidation of Union, and on the other the emergence of various conflicting interests battling for a share of power. World War One provided temporary relief from the strains of an increasingly tense society, though only after the Afrikaner rebellion had been put down and major strike actions had been crushed. War also stimulated the expanding manufacturing sector, so that between 1915/16 and 1919/20 the gross value of output had more than doubled from £35,7m to £76,8m and the number of employees had risen by 53 per cent.[67] These years also witnessed an intensifying conflict between capital and labour, within which a division between white and black workers was greatly extended with the growth of a strongly racist ideology. At the same time competition between fractions of capital increased.

The specific manner in which these dynamics played themselves out gave rise to a growing alliance between capital and white labour, with the national capital fraction best able to utilise Afrikaner nationalism in the competition for hegemony. Colonised workers, and blacks in general, were in consequence increasingly forced to transform their resistance into urban and industrial action against labour controls and wage policies. Little support came from white colonials other than from a few radical trade unionists and politicians towards the end of the decade. The SANNC and its various member organisations found themselves increasingly having to respond to labour issues rather than matters concerning political and social access to the dominant society, though these latter concerns did not disappear. In the reserves, continued alienation from the land and declining production generated a cheap supply of labour forced for all practical purposes to seek wage-labour on the farms or in the towns, and led to increased underdevelopment and poverty.

The Ambiguous Ecclesia

In this context the churches, as will be shown, reacted with some confusion and seldom did they sustain or deepen any one perspective. Their responses more often than not were like spasmodic jerks, at once in one direction, then in another.

The equivocal approach of the churches hides presuppositions that reflect a particular view of South African society at this point. This view was undoubtedly influenced by humanitarian concern — frequently referred to as 'fair treatment' — yet it was also seemingly incapable of penetrating very deeply into the structures of the political economy and their fundamental impact on many of the humanitarian concerns. In short, a fair judgement would be that the churches *felt* the anguish and resistance of the indigenous people but without being able to speak and act in solidarity with them. The churches understood the need to take some responsibility provided, however, that the colonial 'white supremacist' structures were not radically undermined.

As a result, many concerns ended up only as resolutions directed to the government, asking the authorities to rescind or debate certain pieces of legislation, or to provide relief for those most visibly suffering. Questions such as the extension of Pass Laws to women and children in the Orange Free State were dealt with by this means;[68] so were hardships on farms and house raids by police in the Transvaal;[69] so were advances by mine recruiting agents to blacks in reserve areas whereby indebtedness was incurred forcing them to seek wage labour.[70] Other resolutions dealt with exploitative wages, [71] and ill-treatment and inadequate representation of blacks in law courts.[72]

Clearly also of concern were accusations that the churches, out of touch with the working classes, by and large directed their appeal to the leisurely and the comfortable. Thus the *Methodist Churchman* noted that 'the sons of toil are mainly conspicuous by their absence from church worship'. It was also noted that various ministers of religion present on the invitation of labour representatives at a major meeting in Cape Town concerning the 1913 Rand strikes suffered the ignominy of being branded as a 'class alienated from the working man', having 'no sympathy with him in his struggle for what he believes to be his right'.[73]

Indirectly one gains the impression that the Church, undoubtedly convicted in the eyes of at least some significant bodies of workers, may not yet have stepped outside the ideological constraints upon it. Certainly, the attitude of the Rev JH Riston, on an inspection tour of South Africa in 1913 and later president of the British Wesleyan Conference, betrayed no understanding of black workers. Referring to the roughly 225 000 black mine-workers as 'heathen' who are like 'oxen pulling at a yoke, and duly fed in return for content', he saw not exploitation and repression but 'raw material' upon which 'the Church should concentrate its forces'.[74] In similar fashion, the disruption by African strikers at Jagersfontein mine in the Orange Free State in 1914 and its subsequent closure which put large numbers of people out of work produced only the complaint that missionary activity was thereby severely disrupted.[75] Equally oblivious to the life of the black worker, the General Missionary Conference in 1912 felt that conditions on the mines or in the location did not seriously hinder Christianity; many even felt that the strenuous life at a mine improved the men.[76]

Other indicators of the attitutde and practice of the churches include a declaration of 'indebtedness' to De Beers Consolidated Mines for helping establish religious work in the compounds, thus generating 'morality' and 'loyalty' among the workers.[77] On the Rand, two major church bodies, outraged by illicit liquor traffic, between them went so far as to seek the extension of the closed compound system to the Reef, to have compound police replaced by government police, to fence in compounds 'with corrugated iron or wire entanglements, such fences to have but one or two gates guarded by special police', and to have 'open spaces between such fences and the compound proper to be lighted and patrolled at night'.[78] Again, no sense is evident of who was being kept in by such methods and under what conditions. On the other hand, the Board of Missions in Pretoria and the Wesleyan Conference had criticised township ('location') conditions, calling for State aid, use of revenue derived from blacks for housing and facilities and proper siting.[79]

Manifestly, the churches were morally obligated to their large black membership (though not financially). They were frequently in a position to hear complaints, speak on behalf of the complainants, and even provide limited aid on occasion. But in the last analysis they were dependent on those same powers which produced the problems which concerned them. They were dependent not only in a material sense (documents throughout the period attest to financial dependency on settler communities, large capitalist donors, and remittances from British churches and individuals who wished to see 'civilisation' and 'industry' advanced), but on the ideological plane as well (shown in moderate reformism, a fear of effective resistance, and an overly weighted concern with social morality).

Loyalty to 'Throne and Empire' remained a common article of faith, especially during the World War. Simultaneously, the belief in segregated territories where Africans could 'develop in a natural, unforced way on lines suited to the genius of their race' indicated the ongoing colonialist thinking spawned by earlier events.[80] Within this milieu it proved natural to think of African labour under 'proper guidance and control, with firm and just treatment and strict discipline' as the means of prosperity.[81] It could not have been more bluntly put than in an editorial of the *Methodist Churchman*:

> The Native is, we firmly believe, one of the best assets this country possesses. We need him to assist us to develop its vast resources, and he will help us, if we allow him, to make it a country in which an ever-increasing number of Europeans (sic) will live in comfort.[82]

However, the 'asset' on occasion proved to be a doubtful one when he or she took to forms of urban resistance. In the rapidly growing Witwatersrand industrial hub, for example, depressed wages, times of crisis, unemployment, marginalisation, and repressive labour controls created a reaction in many blacks which took the form of social banditry. But such attempts to wrest some form of equity in a largely inequitable world were of course seen by whites as criminal, helping to reinforce their already present racist tendencies. This was especially true of whites whose own living situations and incomes were not secure and threatened by recession or inflation.

It is in this context that the renowned 'Black Peril' scares of the late nineteenth and early twentieth centuries occur. A prime target for spurts of outrage was the African 'houseboy', a domestic servant whose job situation was never free from manipulation. Here contacts between white and black domestics, or between white mistresses and black servants, could and did provide fuel for the fire. Often the contacts led to serious relationships. But on a few relatively rare occasions accusations of rape — and in a couple of celebrated cases, assault — arose. Then the 'Black Peril' cry broke loose. As van Onselen has argued, class and economic factors were usually behind these scares. There are also indications that reduction or withholding of servants' wages sometimes led to reaction, or that a threatened reduction of staff in a domestic household with servants of both colours led to white domestics accusing a black domestic of assault with the inevitable result of the latter losing the job.[83]

In any event, by 1912 the waves of 'Black Peril' scares reached a climax, fanned by a sensationalist press. The *Rand Daily Mail* organised the largest political petition yet on the Witwatersrand, and largely for this reason a government commission of enquiry into assaults on women was set up. At more or less the same time, the 'Black Peril' on the Rand (that 'University of Crime') so alarmed the churches that a commission was set up to investigate the matter and report to the General Missionary Conference. The composition of the commission, a fascinating and motley collection of churchmen, magistrates, businessmen and farmers, lawyers, educationalists, prison and police officials, inspectors, editors, public servants and 'eight Ladies'(!) reflected a palpably bourgeois orientation. Perhaps then their findings were to be expected, but they are nevertheless eye-opening.[84] Among many lesser reasons (in what appears to be a ranked order of importance),

> . . . the main reasons for the criminal instinct on the part of the Native is given as:
> (1) Criminal Instinct 40%
> (2) Undue familiarity and thoughtlessness
> on the part of women 25%
> (3) Alcohol 14%

Several African leaders, some with strong church connections, made it clear that the 'Black Peril' catchphrase too easily concealed oppressive conditions or served white political ends (it was even used in part as ideological justification for the Land Act). The problem of white men seducing black women, a 'White Peril', was neatly ignored. Black domestics who faced the insecurities inherent in their situation increasingly took matters into their own hands, forming the protective and retributive bands of the *Amalaita*. Highly organised and operating largely at night, they variously 'dealt with' employers who unjustly treated their servants. They also organised resistance against police and passes (including forgeries of passes). Moreover they gave 'mere servants' an organisational home and a role with a purpose and dignity. In this sense, 'the Amalaita should be seen as the "houseboys" liberation army fighting to reassert its decolonised manhood during one of the first major waves of South African proletarianisation.'[85]

In similar fashion, the compounds, locations and prisons full of pass offenders and suchlike, also produced pressures upon African work-seekers which led to the establishment of retributive gangs. For various reasons these gangs rapidly turned upon their own, rather than upon the system which gave them birth. Thus they ultimately remained an unconstructive, frustrated form of resistance.

By far the most famous of the gangs, the Ninevites (also known as 'Umkosi wa Ntaba', the Regiment of the Hills) were so named because their leader Nongoloza had read 'about the great state of Ninevah which rebelled against the Lord and I selected that name for my gang as rebels against the Government's law.'[86]

Established on the Rand before Union, organised along parliamentary lines, and operating both within and without the prisons with branches even at Bloemfontein and Kimberley, the gang 'offered a serious practical challenge to a repressive privileged white state'. Particularly threatening to the state and mine-owners was the fact that this extra-legal 'army' was seriously undermining law enforcement and control in the compounds as well as in the cities, especially as the pass laws and contract regulations produced 'a very distinctive labouring population, one characterised by its high degree of nominal "criminal" experience'. It was these 'landless labourers seeking to return to a peasant life that was being rapidly destroyed; urban bands with a form of rural consciousness resisting proletarianisation' that also gave rise to the misplaced belief in an inherent black criminality.

It would be too much to expect the white-dominated churches to have had any insight into these matters, or to have understood why African leaders did not regard them in the same light. The ideology of domination had been deeply embedded, and the most that was likely to come forth from colonist Christians was a paternalistic ethic of responsibility. Thus, for example, commenting on the unsatisfactory character of domestic labour, the *Church Chronicle* accepted the charges that Africans were troublesome, independent, unconscientious, sulky, impertinent and without obligation to their masters or mistresses. Nevertheless, it said, the Church had in its new context 'duties and responsibilities' towards the 'child race' on the basis of in loco parentis.

These 'children', however, were by no means incapable of looking after themselves. Besides the multiple forms of unorthodox resistance that began to emerge, more orthodox political leaders were emerging. In particular, many more articulate beneficiaries of missionary education and the few who had managed to acquire some economic foothold in the colonial economy were increasingly frustrated by the limits placed upon their upward mobility through racial legislation, and they founded a variety of political groups oriented to African nationalism.[88]

The founders of these bodies were usually teachers, ministers, editors, lawyers and doctors, who 'though unwilling, and perhaps unable, to alienate themselves from the poor and the oppressed, . . . did not escape from the compromises that are forced on leaders without power who seek to reform but never overthrow an evil social order'.[89] Many of them were obliged by the very nature of their positions in the South African social formation to serve those who had remained their masters. This is perhaps most lucidly observed in the statement of the executive of the South African Native Congress (Transvaal) to Joseph Chamberlain in 1903:

> The black races are too conscious of their dependence upon the white missionaries, and of the obligations towards the British race, and the benefits to be derived from their presence in the general control and guidance of the civil and religious affairs of the country to harbour foolish notions of political ascendency. The idea is too palpably absurd to carry weight with well-informed minds, and tends to obscure the real issues and to injure the people as a class.[90]

It was not to be very long however before the 'palpably absurd' idea of at least an equal say in the life of the country found an organisational focus. The Act of Union and the effective exclusion of blacks from formal political activity in national affairs soon provided the key impetus to the forming of the South African National Native Congress (SANNC).

The SANNC stemmed from a proposal by Pixley ka I Seme to form a 'Native Union' in symbolic and political opposition to the Union of South Africa.[91] Though Tengo Jabavu opposed the move because he thought it would gain the disapproval of sympathetic whites, the SANNC was established in 1912 at a widely representative, historical meeting at Bloemfontein, an occasion receiving no coverage in any white South Afican newspaper, nor in Jabavu's *Imvo*.[92] Deliberately catholic in its orientation, the new body through combination and coalition sought to force a place for blacks in the colonial system, and to that extent presented a moderate but nevertheless significant threat to settler domination. A major early strategy involved sending delegations and making appeals to Britain and other foreign powers, but Britain in particular would not allow 'the alliance between Afrikaner land-owners and British investors, mine owners and industrialists' to be weakened.[93]

For long the SANNC proved to be a momentous movement of considerable importance but without real teeth, a reflection of its predominantly 'middle-class' leadership whose primary concern was often that of upward mobility within the prevailing political economy.[94] Yet it represented a crucial part of the social equation in the period under consideration, to be over-shadowed later only by black workers' movements (and, of course, as time went on the SANNC, renamed the African National Congress, was to become increasingly potent).

Yet the political activity of the SANNC, a body heavily influenced by Christianity through its leadership (and many prominent members), gained relatively little attention or sympathy from the churches. Many of its arguments were based on well-developed appeals of Christian morality. Its tone was for long rather moderate. Influenced by Booker T Washington and WEB DuBois (and only later by Marcus Garvey), the SANNC first sought the gradual extension of civil liberties enjoyed by whites to those qualified, and equal economic opportunity for those of sufficient prowess.

Thus for the early SANNC, 'freedom involved neither national independence nor a socialist revolution, but freedom for individual achievement and a non-European contribution to the wider society'. Despite this moderate, Christianised and eminently British liberal thrust, the SANNC had little force in Church councils, usually finding friends among a small group of whites. Perhaps the SANNC did not develop an effective, appropriate strategy to gain wide support in the churches. But eventually the Rev Zaccheus Mahabane, at one time head of the SANNC, was forced to conclude that white Christian practice mostly bred cynicism among Africans, while John Dube, a Congregationalist, finally acknowledged that things had deteriorated to the point where Christianity was 'an offensive smell to a large number of Africans'.[95]

In summation, the proletarianisation of the indigenous people of South Africa, the particular nature of this process, the highly exploitative wage structures, the extensive controls over labour, the concomitant process of underdevelopment in the reserves, and the resultant social problems of dislocation and ill-health in the towns, presented to the churches a complex set of phenomena which they were not able to assess critically nor to respond to adequately. However, like most if not all white-dominated institutions benefitting directly or indirectly from the situation, Church leaders perceived the threats involved in the proletarianisation process, especially if some reasonably secure outlets to Africans were not allowed and some social mobility not possible for them in the total society. For this reason, though territorial separation was already in practice and clearly served a major purpose, the Land Act appeared to many too restrictive and formal, closing down avenues of access into the dominant political and economic system and raising the temperature of resistance to a dangerous level. On the other hand, law and order remained supreme, and loyalty to the state a high value. Once again this ambiguity hung like a millstone around the necks of the ecclesiastics, remaining unresolved. Moreover, even moderate African political organisation and activity (the SANNC in particular) were treated by most with a heavy dose of caution where there was any acceptance at all.

All of these observations hold true for the material investigated during the period under scrutiny, but a significant divergance does appear at one stage. From the end of the World War, the churches suddenly paid unusual and insightful attention to labour, in particular black workers, Hints of such a change are contained in reactions to the Native Administration Bill of 1917, widely viewed as not in accordance with traditional British principles regarding treatment of a 'loyal aboriginal population'.[96] The possibility that the Russian revolution stimulated a new consciousness is partly sustained in one journal which described the Bill as governed by the motto 'isolate and repress' and thus designed to lead 'a form of forced, or serf, labour'. An added comment condemned the Bill as a 'crying shame . . . in the very year in which Russia has obtained her liberty'.[97]

However the overt expression of a new attitude came into full bloom only the following year, together with the upsurge of African industrial action and the Status Quo Agreement protecting white workers. Inflationary pressures, hitting black labour the hardest, probably added to the clearing of the ideological clouds. In an open letter to Smuts, Bishop Furse of Pretoria called for a recognition of the contribution to the economy of blacks, commenting that exploitation, bitterly resented, had real meaning for them and rightly so.[98] In like manner, the Provincial Missionary conference criticised continued exploitation, and the Board of Missions sought fair wages lest serious trouble arise.[99]

Another example of the new attitude is found in a Methodist Conference resolution on 'Present Day Problems'. This stated its implacable opposition 'to every form of oppression and to all artificial inequalities and disabilities', and sympathised with the desire of workers for a 'worthier share in the products of their toil'; the conference thus pledged itself to 'the furtherance of every legitimate movement and effort to that end.'[100] The most practical expression of an attempt to connect church life with the experiences and aspirations of workers came from Canon Hodson in Durban who held periodic conferences to facilitate dialogue between what were obviously considered to be two groups. Topics from the floor were usually debated, among them 'spirituality', the indifference of the Church to 'gutter people', the 'unscientific' and 'superstitious' nature of Christianity, hell, socialism, bishops (negatively viewed), and the Archbishop of Canterbury's income. The Anglican newspaper, reviewing these events, concluded that the Church should support 'the rightful ideals of labour'.[101]

Earlier the same journal had published (and indicated support for) an article by the Rev AF Cox on wealth and Christianity. Here capitalism was declared 'a crime against society . . . It does not matter whether the capitalist is a philanthropist or not — personal character has nothing whatsoever to do with the matter'. In a fascinating and bold critique of philanthropy the article proceeded to analyse the 'giving away' by the wealthy of large sums of their money';

> Put into bold language it consists in withholding the rewards due to one class of men in order to hand (part of) it to another class which never earned it. The Church has a very obvious duty . . . But this duty does not consist in exhorting the rich man to give away his wealth nor of specifying exactly how it should be disposed of. The whole *system* of wealth production wants altering.[102]

Such rather astonishing and improbable pronouncements were all but unheard previously in the Church, at least in South Africa; they virtually drop from the clouds in Zeus-like thunderbolts. Canon Hodson and the Rev Mr Cox seem to have been well-known for their more radical positions, yet they were not entirely abnormal as the resolutions of various church bodies testify. Serious ambiguities could be discerned in official positions, however. These included a propensity to support the stratification along class lines of African society (a perspective inspired by Tengo Jabavu), to blame white workers *per se* for the exploitation wages of blacks, and to regard the Church's role as impartial 'between master and men . . . without bias, because the Christian ethic applies to all classes of society'.[103]

A full assessment of the dynamics involved in what impresses one as a notable transformation in the attitudes of the church after war must await the consideration of developments in the following decade. For the moment suffice it to acknowledge a novel approach, while noting that little evidence of any practical outworking of this tack is evident at this stage. However, insights may be gained in turning to the Church's response to the active resistance of others in the period.

Quite remarkable in the first instance, is the almost complete absence of significant references in archival material to the African strikes of 1918 and 1919, to the formation of the ICU, to SANNC protests, and to the massive pass campaign in March 1919. One must accept the impact of these events; yet the churches show a lack of concrete interest in the historical moments these events represent, indicating a shallowness of both reflection and action in their declarations. In fact, the only weighty statement on black unrest on the Rand comes from the Methodist Conference which deplored 'the state of unrest prevalent among the Native section of the population' and expressed its view of 'the greatest need for immediate action by the Government'.[104] One other noteworthy comment printed by the *Christian Express* concerned the municipal workers' strike (1918). It pointed out the role of ISL propaganda, low wages and the pass laws in fomenting the strike, and criticised the harsher measures taken against black workers compared to the treatment of white workers.[105]

In contrast to the post-war activity, a relatively large number of references to serious conflicts appear in church records prior to the war. These include the Indian passive resistance campaign, the 1914 Afrikaner rebellion, and the 1913 and 1914 strikes.

Gandhi's first *satyagraha* campaign, initiated in 1907, continued into 1913. Though some gains were made, the position of Indians in South Africa remained tenuous for the next 50 years. At the end of Gandhi's campaign strikes broke out at the Newcastle coal mines and Natal Indians marched in large numbers into the Transvaal. These events attracted worried notice among church bodies, some concerned with the debilitating effect of the 'outburst' on Church work.[106] Others, while explicitly dissociating themselves from the passive resistance movement, were yet desirous of a repeal of the three pounds tax on ex-indentured Indians which was one of the contentious matters.[107]

Arising out of the decision to invade German South-West Africa in 1914, and spurred on by the government's mishandling of the affair as well as unfortunate incidents such as the shooting by government troops of General de la Rey, the Afrikaner Rebellion flared briefly.[108] Led by Boer generals, perhaps capitalising on the resentment of landless 'poor whites' (estimated in 1916 at 100 000) and inspired by renewed republican visions, the Rebellion received no sympathy from the English-speaking churches at all.[109] Blacks meanwhile were praised for their loyalty to the government during the whole affair.[110]

When mineworkers struck in 1913, producing a general state of unrest on the Rand, both the Methodist and the Anglican newspapers carried considerable editorial comment. The positions they held clearly mirror the analysis previously discussed. While sympathising with 'the legitimate claims of labour', strong disapprobation of heavy conflict was forthcoming, warnings beings directed in the first instance against workers. Accompanying such censure came the call for harmony and partnership between capital and labour. An infusion on both sides of a 'Christian Spirit' was seen to be the only final answer to labour problems.[111] Quite obviously, especially when one considers the crudely and cruelly exploitative nature of capitalism in South Africa, such views reflect not a conscious bias but an unequivocal ideological base in the bourgeois world of moderation, toleration and gradual reform which would slowly change but not shake the system. Archbishop Carter, in a private letter, discussed the crushing of the 1914 strikes in words which make the point clear: regarding the use by the government of what some called extreme measures, he declared 'I don't believe that labour generally in this country is discontented or has any reason for discontent'.[112] Possibly he thought only of white labour in this context; even so the point remains.

The questions implicit in these and similar events received a fairly sophisticated and critical treatment from Canon Hodson in his reply to a number of earlier articles in the *Church Chronicle*. This occasioned an interesting debate of considerable value to the present discussion.

Hodson, certain that previous writers would not 'press Christian principles in the matter beyond a certain point', regarded a non-committal policy in the industrial issues as 'suspicious on the broad principle that it does not entail suffering: we take sides just as much by our silence as we do by our words', he wrote. After analysing the nature of capitalism, the resultant generation of conflict between rich and poor along class lines, and the non-accidental appearance of large-scale unemployment, he ironically points out that the riots in Johannesburg resulted in a net gain in human life. While 21 people died in the streets during one week of strike, an everage of 24 people a week died in the mines. Consequently, when the Church refused to take sides, he wrote, 'the working man turns away with a snort of contempt'. The result of such policies, despite their verbal affirmation of 'high Christian principles', was in his opinion a Church that 'has nil influence in these matters with either capital or labour'.[113]

Such views, as may well be imagined, were not popular. Wilfred Parker came to the attack against Hodson, decrying his call for the Church to opt for a clear position in industrial conflict and not a position that stood above conflict and pointed to 'merits and faults' on both sides. Anything else would have been a compromise of the Church, thought Parker, and moreover would require a real knowledge of the technicalities of industry in order to be defensible.[114]

Parker's position appears to have been representative, at least in the public record; the contradictions within in are only perceived by the earlier mentioned Canon Hodson and the Rev Mr Cox. In a sense this debate over workers summarises the response of the Church to increasing proletarianisation. It serves to highlight the existence of a small pocket of penetrating criticism within the churches in relation to the political economy. It illuminates by contrast the inability of most to escape their ideological captivity to the status quo. It also demonstrates once again that a critical analysis of the Church's role is not post-historical luxury, but a contemporary possibility.

Notes

1 C Bundy (1979), pp25—8 & 95—96
2 *Ibid,* p129.
3 With respect to natural causes, the rinderpest epidemic of 1897 was followed after 1910 by the increasingly damaging spread of East Coast fever.
4 C Bundy (1979), p108 & pp131—2.
5 E Roux (1964), p68; also E Webster (1978), p10. It should be noted that the Glen Grey Act was not everywhere applied, and that in some areas where it was applied (eg Pondoland) local opposition and administrative difficulties made many of its tenets ineffective (cf W Beinart, 1982, p43). Nevertheless, the principles of the Act remained to be expanded and developed in other ways as time went on.
6 See F Wilson, 'Farming' in OX: p169; M Wilson, 'The Growth of Peasant Communities' in OX: p58, also complare figures in C Bundy (1979), p223.
7 W Beinart (1982), p111ff.
8 C Bundy (1979), p240.
9 SANAC Report, para 209, p40, Lagden Papers, July 25, 1907.
10 GMCSA: Summary, p89.
11 T Karis and G Carter (1972), vol 1, p35.
12 CE, August 1, 1907, pp122—3; July 1, 1906, pp155—6; and November 1, 1906, p223.
13 C Bundy (1979), p213.
14 F Wilson, 'Farming', in OX: p156.
15 T Zini, 'The Squatters Bill', *Imvo Zabantsundu,* March 19, 1912, cited in T Karis and G Carter (1972), vol 1, p82.
16 C Bundy (1979), p213.
17 W Beinart (1982), p123ff.
18 C Bundy (1979), p221.
19 A general description of Jabavu's close relationship to the Cape liberals and his gradual loss of face among blacks can be found in E Roux (1964), pp51—77; see also P Walshe (1971), pp21 & 34.
20 TMC, June 16, 1913.
21 CE, December 1, 1913, pp187—8.
22 TMC, November 24, 1913, emphasis in original.
23 SAMSR (32nd), 1913, p2.
24 Minutes, November 1913.
25 See Minutes of Conference, 1914, p126 and 1917, p 126; see also TMC, March 9, 1914; and the SAMSR (34th), 1915, p14.
26 TMC, May 25, 1914.
27 TCC, July 30, 1914.
28 *The Church Missionary Review,* CMS, London, February 1917, pp89—90.
29 CE, May 1, 1914, p67; October 1, 1915, pp148—9.
30 *Ibid,* July 2, 1917, pp103—4.
31 *Ibid,* October 1, 1912, pp159—60.
32 OX: p30; also H Houghton (1967), p142.
33 F Johnstone (1976), pp33—4; S Moroney, in E Webster (1978), p34.
34 E Katz (1976), pp70, 56 & 448—9.
35 F Johnstone (1976), pp25, 50, 55 & 65.
36 E Katz (1976), pp64—5.

37 HJ Simons and RE Simons (1969), pp44—5.

38 D Ticktin (1976), p1—8, p22

39 D Welsh 'The Growth of Towns' in OX: p205.

40 See F Johnstone (1976), pp76ff.

41 Cited in T Karis and G Carter (1972) vol 1, pp24—5.

42 H Houghton (1967), p141.

43 E Katz (1976), p26.

44 F Johnstone (1976), p87—8.

45 See P Rich, in P Bonner (1979), p97.

46 See E Webster (1978), pp15—16; and R Davies (1979), p131.

47 E Roux (1964), p145.

48 *Ibid*, p127 & 124; also E Katz (1976), pp232—3 & 241.

49 R Davies (1979), p127.

50 E Webster (1978), p11 and R Davies (1979), p25.

51 See F Johnstone (1976), p169; E Katz (1976), pp381—429; E Roux (1964), p145; TRH Davenport (1977), p183.

52 A O'Quigley (197?), p3.

53 E Katz (1976), pp462—3 & 360.

54 F Johnstone (1976), p105.

55 E Katz (1976), p324; 'The Workers Charter' is published in full in the same work as appendix C.

56 TRH Davenport (1977), p184; see also A O'Quigley (197?).

57 F Johnstone (1976), pp95—7.

58 *Ibid*, p83; Johnstone demonstrated the effect such a practice would have on the profitablity of 52 mines using 1913 as a cost-calculation base.

59 *Ibid*, pp120—1; also pp80—1.

60 R Davies (1979), p127.

61 On these various events, see E Roux (1964), pp117—121 & 130—1; F Johnstone (1976), pp173 & 177; HJ Simons and RE Simons (1969), p220; OX: p445

62 F Johnstone (1976), p178.

63 *Ibid*, p195.

64 E Katz (1976), p194; and HJ Simons and RE Simons (1969), p152.

65 E Katz (1976), p426; and E Roux (1964), p129.

66 HJ Simons and RE Simons (1969), p193.

67 L Bozzoli (1973/4), pp69—70.

68 Minutes of Conference, 1914, p93.

69 Diocese of Pretoria, Native Conference, Minutes, September 1, 1916.

70 CE, May 1, 1914, p67.

71 GMCSA: Summary, p89 (1912).

72 Minutes of Conference, 1918, p134.

73 TMC, July 18, 1911; and July 28, 1913.

74 *The Rand Methodist*, November, 1913.

75 SAMSR (33rd), 1914, p18.

76 GMCSA: Summary, p71.

77 SAMSR (31st), 1912, pp24—5.

78 GMSCA: Summary, 1912, p77—8; and Board of Missions, Diocese of Pretoria, Minutes, 1915.

79 *Ibid*, Minutes 1913; Minutes of Conference, 1911, p104; see also GMCSA: Summary, 1912, p89; and CE, November 1, 1912, p182.

80 TCC, March 6, 1913.
81 TMC, June 18, 1917.
82 *Ibid,* May 18, 1914.
83 C van Onselen (1982), 'The Witches of Suburbia', p45ff.
84 GMCSA: Summary, pp77—9 (1912).
85 C van Onselen (1975/6), pp54 & 59.
86 C van Onselen (1975/6), p80ff.
87 In GMSCA: Summary, pp77—9, (1912).
88 See for example, CC Saunders, 'The New African Elite in the Eastern Cape and Some Late 19th Century Origins of African Nationalism', (1969/70). P Walshe (1971), p1—2, makes similar points in respect of the SANNC.
89 HJ Simons and RE Simons (1969), p116.
90 T Karis and G Carter (1972), vol 1, p18.
91 E Roux (1964), pp110—1. P Walshe (1971) is the standard history of the formation and development of the SANNC, later the ANC.
92 T Karis and G Carter (1972), vol 1, p61.
93 HJ Simons and RE Simons (1969), p219.
94 See for example, comments on two major blocks in the SANNC, the Transvaal Native Congress (P Bonner, 1980, p3), and the Natal Native Congress (D Welsh, 1971, p299).
95 P Walshe (1971), p12 & pp162—3.
96 Minutes of Conference, 1971, pp126 & 149.
97 CE, June 1, 1917.
98 *Rand Daily Mail,* March 20, 1918.
99 Provincial Missionary Conference, Minutes, September 1918; Diocese of Pretoria, Board of Missions, Minutes, 1919.
100 Minutes of Conference, 1919, p135.
101 TCC, December 11, 1919.
102 *Ibid,* October 16, 1919.
103 CE, November 8, 1918, p166; TMC, April 29, 1918; CE, October 1, 1918, p150; and TMC, March 31, 1919 (quote).
104 Minutes of Conference, 1919, p136.
105 CE, October 1, 1918, pp148—50.
106 SAMSR (32nd), 1913, p2.
107 Provincial Missionary Conference Minutes, November 1913; see also TMC, November 24, 1913.
108 See TRH Davenport (1977), pp184—6.
109 See Minutes of Conference, 1915, p137 and 142; *Transvaal and Swazi District Directory,* 1915/6, p1; CE, May 1, 1915, pp69—71;
110 SAMSR (33rd), 1914, p18.
111 TCC, August 7, 1913; TMC, August 1, 1913.
112 Archbishop WM Carter, ALS, January 16 and January 29, 1914.
113 TCC, 'Social Unrest, Class and Christianity', August 21 and September 4, 1913, *passim.*
114 TCC, October 2, 1913.

CHAPTER FIVE

Reaction and Reform: 1920—1930

> I will never forget the cruel and terrible history of the demand for cheap labour. Modern industry since the industrial revolution has shown itself again and again to be anti-social and inhuman in its passion for cheapness, and to be ready to plead economic necessity to justify the exploitation of the worker.
>
> Bishop of Pretoria, 1922[1]

> ... it was the period ... when the Church really discovered what its function was in social and political affairs.
>
> Peter Hinchliff[2]

Crisis and Contradiction, 1920—1925

'It is a melancholy truth', wrote WC Scully, for 40 years a civil commissioner and stipendiary magistrate in the Cape Colony, 'that South Africa has no policy relating to the native or the Coloured man'. Scully was sufficiently sensitive to add that what policy did exist was aimed at 'getting them to work as hard as possible for the lowest possible wage, and keeping them from having any hand in the shaping of their own — so far dolorous destiny'.[3] Such sentiments virtually filled the pages of church newspapers, journals and reports at the beginning of the new decade, testifying to a sudden awakening on the part of the Church to the economic plight of the African working class, and producing an upsurge of interest in socialism at the same time.

The historian of the CPSA describes it as a period when 'the championship of the underprivileged was the great ideal', when many in the Anglican Church shared 'a muscular Anglo-Catholic, vaguely socialist Christianity that would not be suppressed'.[4] The *Church Chronicle*, for example, carried a series of 'Essays in Socialism' through the middle months of 1920, the Methodist Conference laid out principles for the relation of Capital and Labour, the *Christian Express* debated the issues, and many leading individuals called for a new deal. Why this startling shift in official viewpoints, this rather dramatic critical spirit at this point? Why the apparent move from dependency on the ruling class and its ideology to a 'vague' alternative?

A Time of Turmoil

No judgement on the matter can be made without first referring to the then recent and powerful impact of massive industrial resistance. This was the time of 'the largest number of workers on strike in South Africa's entire history', comments Johnstone, referring to the period 1919—21.[5] Of the 66 strikes during 1920, two were especially momentous. The first involved some 70 000 African mineworkers on the Rand (it also received SANNC support); and the second, led by Samuel Masobala at Port Elizabeth, ended with 21 killed.[6]

The precipitative cause of the African mineworkers' strike in 1920 was their earlier exclusion from wage increases on the mines. High levels of inflation also contributed heavily to the discontent of workers: the retail price index had increased by over 50 per cent between 1916 and 1922 while 'black wages, unlike those of whites who received war bonuses and cost of living allowances, remained relatively unchanged'.[7] African mineworkers in particular bitterly resented the high wage gap between themselves and white workers, especially in relation to the amount of work performed.

The 1920 strike was a consequence of the distinctive features of African wages, namely, 'their ultra-low level, the stabilisation of this ultra-low level over time, and their falling real value'. It affected 21 mines.[8] White labour leaders gave no support, and the only achievement of the strike was a reduction in prices in Rand stores.[9] But fears of what lay behind the strike were great and were expressed not only by whites but also by leaders of the aspirant black middle-class, small as it was. DDT Jabavu, son of Tengo Jabavu and influential in the churches, for instance confirmed the economic roots of the problem but disarmingly went on to attack the rise of 'Bolshevism' as a danger, for here he saw two most alarming features, a drive to fabricate an independent African religion and united resistance to economic enslavement. Pointing to the role of 'agitators', he attacked their brand of socialism (which he opposed to the 'harmless commonsense system' advocated by Phillip Snowden and Ramsay Macdonald in their books) and called for counteracting forces, including the production of 'well educated Native leaders trained in a favourable atmosphere'.[10]

Clearly it was no coincidence that a critical spirit should arise in the year of the African mineworkers' strike. The previous two years had already seen over 100 other strikes. One churchman concluded that 'there is nothing to be gained by fighting trade unions but everything to be gained by working with them'.[11] Later the CPSA newspaper analysed the root cause of all the restlessness and discontent to be 'the realisation of the worker of the position that is due to him as a human being'.[12] And in July 1920, the Natal Missionary Conference heard from DDT Jabavu a long paper on the cause and cure of the widespread discontent and unrest. 'Feelings . . . are seething like the molten volcanic lava in the breasts of these inarticulate people,' he declared, pointing to wages earned as the immediate cause of the trouble. He criticised taxation without representation, the unification of whites against blacks in the Union Act, the Land Act, the failure of all appeals for restitution locally and internationally, a host of other laws including 'the most signal way to repress and humiliate another . . . the system of the Pass Laws', and finally the felt injustice of the Department of Justice.[13]

Meanwhile anti-colonial sentiment was growing, giving impetus to resistance directed along black nationalist lines (often this was influenced by American movements, particularly Garveyism). 'It is the law of economics as well as that of psychology', wrote SANNC leader and Africanist James Theale in an article on Christianity and 'Native Policy', that 'the beneficiary of a system will not antagonise it.' Discussing the calling of the Dutch Reformed Church-sponsored 'European-Bantu Conference' of 1923 (a result of the pressure of the 'awakening' of Africans, Theale felt) he attacked the practical hypocrisy of the mission churches as well as the 'good boys . . . none other than the men of our own race . . . luminaries . . . graduates', whom he believed to have become 'beneficiaries of the system'.[14]

The 'awakening' of a critical spirit at this time appears in fact more like a slumbering fall from an overturned bed than a fresh alertness naturally emerging from church worship and proclamation. Anxiety is also evident: 'I am afraid and disturbed by this attitude of our Christian natives and better educated ones . . . it is very grave and unsatisfactory', confessed one gentleman of the cloth.[15]

Crisis was in fact producing criticism. Even so, limits to the critical spirit were defined by law and order above all. Even the massacre at Bulhoek of Enoch Mgijima's Israelites (a millenarian independent Church grouping), though regarded as somewhat unnecessary and tragic, was felt by Archbishop Carter to be an inevitable result of threatening behaviour against the government.[16] Similarly, the churches by and large responded to the Rand Revolt in praise for a government 'brave, fearless and honest', simultaneously lauding the loyalty and the respect for law and order shown by blacks.[17]

In short, the Church battled with itself, in the midst of unavoidable turmoil, as it sought to discover what its social function was. Did it finally do so, as Anglican historian Hincliff seems to think?

Renewed attention was paid to land issues, some seeing this as the very essence of the problem.[18] The South African Missionary Society saw the deterioration in the rural areas, appearing in the 'mournful tragedies of drought, pestilence, starvation and death', as a serious menace to 'our fine labour supply'.[19] But the more general view also mirrored a belief that blacks were 'robbed of their land and thus, ipso facto, of freedom as well'. In appropriate imagery, *South African Outlook* (SAO, previously the *Christian Express*) warned that 'we are engaged in sowing a most appalling crop of undying (and justifiable) hatred. God knows what the harvest will be, and when; but we shall undoubtedly reap'.[20]

But land problems concerned not only expropriation of space; by 1920 there were roughly half a million farm workers whose conditions of employment were comparable with, perhaps worse than, mine workers.[21] The effective price paid for farm labour was believed to be equally exploitative. Womenfolk of male farm workers were in practice required to add their labour to the production process without compensation. Wages were sufficiently low on many farms to induce stock theft to supplement food supplies.[22] These matters too were taken up by churches, most notably Lovedale Mission. Sometimes considerable sympathy arose for the aspirations of the colonised people, one observer even remarking on the rise of Garveyism ('Africa for the Africans') as popular evidence of white oppression.[23]

One may note further evidence of the relatively strong interest of the churchmen in the effects and practices of a colonial form of capitalist exploitation at this juncture. Undue taxation of blacks was attacked, especially as it was administered without representation or a just share in benefits; recruitment practices and the migrant labour system came under fire once or twice; the 'dog tax rebellion' of the Bondelswarts people received astonishing support from some (though their cause was favourably contrasted with the Israelites of Ntabalenga who were thought to be stirring rebellion among blacks throughout the Union — an illuminating indication of the limits of criticism). The Bloemfontein riots of 1925 were regarded as a demonstration of 'the evils and dangers of the popular white policy of segregation', and the subsequent treatment of blacks as unjust. And the legal system, especially in the rural areas, was thought to be wholly unbalanced against blacks, with punishments and fines out of proportion to offences and earning capacities, improper favouritism to colonials, widespread perjury and loaded juries being common features.[24]

When the political fabric of the whole country was being shaken, the material contradictions inherent in the political economy created strains that threatened to overwhelm the structure already in existence. The Church found itself forced to face the situation critically by virtue of its tenuous position in the society between those upon whom it depended — the dominant groups — and those who claimed its attention from within, the large body of black membership. But those same material contradictions intruded upon the Church, generating incongruencies that bring into question the nature and depth of its criticism. Thus, whereas on the one hand labour and labour issues were to be taken seriously for the first time, on the other no coherent understanding emerged of what this meant. The reaction of the churches to the Rand Revolt exhibits the ambiguities most directly.

Contraction of the gold-mining industry since 1914 had led to the point in November 1921 at which seven mines were running either at a marginal profit or at a loss; one month later it was 15. Rising costs, inflation, and a return by Britain to the gold standard at pre-war parity (meaning a 35 per cent drop in price), combined with a generalised post-World War recession, forced the Chamber of Mines to propose 'a reduction of the wages of the highest paid miners, the abolition of the Status Quo Agreement, and a recognition of underground work . . . to make greater use of native labour in semi-skilled occupations'.[25]

At the beginning of 1922 the mines laid off 2 000 white workers. On 8 January a strike ballot was called. Coal-miners were already on strike and two days later white workers on the gold mines, in power stations and in engineering shops came out. The situation deteriorated over the next weeks until the proclamation of a general strike on 5 March. In short order followed the first white assault on Africans, a widespread uprising including street war, the declaration of martial law and a violent end to it all.

The diverse forces at work during the Rand Revolt have been variously analysed.[26] 'It was essentially an economic struggle over the precise mode of operation of the system of racial discrimination (based on exploitation colour bars) according to the specific and in some ways contradictory class interests of the mining companies and white workers. But it resulted in a profound separation of the bulk of the white labour movement from the black proletariat (even the recently established Communist Party, contrary to its own principles, appeared to support this division).[27] The threat to the interests of white labour, coming as it did from the mine owners on the one side and the competition of many-times-cheaper black labour on the other, produced the fertile ground of an alliance betweeen national capital (in the form of Hertzog's National Party) and white labour, over and against mining capital (in the shape of the newly enlarged South African Party led by Smuts).

Whereas the economic goals of employers were secured in the crushing of the revolt 'through the direct substitution of African workers for whites in semi-skilled work . . . through work extension . . . through technological innovation (the jack-hammer drill), that is through more profitable labour reorganisation, the manner of the resolution of the crisis proved to be politically costly.[28] In the aftermath Smuts — and in a sense, the Chamber of Mines — was to lose control of government.

How did the Church react to the Rand Revolt and the issues involved? Initially, protectionism through the job colour bar was publicly attacked. As the strike got under way a call was made for the raising of African wages to the level of white mineworkers, which would have ended the cheap-labour threat among other things.[29] But such suggestions were not given much notice. As the strike persisted one church paper called for a 'reformed spirit' among conflicting parties, as well as a reformed system.[30] In like manner, 13 pastors of seven denominations on the East Rand published a document pleading for a conciliatory spirit and co-operation between capital and labour, while pointing out the need for workplace reform and a fairer utilisation of profits (though they were very careful to indicate that there was no intention 'to pronounce on the rights of this struggle').[31]

Once the conflict had erupted into an armed battle however, attitudes changed rapidly. Blacks, it was declared, must 'at all costs' be kept out of the struggle between capital and labour. That black workers belonged to the working-class was evidently a dangerous admission in this respect. Furthermore the role of *indunas* and mine clerks who had recently been upgraded in establishing and maintaining control of workers was registered as a tribute to the wisdom of the Chamber of Mines.[32]

The distinction between white and black workers, viewed by some as that between 'the real mine labourers' and a white labour aristocracy, became the basis for differing attitudes to the two fractions of labour as well as to the state which acted at this point on behalf of mining capitalists. White mine workers were increasingly rejected in words and in practice.[33] One vicarage did however attempt a policy of mediation between the police and strikers, thereby simultaneously bringing upon itself the wrath of both the strike committee and mine officials.[34] When it was all over, general relief was expressed at Smuts' handling of the situation, at the 'loyalty' of blacks, and at the quelling of the attempt of the National Party to ally itself with the white Labour Party which now represented a majority of Afrikaner mine workers (this last consolation was of course short-lived).

Taking into account the precious little available evidence that the churches displayed any substantial interest in the actual conditions of workers on the mines once the Revolt was over (at least until the rise of the militant 'new unions' after 1925), and bearing in mind an obvious and growing hostility towards the political representatives of national capital and white labour, the reaction of the churches to the 1922 upheaval parallels remarkably closely the position of the mine owners themselves and mining capital in general. This is true in relation to the competition between national and foreign fractions of capital, to the attack on the privileged place of white labour in the industrial system, to the desirable division betweeen settler (white) and colonised (black) fractions of labour, to the controls over black labour in particular, and to the fear of the rise of socialist doctrines. Moreover, although some church sources 'sided' with black workers in the Revolt, this did not at all imply any serious engagement with their concerns. Rather, their worry was precisely that black workers would 'get ideas' and themselves become more militant, perhaps (heaven forbid) creating a united labour movement.

Therefore, one must conclude that the unstable conditions of the first years of the 1920s, while producing a flurry of critical moments and ideas in the Church, did not, in the last resort, prove strong enough to shake the foundations of the Church's functional dependency on the ruling class. Rather, the general position of earlier decades, for a while in serious doubt, replicated itself in the years after the Rand Revolt. Perhaps this is most conspicuous in the vagueness, the lack of historical specificity, of the Church's brief flirtation with socialist ideas.

What references to socialist ideas exist are generally ambiguous and ill-considered, to say the least. For example, DDT Jabavu stressed that 'socialism of the worst calibre is claiming our people'. It was opposed in his view to Christianity (called by African socialists the 'white man's religion') and it also attacked the South African system as one of 'economic enslavement'.[35] Neither of these features made Jabavu comfortable. Similarly, commenting on the Martial Law Commission Report (1922), *SAO* expressed the hope that a 'human native policy' would soon be formulated to counter the influence of 'Communistic Bolshevism'. And the Provincial Missionary Conference of 1923 heard a confidential statement from Colonel Kirkpatrick, chief of police in Grahamstown, concerning 'criminal and bolshevistic movements now taking place among the Natives', with a request 'to do their utmost to check this movement'.[36]

Evidently, any interest in socialist thought and practice that the Church might have had stopped at the point where it became a tool for the potent organisation of black labour. Consequently one expects that concern for the working class stayed within a particular ideological framework, namely: capital and labour as two necessary counter-balancing sectors of society; harmonious relations between the two sectors as the prime good; a relatively unselfish use of profit on the part of capital and an understanding of the limits to labour power on the part of the workers; co-operation rather than repression or resistance. In short these were presuppositions concerned with system-reform rather than a genuine alternative. Indeed, all these elements appear in church records of the time.[37]

Thus although churches gave some expression on occasion to fairly radical demands — such as the participation of workers in decision-making and management of industry, the idea of industry as a public service rather than a private enterprise, and alignment with the cause of labour — no specific analysis, no particular programme, no unambiguous policy, and no theological clarification appears to have been carried out.[38] Moreover, little evidence may be found of the Church forging a close relationship to labour as such, either black or white, while on the contrary its connections to sections of capital and to the small but influential black bourgeoisie were deepened.[39] The Dutch Reformed Church's growing contact with a sector of settler labour (white Afrikaner essentially) by contrast highlights the middle-class base of the CPSA and Methodist churches. On the other hand none showed any great capacity to relate to black workers.

One must conclude, therefore, that the possibilities for a new debate, for a revised understanding of the Church, its theology, and its role in a colonial capitalist form of society, and for a new practice congruent with such developments, were by and large lost even as they were discovered. Hinchliff writes that

> . . . the influence of theologians like FD Maurice, and the historical crusades of Anglo-Catholic priests in the English slums had a profound effect upon the Anglican Church in this country. The ideal of the priest became that of the Christian socialist, struggling to bring to Faith the poor and underprivileged, fighting their battles in matters of housing, of political and civil rights, striving for social justice, for fair wages and no sweated labour . . .[40]

But here he describes a certain intellectual ideal attached to a practice defined by service to, rather than solidarity with, the dominated. Moreover he does so within the terms and the limits of the dominant class and the prevailing political economy, focusing on the crusaders rather than the resistance of the colonised and of workers themselves. To that extent, insofar as this was also the case with the people Hinchliff has in mind, the ideal remained an abstraction proclaimed by a Church institution still functionally dependent upon the ruling powers; an institution therefore which fundamentally failed to put its organisational, functional and operational weight behind the poor and the dispossessed it verbally championed.

The New Dispensation

The particular conditions of class conflict at the end of the previous decade led to a situation requiring state intervention, a predicament precipitated by the peculiar structure of the mining industry and the profitability crisis of the early 1920s. The effect of intervention was 'to create the conditions for the white wage-earning classes to emerge as supportive classes for the form of the state'.[41]

Long term structural developments and conditions in the political economy of South Africa had produced a convergence of interests between the groups represented politically by the Labour Party and the National Party. In the wake of the 1922 upheaval, they were able to capitalise on the conflicts involved to assert the primacy of their own particular interests. Their election pact represented a fractional class alliance in competition with mining capital and its imperial interests. The electoral victory of the Pact alliance in 1924 enabled the new government to appropriate parts of the mining surplus in order to allow the emergence of a national bourgeoisie based in industry and agriculture, and to protect white labour through special privileges.[42] The industrial policy of the Pact Government consequently sought three things:

> . . . to protect South African industry against outside competition and thus conserve foreign exchange, to protect poor whites against black and coloured competition in the unskilled field, and to protect skilled white workers from undercutting by black competition in the higher trades.[43]

One result of the coming to power of the alliance was the appropriation of surplus value from the mines, still the major source of capital accumulation, for the interests of national capital — in particular for subsidising agriculture and the sponsorship of select, secondary heavy industries (such as iron and steel).[44] At the same time the 'Native Question' demanded a more systematic policy, one which would suit whites, in particular the white wage-earners who formed part of the Pact alliance. Also, the growing militancy of African workers, especially the African mineworkers (who had staged a massive strike), had alarmed both businessmen and politicians. Moreover, an alliance of black and white workers was an unthinkable horror, a possibility not to be allowed under any circumstances.

A new policy able to cope with these challenges had to take shape. Its initial features may be seen in three statutes which 'did more than any other legislation to depress the African's wages, depreciate his status and isolate him from the rest of the working class' — the Apprenticeship Act, 1922; the Natives (Urban) Areas Act, 1923; and the Industrial Conciliation Act, 1924. However, before these came into effect, some solidarity among workers as a whole could be perceived in the white Mine Workers Union's attack on capitalism and their call in 1920 for a worker-controlled economy. In fact, the competition between left-wing trade unions and Afrikaner nationalism for the allegiance of white factory operatives and white unskilled workers continued for some three decades.[45]

Thus the trends of the earlier decades of industrialisation solidified into explicit policies in the hands of the Hertzog government. These appeared most clearly in the earlier Smuts-sponsored Industrial Conciliation Act (Africans were thereby excluded from the definition of 'employees' and thus from any legal recognition as workers with rights); the Civilised Labour Policy (1924: work opportunities and support for unemployed whites were thereby created); the Wage Act (1925: laying down minimum wages for white unskilled workers, but not for black); the Mines and Works Amendment Act (1926: colour bar in mining ratified); and the proposals generally known as the Hertzog Bills, introduced in 1926 (formalising and systematising 'Native Policy' on the lines already established and first enunciated in most aspects by Lagden).

The Industrial Conciliation Act seriously undermined independent union action among white workers, and excluded African workers totally from the negotiating and bargaining process of the new industrial councils while 'coloured' and some Indians were drawn into the system. Those in the councils were able to protect themselves against undercutting, the 'chief bargaining weapon' of African labour, and to enter into agreements prejudicial to consumers and lower paid workers. The total effect of the Act was to extend the pattern of labour organisation established on the mines to manufacturing industries, thereby perpetuating the huge wage gap between white and black workers and giving the former a stake in the white power structure.[46]

Processes of capitalist development affecting blacks did not always discriminate on the basis of skin pigmentation; whites were also negatively influenced. Many rural settlers were forced off the land by some of the same factors pressuring the black peasantry. The rinderpest epidemic (1896—7), the burning of farms by the British during the Anglo-Boer War, the sustained drought between 1903—8: all these factors also played a role in the genesis of a landless, dependent, unskilled body of 'poor whites', estimated by the Carnegie Commission in its 1932 report to have risen to 300 000, all but ten per cent being Afrikaner.[47] Of course not all 'poor whites' were rural victims. Many had managed to establish some economic footholds in urban Johannesburg, especially in the fields of transport riding, cab driving and brickmaking. But later many were forced by larger developments out of the market into wage-labour.

The cost of employing unskilled whites was greater than that of employing blacks, for their families' subsistence and reproduction, unlike most black workers, had to be included, they were not subject to the controls of the forced labour system (such as contracts, compounds, recruiting monopsony), and they had some political rights as colonial settlers. This meant that the mines, the largest employers, found the employment of whites unprofitable, especially given the marginal profit structure of the industry. However, representatives of national capital, desiring an expanded market and a strengthening of their power bloc, saw in the 'poor whites' a possible 'supportive class'.[48] This underlay the attention paid to the 'poor white problem', a concern EG Malherbe cuttingly ascribed to the peculiarity of the South African situation in which 'poor whiteism' rather than poverty as such dominated debate.[49] To this end the Pact government strengthened the colour bars in industry while pursuing its 'civilised labour' policy. In this way unskilled whites could seek jobs and security from the state and the white supremacy parties who defined their problems as racially based and provided racially protective legislation in return for their white support.[50]

Earlier the job colour bars in the mining industry had come under severe judgement in the Hildich-Smith case of 1923, in effect a test of the legality of the bars which were contained in the Regulations of the Mines and Works Act (1911) but not in the enabling Act itself. The bars were consequently declared *ultra vires* leading to a somewhat anomalous and unclear situation. Pressures from white workers pushed the Pact government into formalising the matter in return for continued loyalty. First came the Wage Act, an effective protection for white workers and work-seekers against competition from black labour through minimum wage stipulations; then came the Mines and Works Amendment Act which overcame the earlier anomaly by including job colour bars in the enabling Act.[51] An opposite and widely held view was clearly stated by Smuts on behalf of the South African Party. He felt:

> When you had effective *de facto* racial discrimination there was no need to raise all this feeling all over the country, and thus to threaten the status quo by making it more overt. The position of his party was: 'let us stick to the old colour bar regulations as they have been working in the mines, a course which would lead to no outcry in the country'.[52]

Black reaction to the 'colour bar' was mixed. On the one hand 'limits placed on their capacity for capital accumulation' drew strong and emotional reaction from the bourgeoisie and petty-bourgeoisie (small-business owners, petty commodity producers, professionals and the 'salariat').[53] On the other hand African workers found this issue of far less concern than the various elements of 'the system of ultra-exploitation of labour constituted by the exploitation colour bars of the employers.'[54]

By the end of the decade the topography of the South African political economy could be perceived in bold relief, naked in its oppression and exploitation, a solid mass of laws and structures reinforced by a racist ideology that would be maintained with increasing force from then onwards in the face of regular and mounting waves of resistance.

Religion and Reform, 1925—1930

> And to our Native people we say: 'Be loyal to the Church which has done so much for you. Use all its ordinances and enter into life's relationships with its sanction and blessing. Above all, do not be misled by those who would have you believe that your awakening race-consciousness can be satisfied and your true development secured simply by the improvement of political, educational and economic conditions'.
>
> Address of the Methodist Conference to members
> of the Church, 1929.[55]

> Give the people their rights before they demand them and you will be saved the indignity of being forced, soon or late, to surrender them.
>
> WD Cingo[56]

Consonant with the English-speaking churches' proclivity to reflect the interests and views of mining capital on the one hand, while on the other being bound as a body organised on the basis of voluntary association to respond to the press of its black membership, the last half of the decade saw a growing conflict with the newly empowered Pact government, and a revived concern for the place of blacks within the South African political economy. Arising out of the strong interest displayed earlier in questions of industrial ethics and the relationship of the Church to labour, relatively more notice is paid to labour organisations and the material conditions of workers, though generally within the limits outlined before. But the dominant issue of the time unquestionably was the 'colour bar', with the Hertzog Bills of 1926 providing the primary impetus to furious debate. As a result, for the first time the anti-colour bar (more recently, 'anti-apartheid') syndrome of the English-speaking churches blossomed into firm antagonism against the state, or at least to the particular form of the state governed by the hegemony of national capital.

The struggle of the English-speaking churches to define the role of Christianity in the conflicts of South African society was thus increasingly characterised by a critique of a particular trajectory of capitalist development in favour of an alternative trajectory embodying policies of reform. Consequently, the capitalist nature of the political economy receded as a critical topic, while the major focus of battle became the specific form of capitalism suitable to South African conditions. This remained true of the churches for the next 50 years.

Political Protest

Prior to the election of the Pact Coalition, the Dutch Reformed Church had initiated a widely attended conference to discuss 'Native policy' and relations between 'European and Bantu'. Together with the Pact's policy platform on 'colour', this spurred discussion of these matters among both churches and black political bodies.[57] Amidst numerous warnings about the exclusion of blacks from decision-making processes and from the proper benefits of their labour,[58] various proposals emerged. Some supported systematising segregation policies, others desired their relaxation in order to allow the incorporation of suitably 'civilised' blacks under strict conditions, but all were solicitous of clear policies to manage the 'native question'.

A most notable church figure in support of a segregationist approach which he termed a 'policy of economic differentiation', was Edgar Brookes (though he changed his opinion later).[59] Bishop Karney too saw this as the ideal, but thought it too late to be applied; education, therefore, was the only alternative other than 'extermination'.[60] Similarly, the Rev JWW Owen, having attacked a recent ANC congress for their 'immoderate and truculent attitude', proceeded to praise Hertzog's colour policies, in order to 'set Native aspirants on right lines'. He quoted Brookes as follows:

> 'While we should wish to do our utmost to save them from oppressive or restrictive legislation, while we should strain every move to assist them in progress, social, political and economic, it is not to be expected that we should abdicate . . . in their favour the position in South Africa that is ours by a right every whit as sacred as any which they possess.'
>
> I wish these words could be learned by heart by every Native man who poses as a leader of his people. And the Native people must realise that they cannot do without our help![61]

The bulk of comment from the English-speaking churches turned however on a liberal policy of limited, controlled incorporation of Africans, a concept expressed perhaps most lucidly in the Bishop of George's contention that Africans 'must be made fit to be the Junior Partner in this country, but on our conditions'. He made it clear that this referred only to Africans who were 'clean, intelligent, well-educated, civilised men (sic)'.[62] On this basis segregation policies were roundly criticised.[63] On the other hand the selective inclusion of Africans should occur in relation to their growth from 'infancy to maturity' and a 'willingness to co-operate with Europeans'. Besides this, a dual policy of rural 'native parliaments' and an urban qualified 'separate vote', the Cape franchise policy as outlined by Sir George Grey in 1854, and the Glen Grey Act ordinances, were championed in order to maximise the value of a 'combination of white man's brain and organising power, and black men's hands and sweat'.[64] The key mediating role of educated Africans envisaged in this scheme was supported by leading Africans themselves. They would benefit accordingly. This included the renowned Dr AB Xuma who regarded educated Africans like himself, and them alone, as qualified to 'interpret the European to the African, and the African to the European'.[65]

In short, as opposed to a segregationist 'system of legal peonage' built upon 'reservoirs of labour into which at will employers might freely dip to obtain cheap, unskilled or semi-skilled labour',[66] the English-speaking churches supported something very much like the policy of 'Trusteeship' — a gradual inclusion of suitably 'matured' blacks into 'the responsibilities and privileges of adulthood'.[67] The aim was to produce 'a Bantu citizenship in South Africa, good in character, economically efficient and contented . . . a blessing and not a menace in the land'.[68] Thus, in contrast to legal peonage, a system of legal patronage was proposed, neither approach envisaging any fundamental alteration to economic forces already producing increasing poverty and hardship for the excluded majority.

These issues evince the first signs of a comprehensive opposition of the English-speaking churches to a particular form of the state. Thereafter it hardened into a distinct antipathy tinged with bitterness and hostility.[69]

Opposition to the state *per se* was not of course intended. Rather a competition for political hegemony between the major fractions of capital emerged, as has been argued earlier. The English-speaking churches tended to align themselves with mining capital and foreign capital in general over and against national capital and its alliances. The latter found support among the Dutch Reformed churches who helped promote an exclusive nationalist ideology. Both positions, let it be said, reflected broad agreement about the role of colonised labour; both took for granted the prevailing structures. Their differences lay in the direction in which those structures should be developed, and in the most appropriate policies for managing them. (Note that for our purposes, the matter does not revolve around which of the two options was (is) better, but around the position of the churches in a given political economy.)

The Hertzog Bills signalled the onset of battle and motivated the opposition of the English-speaking churches. Yet — perhaps not surprisingly, given hopes for a consistent, ordered native policy — not all initial reaction was unfavourable. The continued dominance of whites was taken to be a *sine qua non*, but from the middle of 1926 on, rejection of the tenets underlying the bills virtually became a point of honour. Both Anglican and Methodist leaders and publications described and criticised the Bills in numerous ways. The major target was the Mines and Works Amendment Act which legalised the job colour bar in industry rather than leaving it an informal practice.[70] As one journal put it quite succinctly:

> What began as a local, possibly temporary measure and certainly wise and cautious set of mining regulations, that came into force about 40 years ago by the decision of the Transvaal Republic government of that time has widened out and into a law that will depress the status of natives everywhere in the Union. No one had complained of the working of the old regulations; all accepted the necessity . . . But this new law![71]

The most concrete proposal amongst the torrent of disapproval and occasional invective was the calling of 'round table conferences' to include 'Native Chiefs and leaders' with whom consultation might occur prior to the drafting of legislation affecting blacks.[72] The hypothesis that the English-speaking churches, albeit unconsciously, reflected the position of a particular fraction of capital is not undermined by their 'championship' of Africans. As has already been pointed out, they favoured a policy of incorporation of 'civilised' (that is, aspirant bourgeois or petty-bourgeois) Africans, and of 'fairer treatment' for the working class but within the prevailing structures of dominance.[73] In contrast, concern for the black workers *per se* was markedly absent among the churches with the notable exception of a remarkable editor of *South African Outlook*, Dr James Henderson.

Thus, despite massive reaction to the Hertzog Bills (implying a radical solidarity with blacks), almost no attention was paid to the Industrial Conciliation Act, the 'Civilised Labour' policy and the Wage Act (1925). All of these were more potent in maintaining the exploitation and oppression of Africans than the Hertzog Bills, as inimical as the latter were.

With only two exceptions, significant references in church records to wages and wage policy came exclusively from *SAO*.[74] It dealt with such matters as the effects in South Africa of the industrial revolution, unemployment, silicosis and tuberculosis, farm wages, the Native Recruiting Corporation, exploitation wages, the injustices of contracts, the Labour Party, the absence of legal bargaining machinery for African workers, and the 'forced labour' characteristics of black workers' material and legal conditions. Articles were both analytical and critical — valuable work that appears to have been widely respected among the churches and sometimes used as background material for resolutions and declarations, but seldom if at all integrated into the policies and practices of the churches at large.

In general wage minimisation practices, the contract system, the recruiting monopsony, compounds, and pass laws fade out of the Church's public conscience, though the last named was vigorously denounced at the 1929 'Bantu-European' conference.[75] Interest in the compounds was even more abstractly religious than before. No comment was made on the actual conditions of compound life except in acknowledgement of the help of the mining companies, for example, in purchasing 'a portable Bioscope outfit' to show 'scenes and stories of native life and life in other countries as well as nature sketches, educational subjects and humorous pictures of a healthy kind (sic)'.[76]

On other aspects of labour, comments and articles did from time to time appear more widely, particularly in response to the challenge of the ICU and the deterioration of the 'tribal' reserves. But very little of this was of any depth or spiced with much critical insight, so that one is left with the general impression that the prevailing social, economic and political milieu was regarded more or less as the natural order, requiring little discussion in the Church at least, detailed matters of regulating the 'natural' order of state and business not being its concern.

Thorns in the Side

Meanwhile black industrial resistance had begun to develop: with it arose some direct attacks on the churches. This irritated many but did not bring much more understanding or insight into the churches.

Clements Kadalie's ICU rose to the forefront in leaps and bounds during this period. At its climax it was perhaps powerful enough, if not for certain crucial organisational and political errors, to have changed the face of South Africa. Launched nationally in May 1920, within a few years it had a mass base across the country. The exploitation wage structure was recognised by the ICU as the basis for the division between white and black labour, and its attack landed squarely upon the heads of capitalists and the bourgeoisie in general.[77]

One contributor to the *Church Chronicle* was quite certain that 'the ICU is fast becoming one gigantic question to the whole of Christian South Africa, challenging the churches in no uncertain language to come out into the open and face the implications of their belief.' Continuing, he wrote:

> At the back of all ICU propaganda and personalities is the great human cry for justice and 'a place in the sun'; with the unquestionably legitimate demand that every race, regardless of colour, shall be allowed to enjoy the good things it helps to produce. Will the churches move, regardless of the consequences, which may mean deportation or even imprisonment, in helping this native cause where it is right, and rebuking where it is wrong?[78]

How was the challenge answered? Sympathy with many of the aims of the ICU appears to have been expressed in several quarters, especially in respect of the right of workers to organise for collective bargaining and a decent standard of living.[79] Negative criticism, however, always accompanied such sentiments. Among demands made by churchmen who took any interest in the ICU, was that it should not attack whites; that black unions should be sponsored by white unions; that provocative speeches should cease and reform be recognised as a 'bit by bit' process; that socialism should be avoided, drunkenness and vice given up, and decent homes and family life built before the Church could count the ICU as allies (sic); finally, that the ICU should hold itself 'strictly aloof from political activities' and stop 'flouting those who have been responsible for the Native's progressive development from the beginning of the missionary enterprise in South Africa'.[80] With such qualifications coming from even those most sympathetic to the ICU, there could be no hope of any serious engagement on the part of churches with black workers' organisatons or their concerns.

Hostility in fact increased as the ICU prospered, leading a well-known reformist, Father Huss, to complain rather discordantly about workers: 'where at one time I would have been heard with respect, I am faced with bitter antagonism and bombarded with questions.' This he attributed to 'this deadly threat to the peace of the country, the ICU.'[81] The South African Missionary Society went so far as to rejoice in the failure of 'the political agitators of the Kadalie school' to win the allegiance of the Methodist Church.[82] The conclusion is unavoidable that the churches tended to distance themselves as much as possible from organised black labour.

That the ICU did not actually receive the kind of support that positive church statements may imply, in short that solidarity was a word without substance, is confirmed by WG Ballinger, a senior officer in the ICU, in his sad remark to the 'European-Bantu' conference of 1929 that 'friendly Europeans and the better type of Native leaders ought to have taken more interest in the movement and guided it in a helpful fashion'.[83] Once again an exception

was the *South Afrian Outlook* which showed greater sensibilities in its defence
of the ICU against attacks by Durban employers and Natal farmers, charging
the latter with repression and exploitation. In one other instance, in support of
the ICU, a Methodist periodical weighed in against the use of child labour and
unpaid labour on farms.[84]

By the late 20s the ICU had already expelled communists in the movement,
influenced, Roux believes, by the Joint Council of African and Europeans
established earlier in Johannesburg in response to the widespread unrest at the
beginning of the decade.[85] By the end of the decade the ICU was in decline,
their opportunities lost through a combination of a lack of 'a firm base in
large-scale industry (on the shop floor), recognition by employers, and a
record of successful strikes', as well as through elements of 'intrigue, in-
competence, mismanagement and dishonesty'.[86]

Besides the ICU there was a more widespread upsurge of militant trade
unionism between 1928 and 1932, giving rise to a number of new unions.
These 'new unions' arose largely among those employed in the now substantial
secondary industry, and consisted of an inter-racial class alliance among
workers largely founded on a 'considerable overlap of functions within the
labour process between the different racial groups'. Strike action, dormant
since 1922, increased dramatically, in two instances bringing an entire industry
to a standstill.[87]

Thus we have the one salient feature of the decade, namely the growth of
black resistance in the industrial context, its increasing sophistication in the
maturity of the proletarianisation process (not yet complete), and its inclusion
of several class alliances across caste lines. At the same time, contradictions
resulting from the effects of the colonial character of capitalism served to introduce tensions within the working class that were frequently exploited by
capital in general.

Finally, we return to the rural reserves, where conditions in the latter half of
the decade were rapidly deteriorating. The severe impoverishment of blacks in
rural areas, visible in 'diminishing resources, declining agriculture, increasing
population and increasing stock, mostly the usual features of congestion', was
a direct result of colonisation and the exploitation of wage labour under harsh
controls.[88] This did not go unnoticed. A number of references to acute problems of housing, clothing, low crop yields and cattle wealth, diseases, lack of
employment, scarcity of land, heavy taxation, and trade monopolies are to be
found, many of them orginating with Henderson of Lovedale. Various suggestions were made towards land reform, among them tuition in working the land
properly, providing a land bank for Africans, securing additional land, utilising title deeds and trusts to protect ownership, and initiating a national land
policy on rural development.[89]

But despite the heed paid to rural conditions, the call of one Methodist that the Church 'should abandon its attitude of non-intervention in matters economic' (implying that non-intervention was normal) appears to have been answered in a rather incomplete and inactive manner.[90] Thus one missionary council honestly admitted its inability to discover what practical steps sould be taken.[91] On the other hand the Methodist Church did give official support to the 'Native Bill of Rights' adopted earlier by the ANC.[92] Others also pointed to the 'profound unrest among the Native people' arising from what the newspaper *Umteteli 'wa Bantu* called '*sjambok* rule' (rule by the whip). Some thought that industrial education, something missions could undertake, would be best.[93] But in general the practical outworking of church concern, other than in providing support for one or other opposition parliamentarian in formal debate, was close to nil.

Such a conclusion is not intended to disparage the Church, to deny or pour scorn on its well-intentioned efforts. But the evidence of the Church's inability to make powerful and effective its own proclamation in the processes and contradictions of material history, to become self-critical in the best sense of the term, must be faced.

The poverty of church action in the face of enormous challenges may be understood as a direct result of its lack of self-critical awareness, and in its ideological and to a lesser extent political captivity to a fraction of capital which was in competition with national capital and its political representatives for control of the state. At the same time a moderate black aspirant bourgeoisie, desirous of an alliance with liberal forces, pressured the Church in another direction. This raised thorny issues about blacks as a whole, and produced profound ambiguities in the thinking of the Church. Seriously compromised in its capacity to act decisively in solidarity with the more radical black political bodies, the Church found solidairty with workers a virtual impossibility.

Consequently, one sees many promising insights into the nature and extent of oppression and exploitation cut short before they could develop, curtailed before their practical implications were able to drive the Church into seriously challenging the dominant structures or acting decisively in support of the dominated.

In contrast, notwithstanding social-concern departments, archival records towards the end of the decade show a growing interest in apolitical spirituality accompanied by demands that the Church spend its energies on specifically religious tasks.[94] It was thought, however, that it should use what influence it had in pressing the authorities for political and economic reform suitable to a 'civilised' nation.

In sum, the 1920s witnessed several events which encapsulated the trends of the twentieth century development in the South African political economy. Crises were occasioned at almost every point by a rising conflict between capital and labour, and in some cases by the ongoing dynamics of colonial subjugation and expropriation as the process of incorporation continued in the rural areas. Settler colonialism, a unique cost structure in the dominant mining industry, and the growth of national capital combined to produce the main features of a social formation still today largely intact. This was accompanied by a racist ideology through which certain alliances were cemented and overall control over labour and division of labour was confirmed.

It may be concluded that the struggle of the decades that followed took place within a framework and milieu largely determined during the first 30 years of this century. From the Lagden Commission to the Hertzog Bills: this was a time during which the trajectory of capitalist development resulted in the rise to power of national capital, in the incorporation of white labour, in the support of the 'poor white' proletariat for a nationalist state under Afrikaner control, in the flowering of a racist ideology, and in the division of the labour movement. It was a time, too, of increasingly sophisticated and organised industrial resistance accompanied by the march of African nationalism, made visible by the end of the period in the ICU and the African National Congress respectively. It was the time in which the churches struggled to come to terms with the new age — its conflicts, contradictions, crises and controversies — without in the end really succeeding.

Notes

1 'The Kingdom', Diocese of Pretoria, April 1922.
2 P Hinchliff (1963), p216.
3 TCC, January 6, 1920.
4 P Hinchliff (1963), p232.
5 F Johnstone (1976), p126. See also RK Cope, 'Comrade Bill', Ts, Papers, 1941—50.
6 HJ Simons and RE Simons (1969), p220; F Johnstone (1976), p180; R Davies (1979), p179.
7 P Bonner (1980), p5; index calculated on the basis of 1938 prices = 100.
8 F Johnstone (1976), pp180 & 197.
9 HJ Simons and RE Simons (1969), p233; F Johnstone (1976), p183.
10 DDT Jabavu, 'Native Unrest', paper to Natal Missionary Conference, July 1920, in T Karis and G Carter (1972), vol I, pp119—125 *passim*.
11 TCC, January 22, 1920, comment MO Hodson.
12 *Ibid,* August 11, 1921.
13 CE, October 1, 1920, pp153—6, continued in CE, November 1, 1920, pp167—171.
14 JS Theale, 'Christianity, Basis of Native Policy?', *The Workers Herald,* December 21, 1923, in T Karis and G Carter (1972), vol II, p214—5.

15 Rev AW Cragg, Diary entry, September 1, 1921.

16 See for example CE, July 1, 1921, pp104—5; also Archbishop WM Carter, ALS, May 25, June 2 & June 9, 1921.

17 *The Net: Zululand Missionary Association Quarterly*, June 1922; also MCMC, 1922, p107; *Transvaal and Swazi District* (1923/4), p6; TMC, February 5, 1923.

18 TMC, October 8, 1923; *Transvaal Missions Quarterly*, January 1924; MCMC, 1924, p141.

19 SAMSR (39th), 1920, p2.

20 CE, April 2, 1923, p92; May 1, 1923, pp117—8.

21 H Houghton (1967), p47, gives a 1918 figure of about 488 000 wage-earners on farms.

22 CE, April 1, 1920, p63; May 1, 1923, p118; 'Advance', June 1923, p106; SAO, November 2, 1925, p250.

23 *Church Times*, London, July 29, 1925, from a South African correspondent; see also MCMC, 1926, p189.

24 See variously 'The Kindgom', Diocese of Pretoria, July 1921; Native Conference, Diocese of Pretoria, Minutes, 1921; CE, February 2, 1920, p25; SAO, July 1, 1922, pp138—40; August 1, 1922, p161; May 1, 1925, p104; September 1, pp202—3; and November 2, p242; Provincial Missionary Conference, Minutes, November 1923; Bishop A Karney, Johannesburg, Charge to Diocese, Ts, May 1924, and LS, February 11, 1925.

25 F Johnstone (1976), p130.

26 *Ibid*, pp125—136. See also TRH Davenport (1977), pp192—196; H Houghton (1967), pp143—7; RK Cope, 'Comrade Bill', Ts, Papers, 1941—50.

27 HJ Simons and RE Simons (1969), p299; see also the *United Front Manifesto* (SALP and SACP) of 1922, directed against both Smuts and the Chamber of Mines, W Hills, Diary, 1922.

28 F Johnstone (1976), pp138—145, *passim*.

29 TMC, May 31, 1920; SAO, March 1, 1922, pp52—3.

30 TMC, February 6, 1922.

31 *The Star*, Monday, February 6, 1922.

32 SAO, March 1, 1922, pp46—7.

33 *Ibid, loc cit,* p53; *The Church Times*, London, March 23, 1922, a South African correspondent; TMC, August 11, 1924. See also TMC, April 10, 1922; also in the Martial Law Commission Report, 1922, evidence of Rev Oliphant, p524, and evidence of D Snowdon, p125; also Bishop EF Paget, 'Address to Benoni Congregation', Papers, 1922.

34 This was St Dunstan's vicarage; see also Bishop EF Paget, Papers, 1922.

35 CE, November 1, 1920, pp170—1; address to Natal Missionary Conference.

36 SAO, December 1, 1922, pp258—9; Provincial Missionary Conference, Minutes, November 1923.

37 See for example MCMC, 1921, pp128—9, TCC, March 23, 1922; TMC, April 3, 1922; Bishop A Karney, 'Charge to Diocese of Johannesburg', Ts, May 1924; *Rand Daily Mail*, 1925, in Rev WA Palmer, Scrapbook, 1925—1945.

38 TCC, December 23, 1920; September 30, 1920; and to a lesser extent, November 16, 1922.

39 P Hinchliff (1963), makes an interesting observation in this respect, p232; see also Bishop J Williams, St Johns Pastoral Letter, Lent 1922; WC Atkins, 'The Cash Value of Native Education', Pamphlet, Adams Mission Station, 1923; Archbishop

WM Carter, ALS, 6 letters, January 12 — April 6, 1922, in which Smuts and his government receive great sympathy and admiration; and TMC, October 8, 1923; these among many other references which support the point made here.

40 P Hinchliff (1963), p231.

41 R Davies (1979), p32 *passim.*

42 F Johnstone (1976), p152; R Davies (1979), p169; TRH Davenport (1977), p197; D O'Meara, in E Webster (1978), p70.

43 TRH Davenport (1977), p361.

44 R Davies, D Kaplan, M Morris and D O'Meara (1976), pp9—10.

45 HJ Simons and RE Simons (1969), pp319—20; & p327: 'two decades' is the actual statement of the book, but in the light of research by O'Meara and others it is safe to say 'three'; see D O'Meara, 'White Trade Unionism, Political Power and Afrikaner Nationalism', in E Webster (1978&, pp164—80.

46 HJ Simons and RE Simons (1969), p334—6 *passim;* also R Davies and J Lever, both in E Webster (1978), pp67—108.

47 TRH Davenport (1977), p225. Church records show little interest in the 'poor whites' as such, and what references there are tend to be very superficial in their view on the issue, sometimes even contemptuous. See *The Net: Zululand Missionary Association Quarterly,* December 1922; TCC, October 30, 1924; SAO, March 1925, p61; and G Callaway, 'The Native Problem in South Africa', Pamphlet, Oxford 1926, p 7; see also D Welsh 'Growth of Towns', in OX: p176; F Johnstone (1976), pp59—60.

48 R Davies (1979), pp54—65 *passim,* and pp76—7.

49 J Stone (1973), p124.

50 See HJ Simons and RE Simons (1969), p339; also F Johnstone (1976), pp70—1. The effect of this policy may be indicated by the substantial rise in whites employed in private industry in the years following: 1923/4 = 30,7%, compared with 1932/3 = 45,2% (R Davies, D Kaplan, M Morris and D O'Meara (1976), p12).

51 F Johnstone (1976), p145—6 and p69; on p149 he articulates reasons for the acceptance by the mining companies of a limited colour bar rather than their complete removal; see also pp72—4 & 158.

52 *Ibid,* p165.

53 P Bonner (1980), p19.

54 F Johnstone (1976), p184.

55 MCMC, 1929, p208.

56 'Forward', August 10, 1926, p3.

57 TMC, June 11, 1923; SAO, June 2, 1924, pp128—9.

58 See for example TMC, September 22, 1924; Canon Palmer, Address, *Cape Argus,* November 24; 'Forward', October 1, 1925; p1; SAO, May 1, 1926, p117.

59 SAO, March 2, 1925, p62.

60 Bishop A Karney, Johannesburg, Ls, February 11, 1925.

61 TMC, January 18 & 25, February 1 & 8, 1926 *passim.*

62 TCC, October 30, 1924.

63 See for example, 'Forward', May 10, 1926, pp1—2; James D Taylor (ed), 'Christianity and the Natives of South Africa', *Year Book of SA Missions,* 1928.

64 MCMC, 1925, p177; 'Forward', March 1926, p16; DDT Jabavu, SAO, October 1, 1926, p225; 'Forward', October 1, 1925, p3; and 'Advance', May 1926, pp82—3 (last quote).

65 Bantu-European Students Conference, 1930, papers.

66 Rev WW Rider, TMC, November 4, 1929; Rider attacks such ideas.

67 See MCMC, 1952; aslo in CCD, 1952, p10.

68 MCMC, 1929, p177.

69 This is already evident in Tielman Roos' infamous attack on the Anglican Church in 1925, carrying with it the threat of police action: *Rand Daily Mail*, September 7, 1925. See a similar attack by Dr TC Meiser, Member of the Legislative Assembly for Vrededorp, *Rand Daily Mail*, October 28, 1925.

70 See for example. TCC, December 24, 1925; Bishop A Karney, 'Charge to Diocese of Johannesburg', May 1926; 'Forward', January 10, 1926 (p13). June 10 (pp9—10), October 10 (pp1—2) and November 10 (pp1—2. Also the *Transvaal and Swazi District Directory,* 1926/7, p6; TCC, October 28 and December 9, 1926; TMC, 1926—30, *passim;* Bishop A Karney, Ls, February 7, 1927, p197 and 1928, p151; GMCSA: Summary, 1928, pp112—3.

71 'Forward', July 10, 1926, p2.

72 MCMC, 1926, p153; 'Forward', March 10, 1927, p1; MCMC, 1930. p127; CCD, 1930, p7.

73 For example, 'Forward', January 10, 1926, p3; E Smith. 'The Christian Mission in Africa', Le Zoute Conference, 1926, pp90—1; Provincial Missionary Conference, Minutes, November 1928; GMCSA: Summary, 1928, p118.

74 The two exceptions are Bishop Karney, 'Charge to Diocese of Johannesburg', May 1926; and MCMC, 1930, p51. Otherwise see SAO, March, pp61—2, and July 1, pp155—6, and November 2, p248, 1925; aslo SAO, February 1, p33, and July 1, pp151—3, and August 2, pp183—5, and September 1, pp210—2, 1926; also SAO, July 1, p133, 1927; SAO, January 2, p18, and February 1, pp26—7, and May 1, June 1, July 2, *passim*, 1928; SAO, April 1, pp66—70, and May 1, p103, 1930.

75 TMC, February 18, 1929.

76 *Transvaal and Sawzi District Directory,* 1921/2, p1; also *ibid,* 1922/3, pp6—7, and 1923/4, p6; also 'Advance', November 1924, pp210—2; *Church Times*, London, January 1928.

77 See C Kadalie, African Labour Congress, *The Workers Herald,* December 21, 1923, in T Karis and G Carter (1972), vol II, p214—5; and vol I, p324—5.

78 TCC, August 4, 1927.

79 For example, Bishop A Karney, LS, July 19, 1927; SAO, September 1, 1927, pp168—9; SAO, February 1, 1928, pp29—30; GMCSA: Summary, 1928, p117.

80 Bishop A Karney, *loc cit;* SAO, February 1, 1928, pp29—30; Bishop W Carey (Bloemfontein), in SAO, January 2, 1928, p1; Rev A Lea, in 'Forward', January 1928.

81 *The Star,* September 1927, cited in E Roux (1964), pp173—4.

82 SAMSR (45th), 1927, p27.

83 TMC, February 18, 1929.

84 SAO, February 1, 1928, pp31—2; also July 1, 1929, p131; and the Methodist journal 'Forward', January 2, 1928.

85 E Roux (1964), pp161—2 & p166.

86 TRH Davenport (1977), p180; and E Roux (1964), p197, respectively.

87 J Lewis, 'The New Unionism: Industrialisation and Industrial Unions in South Africa, 1925—1930', in E Webster (1978), pp137—8.

88 SAO, July 1, 1927, p127ff.

89 SAO, April 1, 1925, p99f; *ibid,* 1927, p101, and March 1, 1928, pp49—50;

GMCSA: Summary, 1925, pp99—100; *ibid,* 1928, p1117; 'Forward', May 1927, p16; Provincial Missionary Conference, Minutes, November 1928; MCMC, 1930, p151; also 'Forward', December 1, 1925, pp1—3; *ibid,* March 1926, p16; *ibid,* February 10, 1927, pp1—2; E Smith, *op cit,* p121; SAO, March 1, 1927, pp50—2; GMCSA: Summary, 1928, p118.

90 'Forward', December, 1925, p3.

91 Ciskei Missionary Council Report, in SAO, March 1, 1928, pp49—50.

92 MCMC, 1927, p154.

93 'Forward', in January 1, 1928; GMCSA, Minutes, November 27, 1929; Archbishop WM Carter, LS, July 5, 1930; South African correspondent, *Church Times,* London, March 1930; MCMC, 1927, p175, and 1928, p161.

94 A representative example of what could be found more generally in archival material, is the list of major issues discussed by the Provincial Missionary Conference between 1906—1940, as reflected in Minute Books. These included:

Separate church organisation (black and white); clerical structure; finances for missions; Order of Ethiopia; scriptural and doctrinal translation; conversion and evangelism; Mothers' Unions; African marriages; polygamy; liquor traffic; work among Indians and Moslems; Lectionary; women missionaries; religious instruction; 'Native Councils'.

CHAPTER SIX

Church and Ideology: The First Thirty Years

> . . . the conflict between religion and those natural
> economic ambitions, which the thought of an earlier age
> had regarded with suspicion, is suspended by a truce which
> divides the life of mankind between them. The former takes
> as its province the individual soul, the latter the intercourse
> of man with his fellows in the activities of business and the
> affairs of society.
>
> RH Tawney (1926), p274

The foregoing survey of the major elements in the early stages of industrialisation in South Africa provides the context, the foreground within which the
role of the Church is sketched. It remains to take one step back from historical
events, actions and reactions in order to throw light more generally upon the
way ideas in the churches altered and developed with the changing context.

Historically it is clear that the main lines of what we today call 'apartheid'
were drawn in the first decades of this century. Our study of the Church's
response, or non-response, to the dynamics of the period has shown that in
practice the churches were often markedly equivocal. Where clarity of opinion
and practice appears, it was usually in support of one or another of the dominant powers. Class factors, mixed with cultural alienation from the indigenous
peoples, played a key role in this.

In the end, one may justifiably conclude that initial suspicions of the
Church's ideological captivity to the dominant capitalist colonial political
economy, and of a distinct inability to bring to bear a critical and self-critical
awareness of the implications of this situation, have been confirmed in a quite
striking manner. Indeed, very few references were discovered which did not fit
the general pattern, and even these — analysed above at various points — have
not finally escaped suspicion. The method adopted has in this sense proved
rather merciless. However, a clearer picture of the specific religious structure
of the dominant ideology necessitates some discussion of the Church's structure of knowledge, in particular its own self-understanding in relation to the
events and underlying dynamics of the period under consideration. After a

fashion, such a picture summarises the data investigated and the conclusions reached up to now.

1903—1910

Imperial ideas, lauded by Bishop Gaul of Mashonaland as late as 1908, were still deeply influential after the Anglo-Boer War.[1] The term *civilisation* summed up many of these ideals. Its conscious meaning might have differed for missionaries (who saw civilisation in terms of 'Christianity, the abandonment of traditionalism, and education') as compared with other colonists (who meant by it controlled, cheap and freely available labour), but the interests of the two groupings were certainly consistent with each other in most respects.[2]

In a memorandum to Lord Selborne, Sir Godfrey Lagden discussed Christianity as 'the basis of our civilisation' into which the indigenous 'barbarians' must be introduced. At the same time he viewed newly recruited labourers as 'being not unlike baboons', though in his opinion those who had worked for Europeans for ten years or more manifested slight improvements 'in appearance and apparent intelligence'.[3] As crude as these observations were, they reflect a mindset by no means uncommon in the Church documents of the time as well.

Perhaps the most concrete example of what was understood to be civilisation for the African is contained in a report of the Diocese of Mashonaland on St Augustine's mission station at Penhelanga. Here blacks were removed from their traditional kraals in order to bring them under the continual supervision of the clergy. In this context, they learned

> methods of punctuality, obedience, respect, truthfulness, industry and cleanliness. No lax familiarity is tolerated, no indiscriminate hand-shaking or loitering about with books, and no time is unoccupied. Three hours and a half are given to study in the morning, and four hours labour in the afternoon, unpaid.[4]

Along with these marks of 'civilisation' went an education for their proper place in society:

> I may add, we do not address our pupils as brethren, or tell them they are our equals. They are taught that the fundamental law of Christianity is humility, 'to esteem others better than themselves' . . . We try to impress on our people that they are to live by the production of their hands, and will prosper as they learn to dignify and glorify common labour and put brains and skill into the common occupations of life.[5]

In like manner, the Rev Mr Mason in Natal probably went further than most in openly demanding that missionaries should look at things from the colonists' point of view, especially in civilising Africans in their general duty towards what they ought to be — servants, obedient to the government and its various officers.[6] But such thoughts were probably taken largely for granted among the churches' white members. Bishop Gibson thus had overwhelming support from the Provincial Board of Missions for his contention that 'possibly it may be God's will that most of them should always remain labourers, herd men, domestic servants, and the like, and that only a few should come to the front'. Moreover, he added, the Church should not 'force them upwards, she only desires that they should have the gospel and a fair field'.[7]

Such an ideology was eminently suited to the labour needs of industrialists and farmers. While leaving open the possibility of acceptance into the colonist society and its dominating structures for a small number of black bourgeoisie and petty-bourgeoisie, it contained no promise to workers other than that oppression would be tempered by a supposedly 'Christian democratic rule'.[8] On the other hand the functional dependence of the churches on the rulers of the day manifested itself, in the Cape at least, in the public practice by which government officials took part in most religious functions. It could also be seen in Methodist concern to find pastors acceptable to 'the best class of our middle class'.[9]

It is perhaps important to point out that the judgement that the churches were ideologically captive is not merely 'retrospective wisdom'. There is evidence of contemporary criticism that was known and even referred to on occasion, though usually defensively. Thus responding to a broadside from Callaway against his view of missions, Dudley Kidd stood by a description of the missionaries as men 'burning with zeal' who, imagining that 'a divine religion and a ready-made civilisation' were sufficient, 'did not foresee all the strange consequences that inevitably arose from the cross-currents of commerce and politics'.[10] What was not apparent to earlier missionaries however could not be said to be a matter of ignorance in the Church towards the end of the first decade of this century at least. This was not only because of Kidd's widely-read book but also because numerous testimonies to various commissions, statements from black organisations and press, and the voices of black workers had early on made all the important points.[11]

It must not be assumed that the prevailing religious idelogy was static. In fact the hypothesis of its intimate connection to the dominant political economy demands that it reflect changes in accordance with transformations in the political economy. In the early period this is evident in a growing acceptance among the previously 'integrationist' English-speaking churches of segregationist policies, beginning as we have said with the Lagden Commission proposals. Now the call to civilise the African was rethought. Industrialisation and urbanisation created conditions felt to be immoral: drunkenness, hypocrisy, arrogance, lust, immorality, covetousness, and so on.[12]

This view of decadence among blacks caused by contact with the negative aspects of 'white' civilisation matched the contradictory idea that blacks should be separated from civilisation as far as possible, and be returned to their traditional life — or what was left of it. Thus *segregation* now became a common theme. Separate 'Native churches', organically connected to white churches rather than independent groups, were proposed. So were separate ministries, ostensibly necessary because of 'the limitations imposed on us by the prejudices of our people'.[13] This was of course not dissimilar to suggestions made and accepted earlier among the Dutch Reformed churches. Black evangelists were now regarded as necessary to Christianising Africa, for as one cleric put it in a rather unfortunate metaphor, 'the demands are great and the fields as "already white to the harvest".' Thus towards the end of the decade many felt it necessary to develop a definite Church 'Native Policy' to meet the changing situation.

As may be expected, the standard view among the churches on politics and political life as such reflected considerable ambiguity. One sees not so much detachment as opportunism, for example with an early Methodist approval of socialism. But what an approval. On the basis of the Gospel of Jesus Christ, the *Methodist Churchman* stated, it was possible to support the overthrow of 'tyranny, despotism, greed, corruption and every institution and system that unjustly interfered with the inalienable rights of man, or that tends in any way to lower, degrade and coarsen his life.' But then a somewhat remarkable distinction between 'Christian' and 'material' socialism was drawn:

> Christian Socialism differs from what we may call material Socialism. The Watchwords of the latter are 'higher wages, 'shorter hours', 'better conditions', and so forth, all of which may be, and often are, justifiable demands; but in Christian Socialism, character always comes first and environment after. . . . it is the cleansing of the heart and the upbuilding of the character of the individual that lies at the base of the new social order.[15]

This distinction effectively neutralised serious action and repeated the clarion cry of bourgeois religion. In any event, two years after its 'approval' of socialism, the same journal recanted of its belief and deceptive flirtation with the idea.[16] The only other example of an article or document critical of the capitalist economic system from within the established churches came in the form of a reprint of a sermon by the bishop of Birmingham, England.[17]

Not surprisingly, the doctrine of the individual ('nuclear') family (the basic unit in a capitalist production and consumption society), with a 'divinely-ordained' home life dedicated to the 'ideal of self-sacrificing and self-respecting citizenship' and the accompanying 'ideal of Nationality and Empire', also found great favour in the Church.[18]

In conclusion, the data supports the contention that the Church — the Anglican and Methodist churches in particular — did not succeed in this first decade in distinguishing between the ruling ideology of the time and its own proclamation. This is not surprising when one considers that the CPSA at this stage was for many almost a state church (it had intimate contact with the leaders of polity and economy), and that the Methodist Church could be regarded as little more than 'essentially supplementary to the Established Church'.[19]

1911—1920

The years between Union and the onset of the First World War, shaped by an increasing number of wide-ranging strikes as well as the land issue, saw a growing distance from imperial concerns on the part of the churches. Only one significant reference to earlier imperial ideals, and that from a British churchman, colours the pages of church records during the time.[20]

By contrast, Church concerns with social issues increased, perhaps influenced by political currents newly alive in Britain, as well as two major gatherings held there — the first International Missionary Conference in 1910 led by John Mott (father of the modern ecumenical movement), and the Universal Races Congress in London (1911). The concept of 'Human brotherhood realising itself' (even in the form of strikes) and the connection of human action to the theological notion of the Kingdom of God began to grace the pages of the church tabloids and journals.[21] Refreshing as this was, it appears to have remained a minority who reflected on the gospel in such terms.

The Church and its task were most frequently seen as in some sense 'above' conflict (which usually meant verbal appeals to all parties). The 'cure of souls' was still of supreme importance prior to all questions of 'belated social reform', as the Methodist journal acknowledged.[22] The charge that clergy 'sit on the fences in supine slumber', one editorial responded, ignores the fact that the weapons of the Church's warfare are not carnal. Patient endurance of wrong is required in contrast to a 'fierce assertion of rights'.[23] Ultimately, it was felt, all supposed assertions of rights should be foregone in favour of 'the right Spirit, the Spirit of Christ'. This Spirit needed to enter into all human relationships, for all groups and classes were to blame for the state of unrest surrounding the community.[24]In an editorial on the Land Act, the *Methodist Churchman* added the rider *par excellence*, ordaining all things to the wisdom of God's providence: 'Man proposes, God disposes'.[25] Only when one realises how much land some men disposed of through the Land Act, in the process making themselves the beneficiaries and depriving those whose entire economic life was consequently threatened, is it possible to discern the naivete of such thinking, its ideological blindness, and the cynicism it drew forth.

The catalogue of phrases and images that emerge here presupposes a social position of privilege, of access to power, of relative stability and of sufficient material means. The occasional (romantic) view of the labour struggle as a sign of human brotherhood was accompanied by demands that labour's challenge be legal and orderly, respectable and conciliatory.

In short, Church views most commonly were shaped by a position of dominance or at least dependency upon the dominant. Given that such dominance in South Africa was at root demonstrably capitalist, one would expect to discover other indicators of a bourgeois ideology filling the minds, writings and speeches of churchmen and churchwomen of the time. Such is the case.

A whole set of related propositions may be discerned. Free and fair competition governed by 'immutable laws' and functioning in an open market oblivious to anything but purchasing power is propagated as the necessary basis of any critique of the Land Act. 'Service' rather than solidarity should be the key concept in any actions the Church might contemplate. The 'individual' is the special concern of Christianity whereas the transformation of material conditions should rightly be left to political 'reformers'. The Church's task is only to 'arouse the consciences of its members' in declaring certain moral truths and just principles. 'Spiritual' life is regarded as 'the only real' existence. On the other hand, any social work on the part of the Church should be characterised by 'self-restraint . . . patience . . . and faith'. Any untoward conflict, even in resistance to thoroughly bad laws and practice, is regarded with hostility. Finally, though Rhodes' dictum of 'Equal rights for all civilised races south of the Zambezi' was seen as the touchstone of 'justice, Christianity and political wisdom', it is noteworthy that those to be included in the meaning of a 'civilised race' were only those who were 'capable and industrious'.

The actual function of such ideas in restraining those who were exploited and excluded from participation in the circles of social, political and economic power, and in reproducing the ideology of capitalism, is most clearly and ironically displayed in an evangelistic tale concerning the positive effects of Christianity on black workers told by Bishop Gaul at a public meeting. After recounting a conversation with a farmer friend who distrusted Christianised Africans and who was nevertheless persuaded to employ some, Bishop Gaul, to applause from the meeting, repeated the farmer's final judgement:

> 'I have got two of your boys working on my farm. They can say their prayers; but by Jove, they can do their work, too!'[27]

The religious apologetic connected to the ideology of dominance perpetuated and strengthened by the churches was contained perhaps most visibly in a particular notion of mission and evangelisation. This separated the gospel from the historical and material context of the people addressed. It produced as a result an uncritical self-justifying enthusiasm. Only in this way can one understand the otherwise crude terms of the following ringing call from the South African Missionary Society:

> Ethiopia stretches out her hands unto God! Africa cries, with bleeding heart and outstretched hands, for the sympathy, and love and help of the Gospel of Christ . . . The call of a continent! A continent that still lies in darkness and the shadow of Death!
> 'O Christians to their rescue fly!
> Preach Jesus to them 'ere they die!'[28]

A question arises. What explains the continued ideological captivity of the churches to the dominant capitalist milieu in the face of enormous resistance from the indigenous people with whom the churches were so closely associated?

One can point readily and obviously to the close relationship of church leadership to the white community, particularly government officials and leading capitalists, the imperial church connections of at least the Anglican and Methodist Churches, the prevailing view of European cultural supremacy and the structures of control and finance in the churches.[29] But the real weakness lay in the Churches' own internal life. They were white-dominated on the one hand, and whites in the Church at all levels kept themselves at a considerable distance from blacks. Thus despite its large black membership, its sometimes liberal clergy, and a handful of educated blacks who were respected, the Church did not have within itself structures suitable for effectively hearing, let alone understanding, the multiple voices of the oppressed.

Even rural mission stations such as Lovedale were to a large extent separated, in practice at least, from the realities facing the proletariat and the dependents. In an article attacking the views of the *Christian Express* on the Land Act, Sol Plaatje decided to explain why he paid only an extremely brief visit, his first, to Lovedale during a tour of the country. His elucidation points to the somewhat protected situation of mission stations:

I think my duty is with the suffering millions of our people, and not among the one thousand on the Lovedale Estate, who are well-fed and well cared for. I have satisfied myself that they need no outside assistance. Even Section 8(h) of our latest plague, the Natives Land Plague (sic), 1913, attests that they are impregnable under the protection of the missionary agents.[30]

By contrast, the testimony of Bishop Gibson of the value placed in missions by the Witwatersrand Native Labour Association (for mine-labour recruitment) is illustrated by at least one recorded occasion when the Association made a substantial donation to the work of mission, another indicator of the 'captivity' of the Church in the overall system.[31]

As might be expected, after the Land Act and during the World War years a resurgence of imperial idealism made itself felt for a while. Particular pride in the loyalty of 'our native people' was expressed.[32] However with the end of international strife and the increasing tempo of national unrest, new elements intruded on the churches. Earlier we referred to a new sympathy for labour. That such a development was novel is indicated by a London reporter's comment on the Pretoria Diocesan Synod of 1915: he expressed surprise at 'a touch of socialism' among certain clergy, and one instance of 'almost passionate affection' for the working classes.[33] The *Church Chronicle* also critically analysed the mining companies and other capitalist industries as bodies governed by the state, and responsive to public opinion but only via the share market — certainly not moral decision-makers. But despite implying an option for the workers as 'the weaker party', its conclusion was that the present order sufficed because a 'socialistic' solution was 'not immediately practicable, even if desirable'.[34]

After the War, a further note of radicalism crept into the churches. Archbishop Carter in fact charged that a fundamental change in the system itself, from an economy based primarily on a doctrine of competition to one based on co-operation, might be necessary. Moreover, he regarded such a transformation potentially as far more compatible with Christian morality or conscience than the prevailing system.[35] The full extent and seriousness — or lack of it — with which such alternatives were considered emerged more clearly in the next decade.

Finally, one other major trend may be discerned in the latter part of the second decade, one reflecting the rise of manufacturing in South Africa and a strengthening of a black bourgeoisie connected to the churches. With respect to the latter, pressures to include blacks more fully in the hierarchical structures of the churches became more prominent, though — unlike the independent church movement — without suggesting that those structures themselves and white control of them should be seriously challenged.[36]

The ideology of the manufacturing class as described by B Bozzoli wells up in distilled ecclesiastical phrases that could also be found on the lips of successful merchants or rising manufacturers.[37] 'Common sense' behaviour and attitudes were increasingly linked with notions of 'Christain patience', 'moderation and self-restraint', values which middle-class senstivities often found offensively absent from workers and such like. 'Moral greatness' was called for as well, as a sign of the heroic individual. 'Family altars and worship' were felt to be the sound ingredients for a wholesome life in harmony with God and others, but this was a motto expressed in a way that could appeal only to those whose basic material needs had been met. It is not surprising to find in the records an evangelism which understood the kernel (and often the husk) of the gospel as being concerned above all with the internal personal piety of the *solo humanum*, with the 'revival of soul-converting power and of deep and satisfying experience'.[38]

Inevitably such religious code-words, as all the above are, found their way into social issues too. At least one leading churchman proposed a possible breaking of somewhat tenuous relations with the SANNC, not on political grounds but for reasons of the questionable morality of some of its responsible members.[39] The instrumentalist, utilitarian world-view of a manufacturing class may perhaps be discerned in some church support for a plan for the 'scientific study of native problems' by the government and universities, by which was meant the establishment of academic chairs for revealingly and comically named 'ethnological bureaux'.[40]

The dominant ideological patterns in the English-speaking churches by the beginning of the 1920s are thus recognisably similar to those evident in mid-Victorian England when a successful business middle-class influenced by Protestant evangelicalism began to reshape convention and practice. 'Industriousness, tolerance, self-reliance, and self-help, earnest endeavour, liberality of mind': these were the characteristic virtues of the time. 'Piety, fidelity to the pledged word, good faith . . . and charity': these defined the crucial values. The whole could be captured in the concepts of restraint and responsibility, concepts admirably suited to the interests of the dominant group when applied to the poor and oppressed.[41]

Within this framework it would certainly be hard to find place for anything that smacked of resistance, of conflict or of confrontation. An ideological mantle covered the raw wounds of a harsh situation born not of eternal principles but of the acts, decisions and choices of particular groups of people with the means to force their way upon all.

1921—1930

> Our society has come to represent that of the Athens of Pericles — an educated democracy, resting upon the foundation of what, when all hypocritical periphrases are swept away, is really slave labour.
>
> E H Brookes[42]

> It is not enough to enunciate and reiterate the principles of Jesus if conditions exist which make it practically impossible for men to live as brothers. The thing to be done in that case by those who believe in the principles of Jesus is to set to work to alter the conditions and to lift men to the plane on which brotherly relations become a possibility.
>
> JJ Oldham[43]

At the very beginning of the 1920s Senator D Roberts, earlier from Lovedale Mission, was asked what churches might do in the midst of the 'Native ferment'. He replied that committees should investigate land, labour and social problems in depth after which 'they would soon find out the need of doing something definite'. The issues named came up again at the Le Zoute Conference of 1926; here the omission of economic questions from Christian mission was regarded as 'stultifying'.[44] Some two years later James Henderson again declared that 'more than ever before it is necessary for (missionaries) to concentrate their study and effort on the material life and the economic position of Native people'.[45] The Natal Missionary Conference heard the same thing from the Rev Ray Phillips in 1929, and that year the Methodist Conference supported the idea of a properly informed Christian opinion.[46]

It might be expected that such opinions, in the light of the events of the decade, would receive immediate and substantial backing. In fact, by the end of the period, Phillips could claim that 'the only man in South Africa who has taken time and energy to look carefully into the Native economic situation with its accompanying social effects' was the self-same Dr Henderson. A fully-backed agency was needed to rectify the situation, as Henderson's *Outlook* recognised.[47]

But only much later was the Christian Council established, in part to meet this demand. While doing much good work, the task it undertook was seldom integrated into Church life as a whole. The transformation of individual men and women continued to be central to the gospel preached in South Africa, but the transformation of the world which so deeply shaped these same men and women remained at best an addendum to the task of the churches.

The historical reasons for this state of affairs have already been discussed. It remains only to bring to the fore the language patterns sustaining the Church's view of itself and its context to determine the kind of knowledge by which its interests were upheld — and hidden.

The turmoil of the early years generated an unusually anxious drive to expand and intensify the 'social mission' of the Church.[48] 'Christian Socialism' became something of a fad, stimulated largely by the influence of British writers such as FD Maurice and by the links of the Methodist Church in Britain with the growing Labour Party. A much discussed book by the Rev GC Binyon emphasised the gospel identification with the 'poor'. This book described class war as a conflict engendered by those who perpetrate exploitation, interpreted socialism as atheistic 'only in the sense that it cannot be associated with the worship of a God who is not concerned with social justice', called for the 'scientific spirit which analyses the wrongness of society and prescribes the needful changes in economic language', and related the worship of the Church more closely to the common life of the world.[49]

Certain others spoke along the same lines. A fascinating judgement from a most unlikely source pronounced the Church to be bound together with capitalism in an 'unholy alliance' while needing to maintain a hold among blacks, 'because without a very strong influence in that direction, it loses its market value, and capitalism will then cease to support it, having no time for useless or obsolete factors'. The commentator was Donald Snowdon, a Methodist lay preacher on trial with three others for playing a leading role in the Committee of Action during the 1922 Rand upheaval. These four described themselves as 'members of the Boksburg Gaol Congregation of the Wesleyan Church'. They addressed a memorandum (at first suppressed by prison authorities) to the Methodist Conference of 1922, protesting against the Church's alliance with state and capital in the Rand Revolt, and backing their protest with a brief but biting theological argument.[50] In gaol Snowdon had attended church service twice each Sunday.

> Yes, in goal. To worship? Oh dear no. But to study the type of parson and critically analyse his sermon. What was the usual theme? Love your enemies, bless them that hate you. And love all sections, the Corner House (mining company headquarters) included. But Jesus gave humanity quite a different message. He commanded us to hate sin, and what is capitalism but sin? . . . Because if you live for profit you lose your soul.
>
> The Church is a tremendously important factor, both in opening up new coun-

tries and controlling a country's labour supply, whether black or white.[51]

A theology not far from Snowdon's continued to be heard from odd corners throughout the next years. Sometimes it came from those more likely to gain acceptance in the Church — among others, Bishop Karney, DDT Jabavu, and the 1930 Synod of Bishops.[52]

It is therefore tempting to draw the conclusion that significant strands of radically self-critical consciousness and social action existed within the Church. In fact at most one may say that a tradition grew up alongside the established perspective containing hints, clues, and challenges, a tradition accorded honourable mention in the occasional battle but never incorporated into the grand strategies of war. Direct and circumstantial testimony rather tends to confirm Snowdon's sharp charges.

Far more prevalent in the records, and congruent with most activities, one finds an emphasis on the specifically religious or moral task of the Church. Spirituality, prayer, an adequate idea of God, relief from fear, individual worth, moral behaviour, feelings of the heart, righteousness, the Church itself — these were the terms of reference for the role of the Church in the transformation of the world; these were to be the guide and goal of all activity.[53] Not surprisingly, therefore, when the General Missionary Conference met in 1932, its focus was exclusively 'religious', though the four years since its previous meetings had witnessed momentous struggles and other events in the political, social and economic life of South Africa.[54]

In the late 1920s renewed emphasis was placed on mission work, but with little critical evaluation of nineteenth century missions. Although the nature and depth of oppression was by now fairly well established as a matter of public knowledge, the role of mission in assisting the administration of government, law and order, and its various attempts to regulate behaviour, continued to draw public praise.[55]

Besides evangelisation, mission activity now also focused on health care, education, hostels and workshop industries. Unquestionably, this work had great value, particularly in making available to some indigenous people an adequate education for an industrial era and providing an infrastructure of medical care in many areas otherwise without much help. The bulk of missionary reports also demonstrate, however, the hypothesis that education generally was directed towards a particular place in society, one of service to the ruling elite. Access into that elite was possible, but only for those sufficiently qualified. Thus one notices that blacks did not control the organs or finances of the churches, whites always retaining final authority (with the one exception of the Order of Ethiopia, but even then its finances were controlled by whites).

The role of missionary conferences also declined at the time as local congregations were established. The minutes of the Provincial Missionary Conference of 1933, in a moment of profound self-evaluation of over a quarter century's work, concluded that this 'bloated debating society' (itself) had proven 'strangely ineffective and barren of practical results: time and again pious resolutions have been passed and forgotten, subjects have been discussed which would have been more profitably dealt with locally, and committees have been appointed which never met'.[56] Here was a painful confession of the passivity of the Church despite many noble words, by implication an admission of captivity to the status quo.

In other respects the Church showed its colours firmly nailed to the mast of capitalism and a bourgeois ideology. Eschatological expectation often took the form of preparation for the 'hereafter'. Concern for workplace alienation and the impecunity of labour seldom arose, for the morrow was God's concern. Values of 'cleanliness, industry, honesty, health and brotherhood', of the consumer market, of thrift, of personal piety, and of home religion were widely espoused.[57] A women's association heard, without any apparent awareness of the implications, a priest declare that 'the natives can teach us good things, such as cheerfulness even at the end of a long day's work on the road with nothing to eat. We know, too, their amazing patience.'[58] 'The desires among Africans for liberty was natural,' said the Methodist Conference, but they should 'make haste slowly'.[59]

On the Rand, mine companies continued to welcome and help the work of missions. The 'native problem' remained a prime item for discussion, and 'white superiority' slogans raised their head on occasion. Behind unrest lay 'agitators', some proclaimed, while others thought the problems to be a result of progress in South Africa, progress engendered by a 'silent Christian spirit' present in the process of changing the society.[60]

All of these things are indicators of the ideological framework within which Church practice and theory (theology) took place. They are consistent with the general hypothesis of functional dependency on the ruling class. One consequence was a gross misunderstanding of the growing poverty of blacks. One may cite the pride about the 'wonderful generosity' of the oppressed expressed by one gentleman, who showed no signs of shock or anger at the rank injustice and deprivation revealed by his narrative:

> I know one native who walked 18 miles into Jamestown driving sheep which he wished to sell. He had no money, as the farmer had given him sheep instead of money for many months labour. He proposed to sell the sheep. One was to pay his class money, the other to enable him to buy some articles of clothing. On the way one of the sheep died. He sold the other, paid his church arrears and returned without the clothing.[61]

In fact, the story of this unfortunate farm labourer serves as a crude summary of what is more generally evident in all the data investigated: a preoccupation with the life and sustenance of the Church itself, a consonant emphasis on the narrowly religious in thought and activity, a fundamental separation from the existence and material life of dominated groups notwithstanding a frequently expressed concern for them, and an ideological blindness to the historical conditions and conflicts prevalent in the South African context throughout the period.

The credibility of such a verdict rests on the data. It gains force when one discovers that the promise of an alternative tradition in the impetus given by the 'Christian socialism' debate faded into virtual oblivion at the end of the decade, to be replaced by attacks on 'Bolshevism', historical materialism (opposed to spirituality in the eyes of the critics) and communism — epithets by now widely utilised to characterise all that was inimical to Christianity and the Church.[62] Whatever the merits or demerits of these elements as they appeared in the contemporary situation, the Church sank into silence or bitter opposition. Perhaps more accurately, it refrained from exceeding the boundaries of debate set by the ruling political and economic powers. In doing so, it lost touch with the unique identity and role it might have gained had the mindset, the world-view and the economic values of the dominant been cracked open by a meaningful response to the oppressed within its ranks.

The dialogue of the whole gathered community is the foundation of Church theology. But where such dialogue was ruled out, defined by the powerful and privileged, or limited by omission, there one could only expect a truncated religious discourse, a sermon preached from a pulpit on high, an ethereal gospel torn from its lowly, earthy roots.

Notes

1 See J Ellison (ed), *Church and Empire,* 1908, CPSA.
2 D Welsh (1971), p53.
3 Sir G Lagden Papers, ALS, May 28, 1906.
4 Quoted by Lieut Col R Chester-Master, 'Pan-Anglican Papers', Pan-Anglican Congress, 1908
5 *Loc cit.*
6 Rev F Mason, 'Native Policy in Natal', p13ff.
7 Provincial Board of Missions, Ts, 1903.
8 See the later interpretation of 'Trusteeship' in the 'Congress Youth League Manifesto', March 1944, in T Karis and G Carter (1972), vol II, p303.
9 See Rev F Mason, 'Native Policy in Natal', 1906, p30; and TMC, September 26, 1905.
10 G Callaway, 'Kafir Socialism', *East and West*, vol VI, 1908; and D Kidd, 'Kafir Socialism and Missions', *East and West,* vol VII, 1909.

11 For example, see 'Testimony of Rev ET Mpela and Six Others of the Native Vigilance Association of the Orange River Colony', to the SANNC, September 23, 1904, cited in T Karis and G Carter (1972), pp35—6.

12 U Kistner, *Africa Perspective,* no 13, 1979, p68.

13 CE, July 2, 1905, pp98—99; and Provincial Missionary Conference, Minutes, October 1906.

14 Rev JS Morris, Paper, GMCSA: Summary, 1904, p11 (quote); and p15; also Rev A Goodwin, Paper.

15 TMC, November 21, 1905.

16 *Ibid,* January 21, 1908.

17 TCC, July 8, 1909.

18 For example Provincial Board of Missions, Ts, 1903.

19 GM Young (1964), p65.

20 Bishop MR Neligan, 'The Church and the Expansion of the Empire', *East and West,* vol XI, 1913.

21 For example, CR, no 35, Michaelmas Day, 1911.

22 TMC, February 20, 1912.

23 TCC, August 21, 1913.

24 *Rand Daily Mail,* Bishop Furse, Pretoria, on 'Church and Labour', October 14, 1913.

25 TMC, June 16, 1913.

26 References are respectively from: *Ibid, loc cit; Rand Daily Mail,* Bishop Furse, *loc cit*; also Lent Pamphlet, Diocese of Pretoria, 1916; Archbishop WM Carter, 'Charge to Cape Town Diocese Synod', September 1914; Bishop Furse, 'Charge to Diocese Synod', Pretoria, 1913, in the *Transvaal Leader,* October 13, 1913. SAMSR (32nd), 1913, p2; and TCC, May 21, 1914; also SAMSR (37th), 1918.

27 *Transvaal Leader,* November 20, 1913.

28 SAMSR (35th), 1916, p4, Secretary's Report.

29 On this last point, the sociological profile of the churches in these pages would gain from a study of these structures, a task unfortunately beyond the limits of this book though one worth pursuing. Insofar as financial records were read at the time of research, it is clear that well into the period investigated, large sums of money came from Britain in the form of personal gifts and subscriptions (all listed in detail, to the shilling and pence) as well as official subsidisation.

30 CE, December 1, 1913, p189.

31 Bishop AGS Gibson, 'Christianity among the Bantu in South Africa', *East and West,* vol XI, 1913.

32 For example, MCMC, 1915, p141; *Transvaal and Swazi District Directory,* 1916/7, p6.

33 *Sunday Times,* London, October 17, 1915.

34 TCC, July 10, 1913.

35 Provincial Missionary Conference, 1918; Archbishop WM Carter, 'Charge to Cape Town Diocese Synod', 1919.

36 For example, Native Conference, Diocese of Pretoria, Minutes, September 2, 1915.

37 L Bozzoli (1973/4), pp62—7.

38 TMC, February 24, 1919; MCMC, 1919, p135; and MCMC, 1918, pp64—6 *passim.*

39 Archdeacon Lee, Provincial Missionary Conference, Minutes, September 1918.

40 Cape Town Diocesan Synod, 1919.

41 D Thomson (1950), p29; and GM Young (1964), p2 & pp24—5.

42 SAO, March 2, 1925, p60.

43 'The Relationship of Christian Missions to the New Forces Shaping African Life', in E Smith (ed), 1926, p168.

44 TMC, August 2, 1920; and E Smith, *op cit*, p82.

45 In JD Taylor (ed), 'Christianity and the Natives of SA', *Year Book of SA Missions*, 1928.

46 SAO, August 1, 1929, pp150—2; CCD, 1929, p11.

47 SAO, *loc cit;*

48 MCMC, 1921, p128 & 19123, p144; TCC, May 19, 1921.

49 SAO, May 1, 1922, pp98—100 *passim.*

50 D Snowdon, Martial Law Commission, 1922, p1298—9 *passim;* and pp1306—7.

51 *Ibid,* p1297, my parentheses.

52 TCC, August 5, 1920; TMC, September 22, 1924, and February 27, 1928; Bishop A Karney, 'Charge to Diocese of Johannesburg', October, 1928; CT Wood, Papers, 1962.

53 For example: MCMC, 1922, p127, also 1923, p144, and 1930, p151; Bishop JW Williams, Pastoral Letters, 1902—22 *passim;* SAMSR (42nd), 1923/4, pp2—3; TMC, November 10, 1924, and September 6, 1926; GMCSA Summary , 1925, p98; 'Forward', June 10, 1926, p10; Bishop EF Paget, LS, July 31, 1926; Rev EH Hurcombe, Note Book, 1926; *Trasnvaal and Swazi District Directory,* 1926/7, p7, and 1928/9, p5.

54 GMCSA: Summary, 1932, p124ff.

55 South African correspondent, *Church Times,* London, October 1923; GMCSA: Summary, 1925, p101; 'Forward', July 1927, p2; JD Taylor (ed), 'Christianity and the Natives of South Africa', *Year Book of Missions,* 1928; 'Advance', October 1929, p194.

56 Provincial Missionary Conference, Minutes, October 1933.

57 GMCSA: Summary, 1925, p100; SAO, 1925, p92; SAMSR (40th), 1921, p10; Bishop A Karney, Johannesburg, LS, February 7, 1927; MCMC, 1927, p196; Provincial Missionary Conference, 1928; see also SAMSR (45th), 1927, p5; and GMCSA: Summary, 1928, p118.

58 Fr Savage, congratulating the 23rd report of the Women's Missionary Auxiliary, 1925, Minutes.

59 MCMC, 1920, p120.

60 Fr O Victor, 'A Large Room', Pamphlet, SA Church Office, London, 1926; SAO, April 1, 1925, p91; MCMC, 1926, p181; Bishop A Karney, 'Charge to the Diocese of Johannesburg', Ts, September 1927; TMC, February 18, 1929; G Callaway, 'The Native Problem in South Africa', Pamphlet, Oxford, 1926, pp2 & 11; 'The Kingdom', Diocese of Pretoria, May 1923; Bishop A Karney, Diocese of Johannesburg, Ts, February 7, 1923; W Eveleigh, 'Settlers and Methodism, 1820—1920', 1920; SAMSR (45th), p5.

61 'Advance', June 1923, p107—8; see also GMCSA: Summary, 1928, p118, comments by Rheinallt-Jones.

62 SAO, August 1, 1929, pp148—50; *ibid,* September 2, 1929, p160; EH Brookes, 'The Rural Question in the Light of Christian Teaching', Bantu-European Student Conference, Papers, 1930.

CHAPTER SEVEN

The Struggle Within

> . . . the ladder is a perfect symbol of the bourgeois idea of society . . . you go up the ladder alone . . .in the end, on any reckoning, the ladder will never do; it is the product of a divided society, and will fall with it.
>
> R Williams[1]

> We have used the Bible as . . . an opium-dose for keeping beasts of burden patient while they were being overloaded.
>
> C Kingsley, 1848[2]

> Perhaps the consensus was best summarised by the immigrant who declared:
>> I believe but I'm not a *fanatic*. I don't practise it.
>> (referring to his Christian faith).
>
> South African immigrant[3]

Whatever else the first quarter of a century after the Anglo-Boer War represented, there is no doubt that it decisively shaped the trajectory of capitalist development and of South African society for a long time to come. It is thus an auspicious period for an analysis of the role of the Church.

The argument regularly adopted in the past by many commentators to distinguish between Afrikaner and English-speaking churches — that the former express views harking back to a crude racist feudalism, the latter those of civilised liberalism — is minimally valuable, and then only in tracing a history of ideas in relatively abstract fashion. To regard the seeds of 'separate development' (apartheid) as lying in Afrikaner religious beliefs as many have done (one recently)[4] is to miss some things entirely, namely: the role of the British (in the Lagden Commission, for example), who introduced many of the key measures which define modern South Africa; the formative influence in the genesis of segregationist policies and an especially virulent form of racism of the capitalist industrialisation process in a colonial context; and the effect of the unique structure of the gold-mining industry in particular. While the formal policy of separate development (apartheid) may be closely bound to Afrikaner Calvinist ideas, its political origins and economic basis lie elsewhere.[5]

An interpretation of ideas and their history abstracted from the specific material conditions within which they exist and gain substance — removed, that is, from their situation in an identifiable political economy — predominated in the South African Church. A recent publication, while paying lip service to the notion that 'it is just as false to gloss over the economic factor in interpreting South African social history as it is to make this the key to everything else', still makes precisely that gloss.[6]

Why is this so regularly the case? The preceding analysis of the post Anglo-Boer War period attempts to discern the reason for this in the Church's captivity to the ruling class and its failure to find for itself a unique voice and contribution. The lessons, it is argued, are not a matter of past history — they remain to be learnt.

A basic presupposition throughout the analysis has been that the model developed here, if applied, would introduce a systematic set of insights into the ideological captivity of the Church. In a search for explanations, various texts uncovered in archival material have been analysed. The results of this investigation have constituted the foundation upon which the history of the 1903—1930 period has been written. We will now look more directly at the analysis of this archival material, detailing the results of reserach into questions regarded as key to the whole enterprise.

Analysis of Archival Entries

Initially all relevant records in the South African archives of the Methodist Church and the CPSA were surveyed. Extracts of any significant reference to a variety of issues in the political economy were abstracted. The abstracts were then studied for material offering sufficient promise of analytical value, and such further selections gathered onto single-item cards.[7] These entries were then examined according to predetermined criteria, in order to ascertain any emphases and changes in emphases through the period under study, to determine the dominant ideological patterns and constructs including underlying presuppositions, and to correlate the results. Some 30 per cent of the cards, those most substantial in content, were analysed in detail, the others being relatively straightforward. The whole process gave rise to the three-fold division of periods adopted in the historical study. The correlated results of the card analysis, in annotated form, follow. Together they summarise the results of the historical study in a more technical way.

(i) General Periodic Emphases Discovered

Within each of the three decade-divisions it was possible to pick out certain regular themes:

1903—1910	British Imperial presence still strong; late-Victorian ideology dominant; working out of pattern of settler rule and relationship to metropolitan power a major task.
1911—1919	Post-Union crisis and transition in politics and economy, punctuated by World War; white rule basically established.
1920—1930	Ascendancy of national capital to political hegemony, consolidation of earlier trends; incorporation of bulk of white workers.

(ii) Level of Ideology

The debate on the concept of ideology has been discussed elsewhere. It is appropriate however, to make certain distinctions at this point. Fierro has pointed to three broad uses of the term which we will utilise here to make certain distinctions possible in the evaluation of the impact of social environment on knowledge.[8]

1   Ideology as a consciously held system of representations, a mythos defining the matrix within which thought, value and action occur. This may be regarded as a universal phenomenon, for no human is totally without a symbolic life and an active imagination guided by some complex of meanings. In the archival analysis, some items, on the basis of a distinct Christian symbol-construct, give evidence of a consciously held critical distance from the dominant ideology. These are treated as primarily reflecting this first level of ideology in terms of 'consciously valued religious identity'. Here the religious symbol-construct, functioning through conviction, is brought to bear reasonably independently upon oneself and one's taken-for-granted social world. (It should be added that the preceding historical investigation does not treat a system of representations (or a world-view) per se as ideological. Nevertheless, for the sake of convenience, the term 'ideology' is used at this point so as to reflect the distinctions adopted by Fierro.)

2   Ideology as an unconscious degree of determination conditioned by the material base of a political economy and one's position in it. This second level of ideology can only be discerned by imputation, through critical analysis., The historical study of the 1903—1930 period represents an at-

tempt to do just that, and by far the bulk of references fall within this level.

3   Idelogy as the conscious rationalisation of a specific class interest (usually meaning that of the ruling class). This third level reflects a position not susceptible to self-critical changes, for interests here are expressly defended. Items showing this tendency in relation to ruling class interest are thus separately tabulated.

Utilising these distinctions, one is able to gain an impressionistic idea of the existence within the churches of a critically aware tradition, the extent of ideological captivity, and the predilection to defend the dominant elite. Only a limited number of entries were susceptible to such analysis, the others being too ambiguous or inappropriate for any significant conclusions. The results were:

Table 2: Evidence of Ideological Function in
Anglican and Methodist Archival Extracts

	No of Extracts	% of Total
1st level = Critical	11	5,9
2nd level = Base	126	67,0
3rd level = Legitimation	51	27,1
Total sample	188	

Though impressionistic, the distribution clearly supports the judgements made in the previous sections, namely, that the Church was by and large dependent upon or actively propagating the dominant ideology of capital or at least a fraction of capital. Moreover it reflects the presence of a more critical attempt to address the Church and society at large, but a woefully, regrettably small presence, especially when compared to the considerably larger number of entries which reflect a conscious legitimation of colonial settler domination.

(iii) Class Determination

The Church, as has already been said, quite obviously is not a class in itself. Conceivably, however, the Church may play a role in various attempts to form alliances, it may introduce specific class practices into its life, and it may choose to opt for one or other fundamental class, leaving its leadership and direction in the hands of that class.

In the foregoing analysis the conclusion was drawn that the Church exhibits a 'functional dependency' on a fraction of capital in the South African political economy. This conclusion appears to fall into the trap of functionalist sociologies in general, that is, making the open-ended dynamics of history appear merely as a mechanical performance of parts of a total system. The evidence of the archives, insofar as they could be reasonably interpreted, unfortunately strongly tends to sustain the notion of the churches (as institutions) merely fulfilling a rather constrained function dependent upon the larger dynamics of the political economy. Whatever the limits of this interpretation or of the presuppositions that inform it, my view remains that this functional dependency is hard to refute.

The conclusion that the Anglican and Methodist churches during the period investigated were functionally dependent upon the dominant class is a judgement applied to specific institutions at a specific juncture under specific conditions of production, reproduction and class conflict. I thus continue to hold this judgement as meaningful (because it summarises the evidence) and instructive (because it warns us of our own contemporary lack of insight and failures of oversight).

The analysis of the archival entries reveals the following in this respect:

a   In general, even critical entries show little evidence that churches had any solid relationship to the working class, their dependents, or the lumpenproletariat (the 'outcasts' and 'outlaws' of society).

b   Where criticism does arise, especially in opposition to the state, it usually reflects the views of mining capitalists, British and foreign capital in general, or the emerging black petty-bourgeoisie.

c   A predominantly bourgeois ethos is to be expected, as the archival records stem overwhelmingly (in fact almost exlusively) from professionals or clergy in the Church as well as certain political elites antagonistic to Boer authorities.

The last point bears comment. Undoubtedly other views were present among colonised members of the Church but they remained largely unpublished or unrecorded. Written material was bound to come from the whites given their relative abundance of skills and the English medium of almost all official documents. But the thesis of the study is not thereby invalidated. On the contrary, the records convey clearly the dominantly operative mind, structure and activity of the Church, whatever other opinion and desires there may have been. The experience of domination and oppression in the Church itself gave considerable impetus to the independent movements or to outright rejection of the Church on the part of the colonised indigenous people, as we have had occasion to note.

(iv) Denominational Emphases

Besides the records of the CPSA and the Methodist Church, the testimony of *South African Outlook* (earlier *The Christian Express,* published from the Church of Scotland Mission at Lovedale) was taken into account. Each of the three bodies, relative to each other, gave differing weight to the issues studied, thus revealing certain preoccupations.

The *Methodist Church* appears to have regarded the following issues as particularly worthy of discussion:
— Political exclusion of Africans
— Land policies
— Independent Church breakaways
— The compounds mission.

With respect to the *CPSA*, the central matters were:
— Church identity
— Christian doctrine
— White labour
— Marginal people in the urban setting.

South African Outlook commented most often on:
— Resistance
— Recruiting
— Wage colour bars
— Peasantry

Besides these particularly characteristic foci, all three gave considerable attention to issues of black labour and labour matters in general. The Methodist and Anglican churches frequently debated the role of the state as well. Very little attention was paid by any to:
— Trade unions
— Contracts and passes
— Taxation
— Wage structures and housing
— 'Poor whites'.

Similarly the CPSA and the Methodist Church indicated no great interest in wage colour bars, recruiting and the peasantry.

Once again earlier judgements receive confirmation in the impression given by this breakdown of categories, particularly, one notes, in respect of the value of *Outlook (Christian Express)* on several issues. Also the focus of the two denominations on the political process is manifest, while little enthusiasm is evident for considering hard economic matters. This goes hand in hand with a relative lack of understanding of, and opposition to, structures of exploitation, as contrasted with considerable concern for the political exclusion of qualified, suitably 'civilised' blacks.

(v) Period Emphases (specific)

In the analysis of the card entries it became evident that certain issues raised their heads for a while, receded and sometimes returned later. A breakdown of these shifts is indicated here. The specific issues dominating Church records in respect of 'Social Questions' are listed in relation to particular periods.

1903—1910	Missions, state rule, resistance, political exclusion, black labour.
1913—1914	Land, labour (general).
1913—1919	Resistance.
1920—1929	Resistance, labour (general).
1922	White labour.
1923—1930	Land, political exclusion, state rule, missions.
1925—1929	Black labour.

Overall, the implication is that the 1911—1919 period was much less significant in the consciousness of the Church vis-a-vis the political economy than at other times, with the exception of land issues occasioned by the passing of the Land Act in 1913, and the strikes in that and the following year. A fair assumption is that the desire to see a stabilisation of the achievement of Union predominated over other concerns in the first few years of the second decade, only to be overtaken by a consuming care for the progress and outcome of the World War in the latter part of the period.

The following notes are relevant to these specific emphases:

1903—1910:

1   The Lagden Commission is a major topic, mostly approving.
2   Criticism of early independent church growth emerges.
3   The 1907 strikes and Bambata rebellion were major issues.
4   A desire for 'better' locations is expressed as black workers swell the towns.
5   Some criticism of recruiting practices arises.

6   A strong colonial mentality, with emphasis on the Empire, 'civilisation', morality, and the 'Native problem' is manifest.
7   The behaviour of black labourers and the desire for adequate control oven them becomes a major concern.

1913—1914:
1   Land Act is strongly criticised.
2   A positive appreciation of state action against strikes and rebellion is expressed.

1913—1919:
1   Frequent, but ambiguous references to the Indian passive resistance campaign are found.

1918—1922:
1   One discovers a strong interest in socialist ideas and the negative impact of capitalism.

1921—1922:
1   The Bulhoek massacre and the Bondelzwart rebellion generate concern, but law and order are affirmed as prior to all else.
2   A vociferous debate on the Rand Revolt arises.

1923—1930:
1   Continuing interest is evident in the relationship of Christianity to labour and industry, with the emphasis on the 'impartiality' of the Church and the need for harmony between capital and labour, an appeal most often addressed to labour.
2   Demands arise for the extension of individual tenure for blacks, and for general land reform.
3   Great interest is shown in the political incorporation of suitably qualified blacks.

Post-1925:
1   The Hertzog Bills dominate discussion between 1925 and 1928, with at first positive, then largely critical reactions forthcoming.
2   Some economic criticism emerges from certain mission groups, particularly Lovedale.
3   Attacks on Marxism proliferate towards the end of the period.
4   The ICU became prominent in debate, but attitudes were largely negative.
5   First indicators appear of a generalised tolerance for independent chur-

ches, yes almost no interest is shown in building links or establishing contact.

6   *South African Outlook* focuses on the wage colour bar structures.
7   The deterioration of the reserves and African feeding becomes wor-
    risome, especially to Henderson at Lovedale.

The earlier discussions of various events and forces at work between 1903 and
1930 indicate the way in which the issues and emphases arise at any particular
point, but the annotated summary above illuminates changing emphases quite
clearly.

(vi) Symbols and Images; Meaning-complexes; Presuppositions

In this and the next two categories, the analytical intent was to abstract from
the carded items any indications of symbolic representations or catch-words
by which a framework of knowledge could be discerned. 'Knowledge' in this
respect is taken to mean the intellectual and imaginative constructs functioning heuristically to orient, inform and motivate a person's or group's view on
and action in history. From this one may further deduce the material interests
sustained and protected by such knowledge.

In this sense, these three categories seek to allow a developed critique of the
dominant ideology or ideologies in the Church and, as Habermas puts it, to
'take the historical traces of suppressed dialogue and reconstruct what has
been suppressed' in order to decipher the unity of knowledge and interests.[9]
The results of the card-analysis are tabulated periodically with only key words
listed, followed by brief comments at the foot of each column. The key words
are derived from the carded items and indicate a pattern of terminology
peculiar to the period. Certain terms appear to have had a longer life in
Church parlance than others, indicating their greater influence throughout the
decades studied.

Under 'Symbols and Images' are listed terms appearing in the literature
which functioned to summarise an attitude or an opinion. These would tend to
generate in the hearing subject a complex of attached representations which
characterise the public language of the Church in relation to particular socio-
economic issues. (For example, in the same way in contemporary language,
one knows that terms like 'terrorist' or 'freedom fighter' are not merely
descriptive, but summarise differing sorts of feelings, views, etc, in a guerilla
war.)

These complexes of representations, often appearing in the literature as a
composite of phrases and words, are also regarded as being tied into a larger
complex of meaning. Thus a meaning-complex is taken to indicate a broader
category within which several single symbolic representations come together to

inform a way of orienting oneself in the world, at least attitudinally. (Thus to-day, differing goals and purposes are reflected in the terms of 'free enterprise' and 'participatory democracy', at least for those who use these overarching phrases to express their framework of values.) The second set of columns seek to list these broader categories as far as they could be identified in particular entries. Here one is listing terms already functioning as an interpretation of the original text — a second level of abstraction — and to that extent the present writer's own orientation in the study is already critically at work.

Besides these complexes of meaning, it was in many cases possible to ascertain on reasonable grounds what presupposition or presuppositions lay behind a particular text in order for it to be framed as it was within its context (note that 'context' here includes the literary and the socio-economic framework of the selected text). Taken together, such presuppositions also tell one, from a different angle, a great deal about the sets of values and beliefs held by those whose views are recorded in church annals. In the present study they are intended to show the ideological make-up of the churches, at least in their public presentation. Where such presuppositions could reasonably be assumed, they were noted. The third set of columns lists in annotated form these notes. (See tables 3, 4 and 5 respectively.)

(vii) General Comments

In studying Church responses to various issues certain other aspects emerged, not contained in the other categories yet adding some information or further insight. With respect to 'language, meaning-complexes and presuppositions' certain additional remarks are appropriate.

1903—1910:

1 'Civilisation' is still a central idea of mission.
2 Significant later criticism of the basis for Union arises, mostly around the decision not to extend the Cape franchise system nationally.
3 After the Lagden Commission interest grows in utilising African traditional institutions for establishing controls in the reserve areas.
4 Compounds, locations, work conditions, and reserves — all affecting the life of indigenous people negatively — are viewed rather romantically, especially with respect to the role of religion in salving the wounds.

1911—1919:

1 The idea of the 'work-ethic' is strong, coupled with heavy emphasis on the individual as the measure of all.
2 'Moderation' and 'patience' are frequently urged upon the colonised.

3   The authority of the government, law and order, are emphasised again and again.

4   Strong concern is expressed about crime, but in a markedly bigoted fashion.

5   A new missionary thrust arises towards the end of the period and continues into the next.

6   A fair amount of radical social and economic critique emerges, especially towards the end of the period.

7   Some leading blacks (eg John Dube) now begin to regard Christianity in its colonial form as 'a blasphemous fraud'.

8   Increasing attacks upon the churches from workers and the colonised in general are evident; these were responded to rather defensively and without much understanding.

1920—1930:

1   A prevalent attitude: that the Church has no means or mandate to intervene in matters of economic life.

2   On the other hand, growing attention is paid to the application of 'Christian principles' in industry.

3   The ICU is regarded as basically legitimate, but too provocative.

4   Socialism is increasingly regarded as dangerous and unrealistic.

5   In respect of the 1922 Rand Revolt, some churches suggest conflict of management strategies in fact later part of the Industrial Conciliation Act of 1923 (whether they had any direct influence on the Act is another matter).

6   In respect of the Hertzog Bills generally, it is felt that the 'colour bars' should remain informal rather than be legislated.

7   Growing unease with the pass laws emerges.

8   Criticism appears of an unbalanced legal system favouring settlers.

9   Increasing emphasis is placed upon education for blacks.

10 An alliance with black aspirant bourgeoisie and petty-bourgeoisie is more frequently recommended.

11 Attacks on the Pact Government grow towards the end of the period, following along the lines of attacks more familiar today against the National Party Government since 1948.

General comments on the whole period, 1903—1930:
In respect of the following matters there is an astonishing paucity of material or references in church records showing that here at least the official minds (and hearts?) of the Church were not much impressed.

1   *Wage structures:* only one item was found specifically dealing with this

issue, a remarkable fact given the centrality of the matter to the structure of domination.

2 *Contracts:* no reference was found prior to 1932.

3 *Compounds:* these are not at any time seen in any critical light, even mildly so, all references tending to romanticise compound existence even 'in suffering'. The only possible exception was one call to improve Johannesburg compounds to equal those of Kimberley in respect of facilities.

4 *Peasantry:* no perception of rural dynamics and the deterioration of the African farming areas is evident until the late 1920s (Dr Henderson).

Besides the above issues, these were others that were dealt with by the churches, at least to some extent, and which are worth further commenting upon:

5 *African resistance:* one era — that of a traditional military response — appears to end with the Bambata rebellion; from the Bulhoek massacre onwards resistance focuses overwhelmingly on political activity, legal or illegal, until the founding of the liberation armies at the beginning of the 1960s.

6 *State role:* English church opposition on a large scale and a sustained basis against state legislation begins with a *second* look at the Hertzog bills, which were initially much praised for their attempt to establish a systematic and definite 'Native policy'.

7 *State (general):* about 75 per cent of all entries dealing with the South African state focus on the problems of 'colour' (race).

8 *Liquor:* besides items alluded to in the text, many more short references were found concerning the control of illicit liquor markets, prohibitions and the bad effects of alcohol.

9 *Mission:* a quick change in the conception of mission occurs from the middle 1920s on, after renewed calls in the early 1920s for the regeneration of traditional missions. Now a stronger concern for 'economic well-being' arises.

10 *Missionaries:* properly critical views from within the churches on the role of missionaries emerge only in the late 1920s.

11 *Church:* items concerned with economics are emphasised during three distinct periods which coincide with large-scale economic dynamics, as follows: (a) 1913—15 = recession and major strikes; (b) 1921—22 = recession and major strikes; (c) 1928—32 = emergence of black trade unions, rise of British socialism.

Table 3: Ideological analysis, CPSA and Methodist Church:
Symbols and Images, 1903—1930

	1903—1910	1911—1919	1920—1930
EPITHETS USED	re: Africans — 'savages' 'barbarism' 'loafers' 'baboons' Morality Responsibility Good habits	re: Africans — 'heathen' 'menace' 'children' 'Black Peril' 'criminal instinct' 'finest worker' 'an asset' Morality and vice	re: Africans — 'dear heathen boys' 'patient' 'cheerful' re: socialism — 'atheistic' 'revolutionary' Morality and vice
NEED EXPRESSED FOR	Practical industry Well-prepared workers Dignity of labour Cheap labour (NB) White supremacy Character	Well-prepared workers Moderation Self-respect Righteousness Patience	Migrant labour system 'The Good Life' Dignity of labour Fine labour supply Potential consumers Solidarity of race Charity
RESPONSIBILITIES OF GOVERNMENT	Civilisation Home Loyalty Citizenship Property Dominion 'Crown and Throne Empire Against agitators	Pioneers Family Loyalty Uplift 'Natives' Individual is NB Responsible government Authority Union of SA, a divine factor Against agitators Progress	Civilisation Family altar Loyalty Citizenship Individual is NB Bill of rights Trusteeship Reserves needed Against agitators 'Native Question' Colour Bar Living Wage Education of blacks Round Table Conference Welfare Reform Free-market
CRITICAL	Injustice 'Homelands' criticised 'Africa for the African'	Oppression Rich versus poor Class legislation Participatory government	Colonisation 'Rich man's crumbs'
RELIGIOUS	Providence at work Kingdom of heaven	Spirit of Christ needed Africa — raw material for Church	Christ is teacher/ Reconciles Conversion is NB
OVERALL PATTERN	Images of Empire, primitive Africans, exploitation (quite open), and from an early manu- facturing class	Shift to images of crime, middle class virtues and national consolidation	Images now clearly national, religious, middle-class; also a shift to reform of system and a selective incorporation of blacks

Table 4: Ideological analysis, CPSA and Methodist Church:
Meaning-complexes, 1903—1930

	1903—1910	1911—1919	1920—1930
TRADITION	*Victorian *Colonial Free Trade	*Dominion and Empire Colonial exploitation Class a 'natural divide'	Segregation White unity
SOCIO-ECONOMIC SYSTEM	*Capitalism in general Liberal democratic Social democratic Bureaucratic Recruitment controls System reform	National Capital *Bourgeois rule Liberal democratic *Social democratic Affirmation of Union	National Capital *Bourgeois rule *Liberal democractic Social democratic System reform Incorporate qualified blacks Balanced economy
ETHICS/ATTITUDES	Division/control of labour force Security Stability of property *Inferiority of blacks	Harmony between Capital and labour Uphold state authority Individualist Assimilation	Harmony between Capital and labour Law and order Human rights Inferiority of blacks Danger of black culture Christian blacks best

IMAGE OF CHURCH	Bourgeois
	Liberal Evengelicalism
	Impartial, 'above'
	conflict
	
	Imperial support
		Bourgeois
		*Liberal Evengelicalism
		Impartial, reconciling
		  should not get
		  involved
		Souls important
		Intentions always good
		Concern—people not
		  systems
			Bourgeois
			*Liberal Evengelicalism
			Impartial, universally
			Kingdom of God
			  policies
			Charitable organisation
			
			*Concern—spirituality,
			  not worldly struggles

OVERALL PATTERN	Victorian capitalist and mercantile expansionism is dominant, accompanied by a colonial mentality, and Imperial Church, and a crude policy.	The national state (Union) is in the foreground with evidence of emphasis on consolidation and the virtues of a local bourgeoisie. Crude colonialism is much muted, and some social democratic thought is more strongly present.	There appears to be a clear shift to system reform along the lines advanced by local capital needs. Some evidence of a growing crisis mentality, but also a capitulation to the separation of the religious from the social realm.

General note: Capitalism and a Church to match are pre-eminent throughout.

*Asterisked items indicate a strong emphasis in the records as a whole.

Table 5: Ideological Analysis, CPSA and Methodist Church:
Presuppositions 1903—1930

	1903—1910	1911—1919	1920—1930
ON BLACKS— GENERAL	Must work for reward Only need basic manual education Females trained as domestics Assimilation? Negative 'Homelands' provide Taxation—NB source of revenue *Leadership should be co-opted Easily run into credit difficulty Christian education NB American education bad Inferior race	Complaints should be made in 'legal, godly' fashion Crime—result of character deficiency Citizenship—a privilege Inferior race	Citizenship—a privilege General leaseholding required *Alliance with the educated NB Inferior, must be guided
ON LABOUR	Control is first priority Influx control necessary Compounds good, but should be improved	Proper case of Labour—prosperity Unionisation suspicious Cheap black labour necessary for white wealth Labour unfair, government fair Farmers have difficulty Farm labour is exploited	Reserve army of labour NB Living wage NB ICU—a challenge, but too hostile Match supply to economic development Black workers need upgrading Workers need white goodwill Farm labour is exploited Racist white workers—problem
ON ECONOMY— GENERAL	*White security crucial Cape colony system safe, best Opportunity and property NB	Stability NB Land Act a problem Private property/ business NB Worker role must increase Economic struggle basic, worldwide	Development NB Land reform necessary *System needs drastic changes Worker role must increase Collective bargaining system NB Capital and labour both must be responsible to community Black and white co-operation NB

ON POLITICS	White rule essential
	System OK, change
	Union not a fair
	  deal for 'good
	  natives'
		White superiority NB
		Conflict to be avoided
		White unity NB
		Link with Britain NB
		*Victorian manners and
		  virtues NB
		Legislation best for
		  'natives'
		Legislation OK if
		  known 'negrophiles'
		  support it
		Negotiation is right
		  method
		Right spirit—harmony
		Individual change will
		  bring social change
			*White supremacy
			  crucial
			*System OK
			White unity NB
			Segregation necessary
			Communism bad
			*Reform, not
			  revolution
			'Colour bar'
			  provocative
			Subject peoples
			  should participate
			  in government

ON THE CHURCH	Stands 'above' society
	*Allied with State/
	  Crown
	Must fit blacks for
	  labour
	Work holy, religion
	  necessary
	Help to blacks
	  unappreciated
	'Saving' blacks central
	*Christianity only answer
	Family NB for Church/
	  Empire
	Missionaries need more
	  sympathy for colonists
		*Stands 'above' society
		*Capitalists and mission-
		  aries have common
		  interests
		Hard work needs
		  religion
		Should relate to
		  workers
		Alienated from
		  workers
		*Christianity-great hope
			Stands 'above' conflict
			*Compounds—NB
			  mission field
			Religion purifies
			  character
			Religious values NB
			Concerned with total-
			  ity of life
			Its work has im-
			  proved situation
			Only Church can
			  really help
			Family—basis of
			  Church, society

OVERALL PATTERN	Strong role of Empire In general, blacks seen as primitive and fit for labour only.	National state authority strong; also relationship to national capital. But conflicts with respect to workers and blacks in general are evident, while calls for moderation increase.	Reformist tendencies strong, in labour, land and political control issues. Church alliance with national capital much stronger despite Hertzog govern- ment. Emphasis on privatised religion to the fore.

Note: Constants — (i) White supremacy and economic security; (ii) Control over labour (necessarily increasingly sophisticated); (iii) Liberal capitalist economy and its values; (iv) Desire to see 'qualified' blacks co-opted or incorporated; (v) View of inferiority of blacks; (vi) Church 'above' society and conflict; (vii) Family and work ethics; (viii) Segregation in some form.

Conclusion

Many of the themes unfolded in the earlier historical treatment of the Church reappear in the summary data of the preceding pages. From a different angle of view they undergird many of the earlier assessments made and 'conclusions reached. It remains to weld these assessments and conclusions together into a structure of explanation, drawing the various elements into a perceivable and usable whole. For this purpose, it is necessary to step back from the particular to the more general, from the local context to a wider relation of religion to industrial society, from the specific historical moment to its preceding conditions.

Colonisation of southern Africa by the British imperial vanguard included the work of missionaries who proceeded eastwards and northwards, breaking ground before other colonial forces or consolidating ground already broken. A symbiotic relationship between Church and Empire was both central and inevitable.[10]

Viewed by one churchman as the 'pioneer period', during this time any resistance encountered by the missions (there was a great deal) could easily be rationalised as the opposition of the 'Devil' against the European 'invasion of his dominion'. However, the unavoidable conquest and subjugation of the indigenous people, accompanied by their progressive incorporation into the colonial political economy as their own economies were altered, made mission work less and less hazardous with time, and inroads easier. Thus, the 'seed time', eventually gave way to the establishment of local churches, conferences, synods and similar organised groups wherein the 'Harvest' could be reaped.[11]

The elements of manifest destiny, conquest and possession formed the stuff of missionary ideology as is vividly displayed in the final comment of du Plessis' famous history of mission in South Africa:

> Let us then endeavour to fulfil our divinely-appointed destiny. 'There remaineth yet very much land to be possessed.' The Conquest is not yet complete . . . We need leaders for the fight; we need soldiers for the ranks . . . We need the sinews of war . . .[12]

But the end of the nineteenth century brought the diamond and gold discoveries, transformed the economic geography of the region, introduced the first major phase of industrialisation, and set up labour supply and control systems matched to the unique conditions of a tight monopoly in the diamond market and a usually strict monopsony on the low-grade, highly capitalised, but immensely rich gold reefs. From this point on the economy of South Africa was locked into structures that would produce a marked degree of exploitation of colonised labour, a white labour aristocracy, and underdevelopment of the rural reserves. That the gold reefs lay in a Trekker Republic generated at first an Imperial war and then a peculiar and momentous competition between national and foreign capital, a competition for hegemony in the face of various recurrent threats from labour.

Thus one arrives at the post Anglo-Boer War period, in a Church milieu characterised by enormous interests in the industrial education of the indigenous people to fit them for 'their place'; by a concern to consolidate 'the restraining and directing influence of the Christian religion' and to educate them 'on the proper lines';[13] finally by a desire to accept a select number of suitably qualified blacks into the dominant system. These elements remain characteristic, reflecting in a new economic environment a continuing debt on the part of the churches to the ideology and the practice of the dominant powers.[14]

The captivity of the churches to the ruling, powers and their functional dependency on the industrial economy, itself connected in important ways to the imperial metropoli, can be understood at a number of levels. The Victorian tradition, a colonial mentality, the structures of the Church itself, the material interests of its white members, and the impact of European immigrants — all played a part in determining the theory and the practice of the Church along lines prejudicial to the colonised indigenous people and the working class in particular. Regularly the Church stumbled through confusion, ambiguity, inactivity, and occasional protest from its black members among whom it desired no loss of influence. Its undoubted contribution to their welfare and to their ability to cope in a new environment imposed upon them, does not undermine or reduce the force of this assessment of the Church in relation to blacks and to the working class in particular.

Studies of Victorian Christianity, especially of the 'church by law established' (the Church of England) and the Methodist group of churches, reveal connections to the ideology and practice of early capitalism in the English revolution that are of considerable significance to the present argument. Young believes that Victorian England rested ideologically on two assumptions that began to fail as time went on: 'that the production of wealth by the few meant, somehow, and in the long run, welfare for the many, and that conventional behaviour grounded on a traditional creed was enough to satisfy all right demands of humanity.'[15]

Conventional behaviour revolved around duty and self-restraint as characterised by the image of the English gentleman. 'Respectability' became an ideal — it captured the whole of middle-class aspirations and many, including John Wesley, were obsessed with a desire to encourage the working class in this direction. In close connection to these inter-related values, the dominant perspective in the churches in relation to the newly developing conflict between proletarianised labour and free-trade capital was one of 'harmony' at all costs.[16] Consequently, 'restraint, tolerance, a live and let live attitude' were prescribed. Religion was regarded as the basis for co-operation on the part for all. When social evils were recognised, pulpit speakers preached 'a personal regeneration to the sufferers and advocated reform by the State', but 'they did not advocate independent struggle by the workers'.[17] For them the relationship between capital and labour was contractual rather than conflictual. From this point of view exploitation could only be defined as an 'unfair' contract requiring an adjustment in its terms but not a challenge to the nature of the relationship.

Methodism in particular served as the religion for both the industrial bourgeoisie and sections of the working class. Its focus was predominantly moral and individual. EP Thompson points out three major means of securing obedience: requirement of service to the Church itself; the cultivation of one's own soul; and self-discipline in labour as a 'pure act of virtue'. He fittingly adds elsewhere that:

> So long as Satan remained undefined and of no fixed class abode, Methodism condemned working people to a kind of moral civil war — between the chapel and the pub, the wicked and the redeemed, the lost and the saved.[18]

In his view the Church weakened the poor from within through an active demand for submission, and through an ideology suited to the needs of manufacturers and aimed at work discipline in the new economic climate. Moreover, in the churches as a whole, active responsibility within the society at large for assisting in various needful situations was conceived of more in terms of service than of solidarity. This distinction is significant and has a special meaning here.

'Service', Raymond Williams has demonstrated, is the concept of intervention arising out of the middle-class; 'solidarity' that out of a working class base. The point concerns the self-perception lying behind the notion of service when it is used by those relatively strongly bound to the ruling classes. Service is then not defined, for example, as in the acts of Jesus of Nazareth. The stories tell that he served his disciples by way of a startling reversal of the master-servant relationship (most dramatically in the foot-washing). The notion of service Williams discovers in the Victorian Church is in direct contrast to this reversal — it is 'from-above-dominated' patronage or philanthropy. It is therefore no coincidence that service was often understood as the 'raising upwards' of those who were regarded as culturally, socially or economically 'below' the standards regarded as Christian in the empire. Solidarity in contrast is the practice which begins with the reversal of the power or authority relationship. Ultimately therefore, 'the idea of service . . . is no substitute for the idea of active mutual responsibility.'[19]

When one adds to these various insights the knowledge that philosophical idealism reigned supreme in the churches at the time, as is witnessed most profoundly in the Victorian regard for the sermon as 'the standard vehicle of truth' and for the written and spoken word as the power for change; when one recognises that 'the clergy as a body stood in a class apart' from workers and peasantry by virtue of their education, their relations with the gentry, and their local power; then it is not hard to discern the connections of the Church to the dominant political economy and the many parallels to the early industrial period in South Africa.[20] In both contexts the churches 'do not as a rule accept the validity of the struggle between employer and employee', they 'do not produce leaders who would articulate and pursue class interests as such', and they emphasise 'traditional values and activities . . . increasingly disconnected from current political issues.'[21]

At first sight these points appear to be no basis for criticism, but rather admirable indications of an independence from any one group or class in society, by virtue of which the Church could bridge gaps between human beings and hold open space for the constructive resolution of conflicts. Stated baldly, this seems fine. But the effect of such a position, especially in highly differentiated, stratified societies, is not at all neutral. More than anything, such a position allows greater sway for the dominant powers, the stronger party (by virtue of access to and control over administration, legislative bodies, media, finances, forces of production, and so on). 'Standing aloof' from such realities may be comforting to the disturbed, threatened or perplexed person or body. But it is also a certain abdication of responsibility in regard to the poor and oppressed. Often it is also a way of concealing the implication of the inevitable symbiotic participation of the Church in its social context, namely, that it usually reflects within itself the same conflicts and contradictions as the society of which it is part.

The impact of an industrial, market ideology and its attendant practice upon the indigenous population of South Africa has also been well documented. Land became increasingly conceived of as 'yet another form of personal property, realisable and profitable in terms of money.'[22] Prestige was measured in terms of the accumulation of goods and of money to purchase them, which meant a stimulus to wage labour and a cultivation of aspirations defined by the manufacturing class. Thus the indigenous society was transformed, rudely if necessary, while the doctrines of work, private property and individualism were made to replace old values. The Church itself became a measure of status, many of the aspirant middle-class associating with it for pragmatic, political or social reasons. Africans who were Christianised were sometimes referred to as *ositshuzana*, that is, the 'excuse me' people, because of their particular concern for respectability as defined by the conquering colonists.[23] This does not imply that there were no rules of etiquette in Afican societies, only that they were different. But that is precisely the point.

The Church in South Africa could not help but be what it was. It could not avoid being structured so that its finances were derived from the dominant class, both locally and internationally;[24] so that its clergy were paid differential wages according to their place in society — white or black; so that only one African priest had reached the rank of canon by 1934 and the diocesan monthly, *The Watchman*, had then yet to carry an article written by an African.[25] Its ecclesiastical system of administration closely followed and often assisted the imperial, the symbiotic relationship between leading clergy and rulers predominating even when the Church felt constrained to protest in the name of its less fortunate members against injustice and inhumanity.[26] The role of women, never to the fore in the material analysed in this study, also demonstrated negatively the fundamental bondage of the Church to the ideas and the praxis of the class upon which it depended.

On the basis of the foregoing analysis one must also situate the Church in a supportive position to the white state in terms of the struggle between the dominant and dominated classes in the 1903—1930 period, even when it protested against the particular form of state assumed under the hegemony of national capital under Hertzog. Here it is clear that the controlling position of whites in the churches was also significant. English-speaking whites as a group for long had the highest average income in South Africa.[27] Their material privilege and relative affluence, once established, was not threatened by the state even under Hertzog despite their increasingly 'embattled cultural position'.[28] As against black South Africans, the prospects of immigrants in terms of standards of living and income and even education were generally very good, entrenching their interests. Many naturally joined the English-speaking churches in South Africa.

One author has spoken of a 'crisis of faith, commitment and hope' in the white English-speaking community accompanied by a 'failure on the part of the churches to meet the crisis in a creative way'.[29] All things considered — the history, the structure, the interests, the practices, and the thought of the Church in South Africa through the period studied — this crisis may be fairly clearly delineated. It lies in the practical and theoretical homage paid to an exploitative and oppressive political economy, in an incapacity for critical and self-critical analysis carried through in a sustained manner, in the refusal to countenance a clear and active option for the poor and the disinherited, in ideological captivity and a fear of exceeding acceptable boundaries of debate, in theologies and theological education inimical to the needs and the situation of workers and colonised people, and in structures of organisation and finance favouring the control of the Church by the skilled, the affluent, the educated, the well-connected, the articulate and the powerful. The testimony of those people and occasional groups who have been different and done otherwise is an honoured one, held strong within the Church itself, but — one suspects — more as a placebo and a gratification rather than a stimulus to renewal from the ground up.

In this sense, the Church struggle in South Africa is not merely a struggle against a particularly disliked form of state (apartheid) — it is a struggle of the Church with itself and within itself. It is a battle to determine who will be where in the struggle for South Africa itself and in the achievement of a just and participatory democracy. It cannot be taken for granted that the Church will end up where it should, honouring in its own life and worship not merely the 'Son of God' but also the man of truth who strode clear-eyed into the centres of religious, political and economic power in Jerusalem and called their bluff.

In this respect the present study seeks to contribute to the formation of a Church which looks for ultimate peace through the penultimate construction and sustenance of a realistic, intelligently assessed contemporary structure of peace.

Notes

1 R Williams (1961), p317.
2 In A Armstrong (1973), p184.
3 In J Stone (1973), p200.
4 J de Gruchy (1979), p33; see also P Hinchliff (1963), p230.
5 Irving Hexham traces the former connection through the Gereformeerde Kerk in his *The Irony of Apartheid: the Struggle for National Independence of Afrikaner Calvinism Against British Imperialism,* Edwin Mellin Press, NY (1981).
6 J de Gruchy (1979), p19.
7 A total of 626 cards were completed, drawn from close on 2000 entries.
8 A Fierro (1977), p245, somewhat expanded here.
9 J Habermas (1971), p315.
10 Note L Hewson's comment on Methodism (1950), p8.
11 These stages constitute the interpretation of missions made by Samuel Clark, Secretary of the SAMS, 34th Report, 1915, pp1—3.
12 JH du Plessis (1911), p408.
13 GBA Gerdener (1958), p243, first quote from Dr Roberts of Lovedale, to the 1904 General Missionary Conference; and p209.
14 Similar developments in the German Missions are traced by U Kistner, Africa Perspective, no 13, Spring, 1979, p63 and preceeding.

15 GM Young (1964), p100.

16 A Armstrong (1973), p92.

17 R Moore (1974), p7 & p11.

18 EP Thompson (1968), p401 & p50; also p390.

19 R Williams (1961), pp314—6 *passim*.

20 GM Young (1964), p15 & pp63—4; see also R Moore (1974), p224.

21 R Moore (1974), pp26—7.

22 DH Reader (1966), pp70—1.

23 A Vilakazi (1962), p139. Vilakazi's study focuses on a more modern community, but there appears no reason why certain aspects should not apply to earlier periods, and many reasons why such an application seems entirely appropriate. See also pp99 & 133.

24 Figures for the CPSA in 1931, for example, illustrate the point, as do Conference minutes and synod records generally; see also 'With One Accord', *Unified Statement,* Church of England Assembly, Britain, 1933.

25 A Paton (1973), p46.

26 See W Crokat, 'Government in the English Church', English Church House, Cape Town, 1905.

27 HL Watts, 'A Social and Demographic Picture of English-speaking White South Africans', in A de Villiers (1976), p63.

28 L Schlemmer, 'English-speaking South Africans Today: Identity and Integration', *ibid,* pp96—7.

29 J de Gruchy (1979), p95.

PART 2

Reflections in Theory —
The Possibility of a Critical Church

CHAPTER EIGHT

Problems of Method

Introduction

When one chooses not to act, one accepts — that is, passively chooses — the status quo. The symptoms of this condition are fatalism, apathy or withdrawal.

Active choice on the other hand, is not without its ambiguities, its potential lack of insight or even, perhaps, its unwelcome consequences. The story is told of a Swiss army captain who in 1938 foresaw the war clouds looming over Europe. He chose to avoid the coming madness by departing to a remote tropical island, there to remain until it was all over. The island was Guam, subsequently the scene of a most savage battle between American and Japanese forces. Such tales remind one of the ironies of all human choices and acts.

Commitment to active choice, and a willingness to confront the status quo on many levels, are the hallmarks of much Christian theology since the early 1960s. Behind this theology lies a belief in the priority of right action ('orthopraxis') over right teaching or belief ('orthodoxy').[1] Large-scale choices are involved and not just moral behaviour. This usually implies an identification of domination and dispossession wherever it occurs, and an option for those who suffer the consequent loss of their human agency, potency and dignity in the particular context addressed. Theologies relevant to 'right action' are therefore often termed 'contextual' and speak of a prior commitment to the poor and the oppressed. A similar perspective operates as a basic presupposition of this study.

Theology is also regarded here as a human mode of thought without divine exemption from the questions and difficulties of all human thought. This means that theology is non-dogmatically open to history (it would be hard to account for the history of theological ideas if this were not granted). Moreover, because right belief in this framework is not accorded any ontological status (being located in history), theology as a discipline and as found in Church records should not be granted any special autonomy nor any godly immunity from ideological critique.

Thus the method used in this study seeks to elucidate the empirical conditions of knowledge and action in the churches, so as to allow a genuinely self-critical theology. Some of the questions raised in the process are part of a well-known methodological debate. Others are occasioned by the unlikely combination of theology with historical materialist analysis.

Historical Materialism

The status of historical materialism remains a matter of contemporary debate; for that matter, so does its meaning. At one stage the academic world in the West had concluded that studies guided by historical materialism were doomed to the backwaters and museums of scholarship. More recently such studies have proliferated and all sectors of the social and human sciences have found themselves faced with a perspective impossible to ignore.

The main epistemological contribution of historical materialism lies in its consideration of the relation of theory and practice, beginning with the classical Marxian declaration that theory cut off from the practical task of transforming the world is false, an abstraction. One may derive from this the notion of the ideological character of false theory, that is, its function in concealing the real material interests of those propagating it in order to legitimate some form of practical domination over others.

To the extent that false theory succeeds in legitimating domination, that is, to the extent that it conceals from any or all groups in society their real relations, it is false consciousness. In this way false theory has practical efficacy, yet it cannot stand practical critique. For emancipatory practice would destroy it by demonstrating its role in legitimating domination (destroying illusion), and by the overthrow of the conditions which produce it (liberation). Falsity and truth are consequently tied in to the question of human activity, and not just human ideas. (It should be noted that the logic of the above notion of emancipatory practice implies the overcoming of all domination, rather than the substitution of one dominating power for another.)

From this basic point of view Marx analysed the dynamics and structures of nineteenth century capitalism, showing (i) in what way historical material forces (forces and relations of production) so central to the genesis, development and organisation of human society produced new, structurally relevant theory (bourgeois); (ii) how this theory functioned to hide new structures of domination (commodity fetishism); and (iii) wherein lay the countervailing forces (contradictions) that would lead to the practical emancipation from domination of all, through the particular agency of those materiallly interested in overcoming their own domination (the proletariat, for Marx).

Prevailing social institutions find their place in this analysis at the level of sustaining the conditions for the reproduction of the dominant socio-economic system, either by legitimation of the system or by crisis management of the system. In this respect religion as a social institution was seen by Marx to be profoundly false, taking away in its theory (theology) the productive and creative power residing in human beings by attributing it to an external agency (God), and thereby making alienation an ontological presupposition.[2] This corresponds directly with the capitalists' conviction that material production and creative power were external to labour, residing not in its agency (work) but in capital and its technology, both owned by the capitalist. Religious institutions were seen to wield their theory of God in favour of the dominant whose power and agency were taken for granted, and for whom the greatest threat lay in the possibility of the dominated discovering their own power and agency. At the same time religion, in its ambiguity, reflected not only the aims of the dominant but also recognised the contradiction of the whole system in the cry of the dominated. Its ability to provide a relatively non-threatening channel by which that cry could be taken up and out of itself, gave religion its social utility within the system.

Whatever the debates on various other aspects of Marx's work, this view of the social role of religion in a capitalist order has retained much of its potency. More recent acknowledgements of the role of religion in emancipatory practice under certain circumstances (eg parts of Latin America) have only modified the Marxian critique. My analysis of English-speaking churches in South Africa is an attempt to determine empirically the validity of this critique.

The key lies in uncovering the relationship between the theory of the Church (in this case, its proclamations, policies and theology) and its social practice. Quite evidently, one must make the distinction between the practice of domination and emancipatory practice. Where does the emphasis lie in the Church? When its theory appears emancipatory, does this lead to practical results, or does it conceal a contradictory practice? Such basic questions immediately come to the fore.

It would be illegitimate to make any final claims to truth (could one ever make them at all) in the use of the historical materialist paradigm. Yet I take its value to be considerable, especially when compared with more common approaches such as what one author calls 'reductionist bourgeois sociology'. In the case of such sociology . . .

> . . .class structure and class relations are reduced to simple stratification; exploitation and domination in society to the simple difference of position and role; and the role of the dominating class, which results from its control of production, is reduced to the intellectual role of the 'political elite'. Social changes are reduced to the migration of people and of social strata; the class struggle, strikes and revolutions are reduced to disintegration and social pathology; . . . and the theory of values is reduced to distinct, and therefore legitimate, 'ways of life'.[3]

Following Korsch, Bottomore points out that besides the question of praxis (reflective action towards the tansformation of society), a Marxian social analysis would be defined by four major features, namely:

1   the primacy of the economic structure (the mode of production of material life);
2   the historical specification of all social phenomena (periodisation);
3   the setting of empirical studies within an historical economic context;
4   the recognition of revolutionary as well as evolutionary social change (breaks in the historical continuity of a form of society, and the role of conflict in social change).[4]

The original philosophical presupposition underlying this schema concerns the nature of society *per se*. For Marx, society is properly understood only when its connection to nature via the concept of human labour is grasped. The developing interaction between real human beings and their environment creates and progressively transforms social relationships, this interchange being defined by the production of the means of subsistence.[5]

Limits are established by what is already found in existence as a given, that is, the prevailing material conditions (which incorporate nature, technological capability, and the form of social organisaton). Therefore one needs to analyse present conditions, their genesis, and their development; that is, one analyses the mode of life and its history.[6] Potentialities reside in the human beings who produce things, whose agency is thereby capable of changing circumstances as they are changed by those circumstances.

Work is therefore the key element in the historical process (otherwise we have only a natural process). Work effects the transformation of human history (ideas do nothing unless they are acted upon). Therefore, what separates the labourer from the product of his or her work without returning its full value, is what generates (a) the conditions of alienation (what was one's own is taken away), and (b) the conditions of domination (whoever takes away that product acquires power not their own). Given these emphases, consciousness and ideas are seen in relation to the material practices which characterise and define a particular historical epoch. Thus the Marxian analysis of ideology proceeds as an analysis of the institutions of society (state, law, education, culture, religion, etc) which embody the forms of consciousness and the ruling ideas of any given epoch.

Two aspects of the Marxian view stand out. Firstly theory and practice, continually interacting, are seen as inseparable in any real historical process (though theory formally may be separable from practice). Secondly, the individual and society are not seen as isoloated entitites but as fully interrelated.

The axioms, when taken together, provide major advantages for any social analysis. The totality of human society is given priority, its developmental character is conceptually integrated from the beginning, and the open-endedness of theory and practice is treated as a *sine qua non*.

Furthermore, in this view society is not regarded as a 'fixed abstraction opposed to the individual' nor is the individual seen to be identifiable except as at least a social being.[7] In fact the very appearance of society as a 'given', as an alien power independent of the will and action of people, is ideological, for the human origin and goal of society are thereby obscured.[8]

The recent attempts by sociologists, economists and historians to investigate South African society from a Marxian perspective are included in the earlier empirical study of the Church. Their work undoubtedly has proved remarkably fruitful in a short space of time, notwithstanding many theoretical difficulties. In utilising this work, I am adopting certain assumptions and concepts related to the methods of historical materialist analysis. Because this is controversial in the context of the Church, it is worth discussing this approach. In any event, methodological precision also requires a crtical attitude to one'e own language — in my case, the discourse of Christian theology. Unquestionably, my use of the historical materialist paradigm does raise a number of critical matters, both in respect of theological discourse and of the motifs of the paradigm itself.

Economic Development

Many people are easily trapped into thinking that a Marxian analysis simply correlates every social phenomenon directly with economic forces and thereby considers it explained. Thus one hears of 'vulgar' Marxism: a crude, polemical view accompanied by a singular inability to notice subtle detail and fine differentiation in society and history.

But Marxist analysis is not necessarily vulgar; among good scholars it is in fact never so. Complex and insightful models exist within the Marxian tradition. It is to one of them that we will turn.

The Church, sociologically speaking, is a religious phenomenon. It is not simply a product of a particular mode of production, but is affected by other variables such as tradition, education, historical location, family and so on. Yet, as with all religious phenomena, the Church is not an autonomous social reality either.[9]

From the historical materialist point of view, the Church and the variables affecting it cannot be understood without reference to the economic base. This is the determining variable, that is, the primary though not sole cause for explanation. This claim is not naively positivist if one asserts a dynamic relationship between the variables as opposed to a simplistic one-to-one correspondence between economic base and superstructure. Relativism is equally undermined precisely in asserting the economic factor as the prime link. The economic factor emerges as the key on the basis of the argument that 'work', a human activity, practically transforms human history and most profoundly regulates human relations. (The neo-classical market with its price mechanisms is the core of capitalist society, not religion, culture or whatever else.) That the historical materialist view takes the economic base as a determining variable allows for a focal point of systematisation, for all other variables must necessarily find their description, at least in part, in relation to the economic factor.

A well-known Hungarian, András Hegedüs, has developed an appropriate model of social structure particularly suited to this study of the role of the Church in South Africa.[10] He rejects a simple dichotomous model of society (eg master versus slave). Consideration of ownership alone is insufficient to determine social structure and can be misleading. Property relations are therefore only one class-forming factor. The differential functions needed for the maintenance and development of society are another. These form the social division of labour, itself characterised by distinct differentiations in the nature of work (such as manual, non-manual, intellectual, cultural, etc.)[11] Factors such as income and social prestige are in turn dependent upon one's position in the social division of labour. Hegedüs makes quite clear, however, that the social division of labour is not defined by lists of occupations, but by a definite type of relation to production. So for instance, an important aspect of one's place in the division of labour is the control one has over one's own work and over the work of others.[12]

The concept of 'economic branch' also plays a key role in Hegedüs' theory. His prime distinction here is between the industrial and agricultural sectors of the economy, but one may include others such as commerce. This concept and the concepts of ownership and the division of labour together constitute the independent variables determining a social structure, for they most strongly determine social norms of behaviour, value systems and states of consciousness. In short, it is in relation to these factors that interests, functions and objectives of large-scale social groups are most clearly visible.

Two other variables which Hegedüs regards as complementing those already mentioned are domicile and educational level. A difference in domicile, especially between urban town and rural village, may influence educational possibilities, manner of living, use of leisure, and other aspects, but it cannot be regarded as an independent social variable (even though its effect on a single individual may be great). Similarly, educational level and opportunity have an effect in engendering mobility and decreasing the stability of generational strata, as well as on the structure of occupations and trades. These are regarded as qualifying the independent variables rather than eliminating their powerful role.

Hegedüs' model takes note of other 'intervening variables' than those directly affecting social structure, treating these as marks of social differentiation quite secondary to social structure. The total picture conveyed by his model encompasses complexity, statistical accessibility and the systematisation of variables together, based on theoretical presuppositions of historical materialism. Among other things, Hegedüs points out that

> . . . We must always distinguish and select the criteria which are to be reckoned with first and which, in the literal sense of the word, get the better of and dwarf others. We should know, therefore, that though there are a multitude of criteria, they do not weigh the same. An understanding of the social phenomena requires above all that essential and inessential features, dependent and independent variables should be distinguished.[13]

Hegedüs developed his model of social structure in a socialist society, namely Hungary. His context allows the complexity of variables determining a social structure to emerge more clearly than in much work done within capitalist societies, largely beacuse the role of ownership is such a powerful determinant in these societies. Keeping this in mind — for the analysis of the South African Church concerns an obviously capitalist society — I find that Hegedüs provides an approach of considerable heuristic value.

The Model Applied

The analysis of the role of the English-speaking churches in South Africa is carried out along lines compatible with the Hegedüs model. Remembering that it is an essentially ideological analysis, the procedures actually adopted may be tabulated along the lines suggested by Hegedüs. In this way we may specify in its complexity the social structure which is the context of the Church in South Africa. Table 6 sets out the system of variables proposed by Hegedüs, and defines these in terms of specific factors present in the South African situation.

No particular attempt is made to specify and analyse secondary factors of social differentiation, for the reason that in an obviously capitalist milieu the great inequalities produced by class factors, and especially by the inequality of ownership, far outweigh factors of age, sex, culture, religion, etc. Of course, such latter factors may be used by conquerors and rulers to re-define who is to retain ownership and who not, how the division of labour is to be constructed and so on. Thus 'race' in South Africa has become a major ideological weapon relegating blacks to the level of unskilled labour, depriving them of ownership, etc. But this clearly does not deny that the structures of domination which 'racism' defines have an economic foundation. Prejudice may be hurtful, but it is nowhere near as directly final as poverty or dispossession.

Besides the specification of structural factors, other criteria are necessary to discern the language patterns which characterised the Church at the time. These are listed horizontally in Table 7. The investigation of church archival material (speeches, reports, letters, minutes, official documents, etc) sought to find responses to a range of key issues in the political economy of South Africa at that time. These issues are listed vertically. The analysis of Church data via this model is therefore intended to elucidate the developmental logic, in a capitalist order, of a particular institution (the Church) in respect of its public ideology.

If, using these various analytical entry points, the results jointly tend to support a particular hypothesis, and if contradictions can be accounted for, then the phenomenon may be said to have been reasonably explained. Given sufficient analytical rigour, one may claim to have demonstrated a particular proposition (eg about the role of the Church in South Africa) arising from a specific methodological paradigm (eg historical materialism).

This study is an attempt to carry out this analytical experiment. The adoption of the historical materialist paradigm depends not only on a judgement about its explanatory power, but also on what one writer has termed a 'methodological suspicion'.[14] In South Africa, religion and religious institutions have been well-studied in relation to politics, education, law, other religious traditions and ideas; yet rarely in relation to economic structure. This leads one to suspect that an investigation of the latter will yield important results (because the hidden relation covers over certain realities, while this concealment prevents self-critique).

Table 6: Specification of factors for the analysis of the
South African political economy

		SYSTEM OF VARIABLES	SPECIFIC FACTORS FOR ANALYSIS
SOCIAL STRUCTURE (including the history of its development)	Independent variables:	ownership place in the division of labour economic branch	classes and class functions manual—non-manual (skilled, semi-skilled, unskilled) / administrative / professional / cultural / control over job mining / manufacturing / agriculture / commercial
	Complimentary variables:	domicile educational level	urban (residential, location, compound) / rural (village, farm, mission land) / migrant (contract, casual) schooled / illiterate / type and goals of education / selection of pupils (non-universal, non-compulsory education)
	Dependent variables:	earnings social prestige	wage colour bars / stipends (Church) colour—caste / elite / supervisory / craft unions
SOCIAL DIFFERENTIATION	Demographic marks:	age sex phyle	
	Marks of cultural differences:	literary taste	(these factors are largely untreated)
	Other social differences		

Table 7: Criteria for analysing language patterns in relation
to political economic issues

KEY ISSUES	date	key terms	symbols/ images	key ideas	necessary presuppositions	actions taken	rites/ formulae	view on labour	view on power	desired 'good'	intention-ality	meaning complex	level of ideology	interests	alliances	class determination
Land																
Labour (gen)																
Black labour																
White labour																
Trade Unions																
Job colour bars																
Wage colour bars																
Compounds																
Contracts and passes																
Taxation																
Recruiting																
Wage structures																
Housing																
Ownership																
Owners/capitalists																
Reserves																
Poor whites																
Peasantry																
Marginal people																
Political exclusion																
Resistance																
Liquor																
State role																
Repression/control																
Independent Church																
Mission																
Church																
Doctrine																
Ideological aspects																

ANALYTICAL ENTRY

Archival extracts are individually analysed (where possible) in terms of the above set of criteria for each issue to which they are relevant (usually only one or two). Secondly, these extracts are collectively evaluated in terms of their source, ie either Methodist Church, Anglican or Christian Express/ South African Outlook, in respect of emphasis on particular issues. Thirdly, a second-level abstraction is made in respect of each issue to determine chronological (period) emphases. Fourthly, periods are correlated with issues emphasied to determine historical shifts. The insights generated by a combination of these methods are what are taken to determine the developmental history of language patterns in the churches investigated.

At this point another issue raises its head. If one is to study the Church in relation to its political economic context via the words of its leadership and spokesmen, is one not already making one's own interpretation of what they said? How can one be sure one is not putting one's own predetermined understanding in the way, thus falsifying what they really meant?

As has already been indicated, I have tried to determine what the context of Church utterances was, what patterns of language were used, and whether there are ways in which these are linked. Thus I have been concerned less with any one individual's specific way of seeing the world, and more with a particular generalised form and expression of consciousness. This cannot be done by analysing people's ideas alone (philosophical idealism) nor by investigating their overt intentions or subjective perceptions alone (psychologism). Subjectivity and ideas exist in relation to a complex social reality. It is this relationship we need to study, including human actions in the poltical economic context, and the langugae humans use to speak of and define their actions.

If, however, historical materialism regards 'work' as the key to understanding human beings in society, including the way in which consciousness is formed, how are we to give any significance to language? Language is obviously not just an expression of consciousness, but itself plays a crucial role in human interaction, and therefore in human action.

One way of dealing with the problem has been to broaden the definition of labour to include intellectual activity and its products. But the problem then is that the practical effect of intellectual work becomes very difficult to distinguish from the traditional idea of the efficacy of consciousness which Marx criticised.

Another direction, particularly well-developed by Jürgen Habermas in recent years, is to define language as act, and language acts as integral to praxis. In this view, labour is not the only fundamental reality of human existence, for the transformation of the world and of oneself by work is accompanied by equivalent transformations embodied in language practice. The goal of social evolution is then not defined in socio-economic terms alone, but also in terms of what Habermas calls 'speech acts' in a milieu governed by a generalised 'communicative competence'. This communicative competence of all people in society is possible only when domination has disappeared, when fully responsible participation of every citizen in all aspects of life is materially present (Habermas calls this the 'ideal speech situation').

What Habermas thereby implies is that the goal of social transformation includes the possibility for every person to participate fully in defining society at both the political and the economic levels. At the political level, language comes to the fore. The ability to participate fully here depends upon one's control over language and its environment, as well as one's access to political discourse.

In other words, a society fully defined by communicative competence would necessarily require proper education for all, effective channels for the exercise of power by all, and a fulfilment of all basic subsistance needs such as food, shelter, warmth, etc. Clearly, therefore, access to (and participation in) power and control in the economic sphere is also a necessary condition, as Habermas is not assuming that such a society is possible merely through the impact of good intentions, freedom of expression, or higher levels of education. The concept of an 'ideal speech situation' has its force in defining the aim of social transformation and in providing a touchstone whereby any current social construct may be analysed and evaluated.

The model developed for the present study follows the clues offered by Habermas. What one sees in Church records are by and large 'speech acts'. What one wishes to determine is the extent to which such speech-acts are firstly, self-conscious via-a-vis their objective conditions, secondly, self-critical, and thirdly, aimed at generating a milieu of 'communicative competence'. The first and most basic test arises in the judgement of the relation of any speech-act to its practical reference. In the simplest terms, one asks: is what you say what you do?

In this case, interpretive analysis cannot rely on the face-value of statements observed. On the contrary, 'face value' is precisely what is under question.[15] For this reason, an interpretive framework is unavoidable; in fact it is necessary. One needs to grasp the meaning of a speech-act through insightful understanding. But a specification in detail of the objective conditions of a statement (or text), and an understanding of its meaning cannot be reduced to a single principle, either by regarding meaning as residing purely in the text irrespective of its context, or by treating objective conditions as already containing the full meaning of the text.

A combination of the two requirements would most adequately generate reliable insights. In respect of objective conditions, LeFebvre has provided a concise detailing of the required task, spelling out the implications as he sees it of dialectical method (as opposed to a method of simple correlation):

> The sociology of ideological forms tries to discover their class meaning in a dialectical manner, that is, at manifold levels both in the past and the present, studying the conditions for their emergence, their points of impact, their rebirths and renewals, their truly representative and their illusion-creating functions alike, the shifts among them, cynical utilisations of them, etc. The critique of ideologies deepens the distinction between appearance and reality . . . The analysis of ideologies finds its proper place in the study of forms that impose a certain order — a relative, precarious order, often put in question — on the constitutive elements of class society.[16]

But this does not finally solve all problems. Such demands as discovering what is 'truly representative', where 'cynical utilisations' of language occur, and so on, imply a judgement on what is true, what is cynical, etc. When a text consciously asserts a perspective of domination, or manifestly legitimates oppression, or expressly idealises an existing order over and against its contradictions, then things are not so difficult. However the majority of texts encountered in the present study are not overtly like this, for domination, legitimation and idealisation are not their conscious intention. One needs to understand the meaning of these texts as something more than a reflection of conscious intention.

The text is the speech-act of a human agent or agency. Such human agent or agency may intend something not directly because of class position or material interest. But their context is nevertheless one of inter-subjective interaction with others beginning with first life, and in this interaction general material interests play a powerful role, often unwittingly shaping consciousness.

If one adds to this Marx's and Engel's notion that language *is* practical consciousness existing also for others and for that reason really existing in social reality for oneself as well,[17] then it becomes possible to assert that the meaning of a text is discernable in its inter-subjective context.

In short, the text may be related to the generalised discourse within which it is situated (both micro-socially and macro-socially) in such a way that patterns of terms, symbols, ideas, and intentions may be distinguished in the social whole with the aim of recognising the locus of the text in those patterns. These patterns will in themselves reflect the types and varieties of consciousness of which they are the practical expression. In turn, these would be characteristic of the social whole at any particular point in its development. Equally, it becomes possible to make relatively accurate judgements about what presuppositions lie behind a particular claim, declaration or interrogation in the text. So, for example, patterns of discourse would be related to the variables of the social structure.

In order to indicate what sort of data are necessarily incorporated, one may cite the case of the Church in South Africa post-1886. Here certain historical conditions were fixed by the prior development of the society, and these inevitably conditioned later patterns of discourse to a greater or lesser degree. One recognises factors such as the semi-feudal character of Dutch colonisation, British trade-route interests, colonial trade in the interior, the state of African kingdoms, their level of technology and their form of economy, British mineral interests, and the actual conditions of resource development.

In short, capitalist industrial development in a colonial setting already characterised by groups engaging in traditional and semi-feudal economies is the primary context of discourse, the 'natural' environment. However, the style and specific trajectory of development depended secondarily on competition for resources and political hegemony among some groups as well as a consolidation of their domination over others. Perceptions of immediate or long-term interest, of possibilites of resistance, and of inter-subjectively defined social forces enter into the equation at this point, and though not determined absolutely by the force of capitalist development, they would nevertheless be conditioned by them.

The total complex, once analysed, would be characterised by patterns of discourse giving linguistic expression to the variety of conflicts, competition, and perceptions contained in that complex. These patterns in turn are the clue to analysing texts taken from Church archives. Thus two requirements — specifying objective conditions and inter-subjective meaning — are woven together to produce a systematic set of operations by which one may proceed to analyse Church documents, and attempt to understand the intentionality of actors/speakers in relation to social structures and their developmental history.[18] Without this the role of the Church is never properly understood. Within this general framework judgements are held to be sociologically sound in the sense of accounting for a system, its functional apparatus, and its historical development. However, they imply a particular goal for human society — a goal of emancipation. I therefore adopt a critical theory that

> . . . involves not only a general criticism of ideologies but also the assertion of a distinct philosophical conception that relates all social inquiry to the aim of human emancipation.[19]

A Concept of Ideology

Considerable confusion may result if the concept of ideology is not clarified at this point. Quite clearly, my investigation of the role of the Church in South Africa has sought to uncover the extent to which ideology pervaded its public practice. Immediately one implies that the less this is so the better. A further implication is that ideology is not fundamentally a psychological condition, but a structural and historical aspect of society.

Because this use of the concept of ideology is restrictive and by no means generally agreed to in the literature of sociology, it is necessary to elaborate and explain it more fully.

As Jorge Larrain's excellent review of the concept of ideology points out, its historical origins lie primarily in the nineteenth century, although earlier notions contributed to its genesis.[20] Bacon's analysis of 'idols' which warp, through their irrationality, the cognitive truth of nature; Holbach's and Helvetius' critiques of the 'priestly deceit' of clerics who sought to restore the political legitimacy and domination of the mediaeval Church in the face of the bourgois revolution; Destutt de Tracy's attempt to found a 'science of ideas' (to which he first gave the name ideology); and Ludwig Feuerbach's criticism of the idea of God as a 'projection of the essence of man' — all of these prefigure the first fully developed concept of ideology in Marx's writings.

Marx himself had of course placed emphasis on the critique of religion as the premise of all criticism directed at destroying people's illusions about their real condition.[21] At a very early stage he enunciated the principle of critique as being aimed not at the motives or psychology of persons, but at objective social reality. In a discussion on political matters in the *Rheinische Zeitung* in 1842, he argued that

> . . . taking this objective standpoint from the outset, one will not presuppose an exclusively good or bad will on either side. Rather, one will observe relationships in which only persons appear to act at first.[22]

But criticism for Marx was never sufficient in itself; that boils down to mere intellectualism. Criticism needs to be situated in the historical process as praxis, that is, it should not simply illuminate the distortion of reality, but seek to transform the conditions which allow such distortion.

Consequently, Marx's notion of ideology cannot be separated from his epistemological claim for the unity of theory and practice as the locus of all genuine criticism. Then ideology is what is overcome in transformational praxis (or revolutionary practice, to use Marx's term). Correspondingly, ideology is related to attempts, conscious or unconscious, to halt the historical process (preservation of the status quo) or to direct it into channels that may alter but not undermine the position of the dominant class (amelioration).'

Marx therefore locates ideology in its specific historical context, identifying its meaning in terms of the practice of a dominant class.[23] On this basis he analyses the specific formation of nineteenth century capitalism not only from the point of view of political economy but also from the point of view of unmasking the illusory representations that hide real social relationships of production and organisation. 'Ideology' is therefore a concept developed in parallel to the concept of 'consciousness' which is itself rooted in human praxis and which takes form in language.[24]

Misunderstandings may arise at this point if one forgets that Marx's struggle to situate the concept of consciousness was waged on two fronts: against materialism *per se* on the one hand, and idealism on the other. The former refers consciousness to an objective, external reality, and thereby loses touch with the 'sensuous human activity' of a subject. Idealism on the other hand makes reality the product of consciousness.[25] Marx subsumes the two under human praxis, itself a social phenomenon. One can thereby analyse consciousness at two levels simultaneously (dialectically): (i) as it expresses itself in the intentional actions which produce material and social life; and (ii) as it is expressed in symbolically structured representations of that activity in language. On this basis one is able to analyse a particular form of consciousness 'whose two specific and connnected features are, firstly, that it conceals social contradictions, and secondly, that it does so in the interests of the dominant class'.[26]

This form of consciousness is what Marx calls ideological. Thus not all errors of consciousness are ideological, for they may not all conceal social contradictions in the interest of the dominant class. Moreover, social structure in its historical development enters into and shapes subjectivity, thus 'ideologising' the subject at the same time. Thus people are not by definition ideologues in the Marxian view, yet they are ideologically constrained, for example, by the forces of capitalism wherever these conceal social contradictions and bolster domination.

Of course, some people may with conscious deliberation develop and use ideological constructs in defence of structures and institutions of domination. This is the realm of manipulative propaganda which reaches its greatest impact under totalitarian or fascist orders. Then language no longer has real meaning, only an instrumental purpose.[27]

Marx's theory of ideology is not a conspiracy theory. But where a social fact, whose genesis and operation can be explained historically, is collapsed into a natural one — giving the appearance of a permanent structure of universal reality, a fatefulness to life — there ideology rears its head.[20] In this way 'ideology fetishises the world of appearance, separates it from its real conditions', making the world as one encounters it into something over which one had no power in general.[29]

Ideology in the Marxian view clearly has critical, negative connotations. Ideological critique is a debunking exercise. This is in sharp contrast to other and later views which take ideology to be a general function of human activity.

The most developed alternative to the Marxian concept is to be found with Karl Mannheim. Mannheim desires to have ideology treated as a generalised reality in human society. All knowledge for him is socially determined, and no one perspective (eg the Marxian) may claim a superior point of view. Consequently, what one really means by ideology is 'perspective'. Mannheim thus turns the concept of ideology as used by Marx into a sociology of knowledge, the former in his view being a partisan weapon, the latter a genuinely scientific method of research.[30]

Mannheim's goal is to make all knowing subjects visible to themselves in the roles otherwise hidden from them by the impenetrability of social conditioning and by unconscious motivations. One must seek self-illumination to the point where 'the inner connection between our role, our motivations, and our type and manner of experiencing the world suddenly dawns on us.'[31]

Significantly, as Larrain shows, Marx did not disavow the social determination of his thought or that of any other person.[32] But he regarded the universal social determination of knowledge as something different from ideology. To repeat, for Marx 'ideology was a distorted knowledge which concealed contradictions in the interest of the dominant class', not a question of the social conditioning of all knowledge. Consequently, from a Marxian point of view, the insistence of the sociology of knowledge upon the social setting of all thought is somewhat misplaced insofar as the concept of ideology is concerned.

I take for granted the social determination of all knowledge. But I also take the critical concept of ideology developed by Marx to be both sufficiently discriminating and analytically potent to warrant its separation from a general sociology of knowledge. Moreover, its connection to praxis, to the overcoming of the conditions of the distortion of knowledge, and to a critique of the interests of a dominant class, enables the Marxian concept of ideology to have a penetrative capability in the analysis of social change and structure which any general or 'perspectivist' theory lacks. The social scientific value of retaining the critical, negative use of the concept of ideology, in the sense described above, is thus regarded as sufficiently high to make it the basis of the present study.

Because the Church is the focus of this investigation and cannot be unequivocally regarded as serving the interests of the dominant class, it is necessary to specify a little more clearly what one is looking for via a criticism of its ideology.

Ideology (in the Marxian sense) firstly is a 'general, speculative, abstract' complex of representations by which one purports to comprehend the world, but on the basis of a restricted praxis. One is 'ideological' when one does not understand this or admit to the limiting conditions and presuppositions contained in one's comprehension of the world. Thus one masks reality and reinforced specific practices in an uncritical manner in order to protect or advance 'determinate, limited, special interests' for the sake of domination.[33]

Secondly, an ideology is not the same as myths or utopias (which Durkheim calls collective representations) except where these conceal contradictions in the interests of the dominant class.[34] Thus the Marxian notion of ideology is not inherently antithetical to imagination and non-scientific truth, though it quite clearly mounts a frontal attack on mystification, that is, making mysterious or obscure realities which are otherwise accessible to undistorted thinking.

Thirdly, ideological practice manifests itself (i) in the limited, interest-bound selection of problems and imputation of their source; (ii) in the effect of the *form* of a text or a statement whose content may otherwise appear neutral; (iii) in the solutions implied by the presentation of a problem; (iv) in a prior recasting of conflictual themes in order to disguise, conceal or deny conflict (the use of the concept of reconciliation in the Church has often been used in this way); and (v) in the displacement of contradictions and the encoding of symbolically structured meaning aimed at achieving consensus on false grounds.[35]

Notes

1 See A Fierro (1977), pp19—20.
2 For this reason Marx regarded the criticism of religion as the presupposition of all criticism; see D McLellan (1971), pp21—2.
3 L Zivkovic, 'The Structure of Marxist Socialism', in P Berger (1969), p124.
4 T Bottomore (1975), pp67—8.
5 K Marx and F Engels (1970), p42.
6 *Ibid,* p58.
7 D McLellan (1971), p126, extracts from Marx's *1844 Manuscripts* and *The Holy Family* (1945).
8 K Marx and F Engels (1970), p54.
9 M Kalab similarly claims that a mature historical materialist sociology 'traces the influence of economics on specific and concrete social phenomena . . . only with all the nuances that differentiation implies, taking the mechanism of mediation fully into account as well as the conditions proper to the society at a particular stage of development.' See 'The Specificity of the Marxist Conception of Sociology', in P Berger (1969), p67.
10 A Hegedüs (1977), Part I; see aslo P Berger (1969), pp128—145.
11 *Ibid,* p10; Hegedüs distinguishes for example, five categories of non-manual workers depending on the quality of intellectual work required, role in hierarchical standardised systems, and degree of control of others' and one's own work; see (1977), p51.
12 *Ibid,* pp48—50.
13 P Berger (1969), p145.
14 J L Segundo (1977), pp8—9.
15 As McCarthy, in his study of Habermas' work, puts it: 'It is not possible . . . to understand action solely through the explication of subjectively intended meanings. The empirical interconnections among actions governed by social norms go beyond what is subjectively intended. And the effective determinant of the actions themselves need not coincide with manifest motives. An approach that remains within the confines of an analysis of structures of consciousness is methodologically incapable of grasping the objective context of social action.' (See T McCarthy, 1978, p160.)
16 H LeFebvre (1966), pp118—9.
17 See A Giddens (1976), pp74—77, for a valuable discussion on these distinctions.

18 T McCarthy (1978), pp182—7.

19 Bottomore and Nisbet (1978), pxiii. Note that following Marx, a distinction is made here between political emancipation (the last form of emancipation within the framework of the existing social order: a state may be free from some constraint without its members being really free from alienation, domination and so on), and human emancipation (the humanisation of the whole of life accompanied by a democratic, participatory and solidary form of social existence). See D McQuarrie (1978), 'Marx and the State', by Ralph Miliband, pp256—7.

20 J Larrain (1979), Chapter One, 'Historical Origins of the Concept of Ideology'; see also 'The Hinterland of Science: Ideology and the Sociology of Knowledge', in Center for Cultural Studies (1978).

21 S A Giddens (1971), p7.

22 See D McLellan (1971), p12.

23 D Howard, discussing this issue via a consideration of the work of Claude Lefort, makes the point that a theoretical formulation of ideology as that which veils the 'real' leaves open the rather crucial questions of what determines the 'real'; see (1977), p255.

24 A Giddens (1971), p41.

25 J Larrain (1979), p38.

26 *Ibid,* p48.

27 See M Jay's discussion of Horkheimer in (1973), p156.

28 S Mohun, 'Ideology, Knowledge and Neoclassical Economics: Some elements of a Marxist Account', in F Green and P Nore (1979), p234. He describes the conflation of social and natural facts in terms of the exchange process:

> For it is exchange which establishes the social links between the different producers, which establishes, that is, a social division of labour, through its determination of which protection processes are profitable and which are not. Yet profit is not produced by exchange; it is only realised in it. Hence the exchange-process does not define the content of social relations — it merely provides them with their context. To confuse context with content is to be blind to (the separation of the worker from the means of production and his consequently enforced entry into the market), and to collapse (the juridical equality of the worker as a free agent within the market) from a social process into a natural one.

29 J Larrain (1979), p58.

30 J Larrain (1979), p109.

31 K Mannheim (1936), p43.

32 J Larrain (1979), p119.

33 H LeFebvre (1966), pp70—1.

34 *Ibid,* pp75—6.

35 These aspects of ideological practice are drawn from unpublished notes on 'Propaganda and the Mass Media', partially reliant on Louis Althusser's work, by E Bertelson, University of Cape Town, 1981.

CHAPTER NINE

Material History as Presupposition

Der Wahnsinn schleicht durch die Nacht
Und nennt sich Recht und nennt sich Macht
Verjagt die Sonne, löscht die Zeit
Und stiehlt uns aus der Wirklichkeit.

Konstantin Wecker, 'Im Namen des Wahnsinns'

Insanity creeps through the Night
Calls itself Right, and calls itself Might
Drives out the Sun, extinguishes Time
And steals us away from Reality's shrine.

(My translation)

I wish now to investigate (1) in what way the specific method adopted for investigating the churches in South Africa, informed as it is by historical materialism, may be considered normative in a revisionist theology, and (2) what kind of implication this may have for the object of theology itself, namely, the Christian mythos.

I have shown at various stages that the reflective processes called for in our model demand a critical intention capable of penetrating the structures of existence in their conscious and their unconscious moments, and of disclosing thereby the unwilled (as well as the willed) repression and illusion which distort and falsify reality.[1] However much as some may find it unwelcome, no serious thinker doubts today that the tools made available by the Marxian tradition are ineluctably part of that kind of criticism, especially when one is considering political-economic social structures.

The question is: why should one adopt a materialist understanding of history, for there are alternatives? This is also the question with which Fierro busies himself, beginning with the proposition that Marxist materialism must be taken seriously as a 'hypothesis' for theology. Quoting Paul (1 Cor 9: 20-22 — 'becoming a Jew with the Jews and a Gentile with the Gentiles'), he argues for a 'real effort to put oneself in (the place of Marxists, Freudians, etc) and see whether faith is possible from their standpoint and if so, in what way exactly'. Even more strongly, Fierro believes it is not the theologian's task 'to discuss the truth or falsity of Marxism or psychoanalysis, or any other scientific theory'. Rather, 'their job is to point up the possibility or impossibility of faith and the further specifications of the faith, on the basis of each of those theories'. Thus an 'historical materialist theology tries to assume (Marx's) theory completely in order to see what sort of faith, if any, is possible on that basis.' At the same time, Fierro defends Marxist theory as 'not just another hypothesis', but 'the broadest and most comprehensive of the theoretical approaches to human historical reality'.[2]

Fierro's arguments in my opinion are not convincing. The contradiction involved in his related assertions about 'historical-material theology' are too weighty, the jumps he makes insufficiently grounded.

On the one hand he believes all theories should be tested, but strangely not in themselves, only for what they may say about the Christian mythos. On the other hand, the reference to Paul would lead us to suspect that such testing arises from a pre-critical commitment. The implication of value-free processes of reflection here is untenable, especially when one is asked to assume Marx's theory completely. How is this hermeneutically possible if one is not Marx, not contemporaneous with Marx, nor with privileged access to the 'true Marx' (for it is abundantly evident that Marxism is not a single, systematic product when one looks at the theoretical productions of the Marxian tradition)? It seems to me not possible to 'put oneself in the place of' Marx (or any Marxist) without being caught up in the need to interpret, evaluate and judge this tradition. Moreoever, if the truth or falsity of a theory is bracketed, it becomes very difficult indeed to know whether one is dealing with something serious or something trivial. Fierro himself immediately proceeds to make some such judgement in claiming that Marxist theory is 'not just another hypothesis'.

Another writer who approaches these issues is Charles Davis in his *Theology and Political Society*.[3] Analogous to Fierro's 'historical-material theology', Davis prefers to speak of 'critical theology' which he situates in the history of critical philosophy, pre-eminently the Hegelian and Marxian traditions. Moreover, in defining modernity as ineluctably 'political' insofar as society and human action have become the central themes of contemporary life, he is in agreement with Fierro. But the distinctions he develops are more precise.

Firstly, one must recognise that an old problem is involved, namely, the dialogue between Christian faith and (modern) reason. The ground of the dialogue however now shifts away from that between science and revelation, or between dogma and historical knowledge, to that between faith and social practice. Thus 'theology in such a context has to find a place as a form of critical reflection upon practice, as critique when carried out under the horizon of faith.'[4] But why is an horizon of faith necessary? What does it contribute to human action? At what point does faith become practically meaningful?

Davis' answer is an important clue:

For the basic derivation of Christian faith we must go back to the qualities of social practice as human action . . . Or to put it another way, Christian faith is grounded when emancipatory social action brings us to the *limits* of human meaning, so that we experience in Christ a transcendent source of hope and liberation.[5]

In short, there is a boundary to be crossed — a boundary between the horizon of faith and the horizon of political life. The intersection of this boundary is where interpretation arises as a composite discourse, pulled but not destroyed by rival demands: a composite discourse between Christian faith and social action theory. Because each individual field of discourse has been defined non-dogmatically (that is, without absolutist claims), the intersection between them is transparent. Neither is exempt from the judgements of the other. As Davis remarks, 'if it was an insight of Marx that theory is not innocent, it is an insight of religion that practice is not innocent either.'[6]

Now we return to the question with which we began: why the historical materialist theory of social action? Clearly this is a different question in principle from: why the Christian faith? The latter arises, if it arises at all, in the form of a fundamental choice, a 'turning' of imagination (we deliberately exclude the sense of 'Christian' in which straightforward socialisation is involved, as for example in: 'I was born a Christian, because my parents are'). Historical-materialist theory may similarly become a 'subject of faith', but that is not its original intention. Rather, it intends a specific, defensible scientific analysis of social processes and thus depends fundamentally on the reflective processes. Historical materialism cannot be fairly evaluated, let alone properly understood, when it is regarded as a religion, just as the Christian mythos cannot be evaluated on the basis of scientific validity. Both paths are forbidden by the hermeneutic of interpretation between the two fields of discourse even as interpretation connects them.

In the end we are led to conclude that there is no ontological imperative demanding the historical-material theory, and should it be adopted, neither is there any reason to do so uncritically. On the other hand there are solid grounds for regarding historical-material hypotheses as potent tools of criticism. At the same time there is not just critique here, but a practical intent including the restoration of human-being and a reconstruction of human history utilising the capabilities of reflection.[7] This necessarily involves — as with all analytical/reconstructive sciences — what Per Frostin terms 'methodological atheism' (whereby phenomena are explained through testable hypotheses) as opposed to a 'theoretical atheism' (whereby one asserts material as the only reality, and thereby negates any theism).[8]

Two further points are worth noting here. Firstly, as Dussel remarks, the attack by Marx on religion can only be conceived of in relation to his general viewpoint which aimed at destroying illusion and falsifications of reality. In other words, Marx was atheistic towards a particular conception of God, a conception which made of God a fetish and which a Christian might label an idol or a graven image were he or she to recognise it. In saying this, we recognise that there can be no analysis of God as such, only of the concepts people have of God — and there is no reason why these should be sacrosanct.[9]

Secondly, the critical challenge from historical materialism does not come in the form of a competing religious mythos, but in the form of usually well-defined concepts (such as alienation, fetishism, knowledge-as-praxis, the material basis for human development, and so on).[10] In fact there is a sense in which Marxism cannot be considered a mythos at all except insofar as some very basic assertions are made on the strength of images of the human being as *homo faber* and *homo politicus*.[11] (This is not of course to claim that no one has tried to fashion a comprehensive religious mythos on the basis of Marxism.)

Recently it has been argued that a reassessment of the Marxian critique of religion undermines the now classical imputation of doctrinal atheism to Marx. This reassessment does not make of Marx a hidden theist, but seeks rather to discern the methodological limits within which his critique of religion should rightly and consistently be situated. Charles Davis points out that Marx's early critique of religion actually does not utilise an historical material framework but exists more in the form of purely negative assertions. Marx never came back to the question of religion, but in a single text in *Capital* he does refer to the need to extend principles established for a critical history of technology to the history of religion. Davis discusses Per Frostin's analysis of the implication of this text and concludes that 'a scientific critique of religion must therefore always rest upon a detailed study of the actual, concrete material conditions of life at every particular time and place.'[12]

The critique of religion in the Marxian sense is then seen to be a particular instance of the general critique of ideology. Its results point not to the destruction of religion *per se* (any more than a critique of the role of technology destroys technology *per se*), but to an exposure of the relationship of religion to the interests of the dominant, and of the role of religion in concealing reality through illusion or systematic distortion. Similarly, as Frostin points out:

> . . . materialism does not here imply accepting that only the material is real — for example as derived from a classical physics definition of material — but it implies accepting that the material and the spiritual are inseparably bound up with each other, so that the spiritual cannot be scientifically dealt with if it is isolated from its material base.[13]

On the other hand, the scientific intent of materialism as here defined is not totally pervasive: thus

> 'The question of the existence of God cannot be answered by a materialistic method.'[14]

A critical theology, for the reasons mentioned above, would accept the critique of religion therefore as belonging to the dynamic of religion itself, insofar as it specifies within the human community of faith (1) sources of experience for emancipatory praxis, (2) the nature of unfreedom and freedom, and (3) the identity of the structures and dynamics of domination and alienation.[15]

But the hermeneutical circle is not complete if we leave it at that. For if historical materialism is to be a presupposition for a revisionist theology (in the minimal sense of being an adequate analysis of contemporary existence), then its implications, critically reflected back upon the Christian mythos, must also be considered.[16] Bearing this in mind, I wish to consider the critical impact upon the Christian tradition of the concepts of praxis, ideology and labour. In each case not much more than directions for further detailed investigations are indicated.

Praxis

The unity of theory and practice, of subject and object, is the central aspect of the notion of praxis. Upon this is built the proposition that all genuine knowledge of history (and of the human being in history) derives from reflected activity, and not in the first place from ideas.

In accepting this, many contemporary theologians point out that one is driven thereby to regard those symbols which emphasise discipleship and mission as most central to the Christian mythos. In turn, discipleship and mission must be historically specified and, in terms of emancipatory practice, related to the struggle of the poor and oppressed. The doctrines of incarnation, crucifixion and resurrection are reinterpreted accordingly. Likewise, study of the New Testament focuses more clearly on the contrasting relationship of Jesus of Nazareth to the poor and the oppressed and the rich and the wealthy respectively, as well as on the role of the 'kingdom of God' parables in shattering normal existence while introducing an imaginative 'turning' towards new existence.

Assman thus declares that faith 'can only be historically effective in the liberation of man'. Elsewhere he adds that 'evangelisation, whose hand-maid theology is, should be the historical articulation of love-in-practice, not the mere annunciation of a message.'[17] In slightly different language Tracy similarly points out that 'rendering Christianity relevant to contemporaries' misses the real problem, which is to 'make our 'Christian self-understanding meaningful in our own life-styles and in our own reflection.'[18]

There is however a warning to be made here. As Fierro argues, one cannot take for granted among the poor and oppressed that Jesus Christ has something to do with their history.[19] Rather, this is something to be demonstrated in the praxis of Christians and not in proclamations from without. Consequently, a Christian contribution to praxis has nothing to do with a doctrinal *a priori* by which alien conditions are imposed upon the poor and oppressed before one makes any commitment.[20] On the other hand, a Christian involvement in praxis does not exist without presuppositions of faith, presuppositions which enter positively into reflected practice as well as being critically reconstructed in the process. Or as Charles Davis says: 'the idea of a spontaneous *ortho-praxis* is a myth'.[21]

Ideology

The critique of ideologies sets out to expose the manner in which language and practice function to serve the interests of the dominant while appearing as the 'natural law' of a particular epoch, thus concealing those interests. The whole of Part One of the present study demonstrates this critique at work on Church practice and language.

But one may go further than was intended there to reflect critically on the symbols of the Christian mythos as well. For example, several writers have pointed out the frequently ideological nature of many concepts of God. Fierro remarks on the way in which the image of God is often conditioned by the class position and class perception of a particular person or group. He draws the conclusion that Christian talk of God is necessarily alienating as long as it emerges from an alienated situation.[22]

From a slightly different angle David Tracy shows that the question of the Christian God is 'fashioned by the aims and methods of one's general theological model'.[23] It remains to add that one's general model is also fashioned by one's specific history and class position. Models do not arrive *de novo*, but as part of a social history and in connection to the interests of a particular group (without which they would not remain meaningful). Consequently one may draw the conclusion that theological talk of God cannot know anything directly about God; and that in 'shedding light upon its ignorance through imaginative illustrations', theology proceeds negatively and critically vis-a-vis the claims it nevertheless makes.[24]

Thus the validity of any concept of God — who may be believed in, but cannot be cognitively known — is judged, in the historical materialist idiom, against transformative praxis. Put another way, doctrine cannot be regarded as exempt from the hermeneutical circle which makes one's values, decisions and primary orientation also matters for critical scrutiny. For this reason the critique of ideology, drawing on the insistence of a unity between theory and practice, destroys the traditional structure of religion as a fixed orthodoxy.[25]

Labour

A central presupposition of Marx was that history is the product of human labour acting on nature to transform it, in the process (and according to the limits of prevailing technology and means of social organisation) reproducing as well a characteristic pattern of social relations. Here we have *homo faber,* the human being as maker. One may rightly treat as integral to modern sensibility the experience of human potency in 'making' or 'creating' things (whatever the ambiguities, this is impossible to avoid in an age of steel, computers, nuclear power, microbiology, and so on).

But if humans fashion history with such obvious and sometimes terrifying effect, what does God do in history? The question is painfully acute in the Judeo-Christian tradition which asserts so strongly that God is the one who acts in history. With momentary relief, one may declare that God and human beings are co-creators and thus leave room for human freedom and responsibility in history. But, as Fierro points out, this formula really changes nothing for it remains a faith claim not yet opened to criticism.[26] The question is whether any reference to God has meaning at all when faced with modern criticism (by 'meaning' I imply 'coherence'; talk of God may of course be *meaningful* to some people without being coherent).

The traditional, classical theistic notions of absoluteness, impassibility, omnipotence and omniscience are under attack here. If the notion of God acting in history is to retain any meaning at all (at least for those for whom the classical and mediaeval patterns of thought are no longer defensible), then new categories for understanding theistic language are needed. Tracy, for example, argues for the use of categories largely derived from process philosophy in which God is understood and conceived of as subject to time, to sociality and to the historical process.[27]

At a less sophisticated level others have begun to speak of God in the Jesus Christ who suffers with them, who feels their suffering, who despairs with them and who celebrates with them. Quite clearly here the sensibility of the poor and the oppressed emerges; ironically there is also some sense of this very human God — though in highly docetic, apolitical form — in the fundamentalist-evangelical notion that 'Jesus walks with me and talks with me'. The central issue in the problems raised here remains that of the meaning of the Christian mythos, an issue not to be avoided by a quick and shallow dive into claims that the knowledge of faith transcends all other knowledge and therefore stands outside of all critique. The issue is then dodged only at the long-term cost of all meaning.

Sufficient has been said now to make the general discussion of theological method a little more concrete. In summary of the whole chapter, it may be pointed out that the method developed here does not allow professional theologians or the clergy to hold for themselves an elevated position above 'ordinary' Christians, either by virtue of training or calling. On the contrary, they are servants of the people with a major responsibility for assisting the 'doing of theology' in the general life on the community as it emerges in emancipatory praxis. In this way powers of imagination and critical reflection may be strengthened among 'the least' of one's fellows, thereby enabling a more penetrating apprehension of contemporary structures of reality and of the Christian mythos.

Professionals are there only to introduce resources as required, and by means of their skills to help in the communal formulation of the general theory of the Church and its mission, for which praxis in solidarity with the dispossessed, the poor and oppressed must remain the sounding board. (We do not refer here to the strictly priestly functions which may be exercised on behalf of the community.) Such formulation will include the process whereby the dispossessed (robbed of their rightful dignity and shared dominion), the poor and the oppressed find their faith both real and liberating as they critically grasp their situation, its demonic character and their hope in the future. With these thoughts in mind, the specific question of the nature and function of the Church will now be addressed, drawing on the conclusions of the earlier analytical investigation of the Church in South Africa.

Notes

1 See also P Ricoeur (1974b), who discusses this point in relation to the 'opaqueness' in the nature of action in modern society which demands that one's best intentions be critically and self-critically worked through lest actions that flow from them produce unexpected and unwanted results which could have been avoided: pp106—13.

2 A Fierro (1977), p365—375 *passim*.

3 C Davis (1980).

4 *Ibid,* p10.

5 *Ibid,* p6.

6 *Ibid,* p26.

7 Paul Tillich considered the whole issue in some depth in a book he himself prized highly, namely, his *The Socialist Decision,* (1977). See especially chapter 6 on 'The Socialist Principle and Problems of Marxism'. See also B Meland (1953), pp32—46, who discussed what is needed to reconstruct the 'Liberal' church if it is to connect its concern for justice, peace and humanity with a much more solid, less idealistic perspective on reality, though he did not specify the use of historical materialism.

8 P Frostin (1978), p155ff.

9 E Dussel, in R Gibellini (1979), pp199—200. Dussel's discusssion extends considerably beyond the minimal statement made here.

10 B Lonergan discusses the distinction between concepts and foundational values at many points in both *Insight* (1957) and *Method in Theology* (1972).

11 HR Niebuhr (1963), p160, sees these two images as among the 'three great symbols of our age', the third being *homo dialogicus*.

12 See C Davis (1980), p125ff.

13 P Frostin (1978), p41, my translation.

14 *Ibid,* p42, my translation.

15 C Davis (1980), p131.

16 A similar point is made by D Tracy (1979), p239.

17 H Assman (1975), p81 & p64.

18 D Tracy (1979), p177.

19 A Fierro (1977), pp333—5.

20 See JL Segundo (1977), p90; also p132.

21 C Davis (1980), p61.

22 A Fierro (1977), p385—7.

23 D Tracy (1979), p175.

24 A Fierro (1977), p411; also p351ff, where he discusses the negative and critical function of theology in a manner which makes it clear that this is one way of describing God-language as limit-language.

25 C Davis (1980), p130.

26 A Fierro (1977), p327.

27 D Tracy (1979), p1333. This whole question is also taken up by L Gilkey (1976) in his excellent discussion of the doctrine of providence: see pp161—187 and p211ff; see also P Tillich (1977), p114 and pp119—20.

CHAPTER TEN

Towards a Critical Ecclesia

> With the drawing of this Love and the voice
> of this Calling
> We shall not cease from exploration
> And the end of all our exploring
> Will be to arrive where we started
> And know the place for the first time.
>
> — TS Eliot, 'Four Quartets'

Introduction

The Church is a human community, and as such can be understood in the same way as any other human community.[1] This assumption lies behind the possibility and the relevance of the earlier analysis of the English-speaking churches in South Africa.

That the results of this kind of analysis are also important for a theological understanding of the Church, that is, for a contemporary ecclesiology, is not always accepted. But, as Gustafson has pointed out, if the question of the truth and the function of the Church is dealt with in terms meaningful only to properly trained theologians, that is, as a doctrinal question rather than one of practical experience, then not much has been explained or understood.[2] In short, a theory of the Church abstracted from the actual life of the Church in society, a theory therefore seeing only some idealised Church, is mere dogmatic assertion, the perpetuation of illusion. Such a theory is thus false.

The proposition that a theology of the Church must take the Church seriously as a human, historical entity may be accepted as a general consensus today. In Church history the high role of non-theological factors in shaping doctrine and practice is unavoidably clear.[3] Moreover, that doctrines of the Church begin from experiences in and with the Church is also evident.[4] The New Testament documents themselves testify to the priority of the real life of the Church which occasioned, for a variety of reasons, a subsequent reflection on its work and its identity, now recorded as scripture. At the same time, the

Church not only reflects on its circumstances but is in a real sense at their mer-
cy.[6] In what way this latter may be true cannot be discerned by theology itself.
Thus the very fact of the human nature of the Christian community drives it
towards taking sociological and other empirical data seriously, for theological
reasons.[7]

Therefore one may agree with de Gruchy that the identity of the Church in
South Africa must be worked out in relation to the concrete realities of the
contemporary context.[8] The significance of entering into such a task is much
less a question of explaining doctrine than of helping to specify the content of
Christian existence in the world.[9] Or, as Moltmann has expressed it, the
sociology of religion must become a theological critique of the Church in
terms of the question: 'How does the Church become *true*?'[10]

Black theology (from its practical basis in resistance to oppression) has since
the late 1960s been the greatest internal force raising the issue of the Church's
identity in South Africa. Thus one has heard frequently renewed debates on
whether to form a Black Church, what the status of blacks in the Church is,
and whether the European-originated churches in any case have any acceptable place for blacks. Yet recently a leading Black theologian admitted that
no adequately developed ecclesiological statement yet exists.[11] Among several
possible reasons for this — not the least being heavy demands made upon
those who are critically engaged and who have the resources — one strong
reason would be the lack of a developed analysis of the concrete reality facing
the Church in South Africa. The same Black theologian points out —
significantly in my opinion — that one may talk of an ecclesiology of the 'have
and have-nots' in South Africa.[12] Yet no-one has properly spelt out what this
central insight implies for a contemporary ecclesiology, except in the now
commonplace but minimal assertion that the Church is the Church of the
poor.

Though Black theology from its beginnings was linked with philosophical
aspects of Black communalism which framed general principles about work
and the use of land, the symbol of 'Blackness' reigned supreme in analysis of
the actual context. Not surprisingly, this de-emphasised tools of economic
analysis while emphasising racism or traditional African economic values. To
this there is a positive side: the refusal to allow certain aspects of domination
to be side-stepped. But there is also a negative side: the neglect of potent
analytical resources able to specify the issues raised by industrialisation and
proletarianisation, by exploitation and underdevelopment.

It is not surprising then that an observer of a recent Church-related conference on Marxism, Socialism and Capitalism in the South African context
should note that the role of the Church in structural change remained a most
controversial issue despite a widespread agreement on the need of the Church

to relate to poverty and issues of labour, and that the conference 'time and again' fell into 'the discrimination groove'.[13] The intimate connection of 'racism' to economic structures is however likely to be increasingly noticed in the Church.[14]

Some would inquire whether the Church has any mandate to be concerned with issues of political economy in the first place. But as Tawney pointedly remarked, 'the criticism which dismissed the concern of churches with economic relations and social organisation as a modern invention finds little support in past history. What requires explanation is not the view that these matters are a part of the province of religion, but the view that they are not.'[15] Others discern in the increasing influence of Marxist thought in South Africa a sign of the failure of the Church. Yet any 'success' would not have diminished the need for an empirical-historical analysis of capitalism. It is correct to see 'self-criticism, repentance and rebirth' as proper responses on the part of the Church to the Marxian critique, but not as if that critique itself could not be positively incorporated and utilised in the Church as such.[16]

Many also argue that the Church is not permitted to model its practice upon the theories of a social system. But this occurs in any case, though presently as if the given structure and order were in some unfounded sense 'natural', the way things are *ipso facto*. Thus, as the social system upon which to a considerable degree the Church in most instances models itself is brought into question by rapid social change, one is likely to see a growing conflict within the Church between groups that favour the *status quo* (especially those who see themselves as guardians of the institution and its relations with society) and those more responsive to pressures for change.[17] The Church reflects the conflict situation that generally obtains in the society.

Thus one may investigate the churches in South Africa as 'part of the problem', that is, as imbued with the contradictions characterising the society of which it is a part.[18] In this vein, various theologians speaking from the point of view of the oppressed in South Africa have called for judgement to begin at 'the house of God' itself, feeling that the '. . . Church in Southern Africa has to admit that she is actually an urgent object of mission'.[19] One notes also the Church Commission report of the Study Project on Christianity in Apartheid Society (Spro-Cas), published in 1972, which concluded that three basic hindrances obstruct mission in the life of the Church. These are:

(1) ecclesiatical self-concern — evidenced in the disproportionate energy, time and money invested in strictly internal affairs;

(2) pragmatic pietism — by which was meant an individualistic, inward attitude to religion fundamentally apathetic to the life of the *polis;*

(3) clericalism — an emphasis on the Church as constituted by professionals and ordinands.

It declared that the structures of the Church itself, 'the form in which its life and mission in the world is arranged', are essentially problematic, but the final recommendations of the Commission proved tame, focusing mostly on attitudinal and educational actions. Their overall weakness is perhaps best demonstrated in the sole reference to the issue of poverty, and that merely a call to church leaders to simplicity of life.[20]

My earlier analysis of the role of the English-speaking churches during the first 30 years of this century produced a more precise structural critique of the Church. This is summed up in the notion of the Church's *functional dependency* upon the dominant political economic system despite its public criticism of certain policies. The evidence pictures a Church, as a rule, unable to accept the validity of the struggle between employer and employee, fearful enough of conflict which might threaten the dominant social order that it preaches personal regeneration and state reform but not independent struggle by workers. This picture in many ways duplicates that of the Church in Britain in the nineteenth century during the first decades of industrialisation there.[21]

A second commission of Spro-Cas, that given the task of reflecting on the economy of South Africa, went much further than the Church Commission. It recognised that the extension of the notion of Christian love into the social dimension called for more than moral or attitudinal action.[22] The Economic Commission concluded that:

(1) the goal of society should not simply be economic growth;
(2) development exists for the sake of humans and not vice-versa;
(3) the great gap between rich and poor should be regarded as obscene;
(4) the sharing of power means the inclusion of workers in decision-making processes (and in the sharing of risks);
(5) equality of opportunity implies equality in access to the means of production (land, human capital).[23]

But the recommendations flowing from the Spro-Cas Commission in respect of actions the churches might take say little about trades unions, strikes, and workers' struggles in general. They remain content with a general recommendation that the Church restructure itself to evince greater solidarity with labour, but without specifying what this might mean.[24] The report of the Economics Commission did lead to several constructive actions in some quarters (on such issues as community development projects, credit unions, and literacy programmes). More significantly for the present discussion though, it did not lead to any great examination of the power structure of the Church itself, nor to any deeper reflection on its implication for a contemporary ecclesiology.

If we take the analysis of the Church's captivity to the dominant structure of the political economy seriously, and if we recognise that characteristic marks of this structure are domination and dependence, exploitation and poverty, then it must be faced that the conflict lies not essentially between Church and state in South Africa, but within the Church. The Church is itself a sign of deep contradiction, at the same time as it proclaims itself, in contemporary terms, the sign of the kingdom of God.[25] The experience of this contradiction has led many to seek an understanding of the Church that contrasts the defective, visible body with its ideal, invisible image. From the point of view of historical materialism, such a procedure is both an error of philosophical idealism and historically unscientific. An image transcendent of the present construction of reality may function in an emancipatory manner (for Marx communism is such an image), but not when it is removed from historical material reality. For ecclesiology, this implies the need to define the Church in full acceptance of its historical material reality (including the fact of its contradictions) before an image of the Church can emerge that is both conceptually valid and generally emancipatory.[26]

A further implication: in a capitalist milieu key contradictions within the Church will also be related to the conflict between classes. Thus we begin to speak of an ecclesiology of the 'haves and the have-nots'. Then the theological question of the unity of the Church emerges (its identity as both historical and eschatological). Secondly, the question of its life and work also arises (its praxis in relation to mission).[27] As Miguez Bonino makes clear, such an ecclesiology will drive (1) towards unmasking class conflict within the Church (in accordance with the recognition that the critique of religion is a moment in the general critique of ideology), and (2), in respect of the emancipatory interest, towards battling the Church itself insofar as it is a sociologically identifiable part of a system of domination or oppression.[28]

The Church in Contradiction

We face a crisis of unity in the Church and in ecclesiology as such. This may be related to a 'lack of cultivated fellowship' among those who by definition are gathered together for a particular purpose.[29] A visible lack of fellowship extends not only between the dominant and the dispossessed, as we have suggested, but also between confessions. In the modern global market economy, pressures of industrialisation, proletarianisation and global communication have forced into the foreground the concerns of a united Church fellowship and an emancipatory Church practice. In the process the painful contradictions highlighted in the visible Church have given rise to a search by many for the 'true' Church, a search that has had both a practical and a theological aspect.

Some of the main responses to this modern crisis of identity have been documented. William Wake, Anglican primate in 1716, believed that one should distinguish doctrinal fundamentals 'in which all ought to agree' from other teachings in which error or difference could be tolerated. In his view the identity of the Church could be re-established on this basis.

In the first part of the nineteenth century, JH Newman and William Palmer, both of the Oxford Movement, conceived of the true Church as comprising three regional branches of the one Catholic Church: English, Roman and Orthodox. In their view the Church was not divided at all, but merely in a state of suspended communication. At about the same time an idea was put forward in the USA for a 'comprehensive Church' based on the selection by all denominations of an already established ecclesiastical system, its imperfections to be subsequently ironed out.[30]

In the 1920s the idea of an international fellowship grew, a fellowship above the conflict between states and particular nationalisms. This idea led to the emergence of the World Council of Churches, perhaps not unrelated to the growth of international socialism on the one hand and to that of the transnational corporations of late capitalism on the other, both of these economic forces creating for the first time a truly global sensibility.

Proceeding in an opposite direction, many sought the 'true' Church not in the uniting of ecumenical fellowships, but precisely in separation from the mass of nominal Christians. This development begins in modern times with the Reformation which yielded various forms of what Durnbaugh calls the 'believer's Church'. Just what form such a Church takes is a matter of perspective. As Durnbaugh's analysis demonstrates, there are those who separate themselves from the 'established' Church in terms of the 'apostolic succession of suffering dissenters' (sectarian definition); those who do so in nonconformity to any doctrine, polity or discipline of the established Church (puritan definition); and those who derive from the radical Reformation with both scripture and the practices of the early Christians as norms (anabaptist definition).[31]

The variety of theological definitions of the Church is as wide, if not more so, than the practical models. There is clearly no agreement on what the 'true' Church is. In an attempt to overcome this, Avery Dulles isolates five overarching theological models of the Church (as institution, as mystical communion, as sacrament, as herald, and as servant). He highlights the strengths, weaknesses and implications of each, and finally argues for the complementary validity of each (though in his opinion some have greater merit than others).[32] Thus he seeks a mutually enriching recognition of the validity of each model in its own way, time and place. We may call this the harmonisation model of the Church.

A somewhat different procedure is to establish a strictly theological definition of the Church. Ecclesial images of the New Testament and later tradition (themselves of considerable variety, as Küng points out)[33] are compared, assessed and systematically related through historical scientific investigations of the relevant texts. Such doctrinal style involves a necessary clarification of the symbols and concepts of the Christian mythos. But this approach too easily and too frequently describes a Church relevant to initiated theologians alone. Its reliance on a history of ideas leaves the historical-material reality of the Church high and dry. Thus the 'visible' Church becomes practically unrecognisable in its theological formulation; here we confront a form of philosophical idealism.[34]

A different form of idealism may be discerned among those whose definition of the Church is deliberately and radically contrasted with their experience of the Church. Biéler, for example, speaks of the Church as a source of development where political awareness comes about; a source of action in the world and a seedbed of social transformation, standing as a sentinel for humanity; a source of reconciliation engaged in the necessary criticism of powers. But then he continues by pointing out numerous ways (19 in all) in which the real historical Church fundamentally fails to be what it should be.[35] A definition of the 'should-be-Church' may function as a form of negative utopianism, that is, as a projection beyond what actually is to describe what ought to be, and therefore as a means of directing criticism and action towards the transformation of the present Church. But unless it becomes clear how such a utopian projection arises out of present historical reality, where its transformative agents are located in the present, and what real possibilities exist for the desired transformation, it remains severed from reality. Consequently an 'ideal' Church never experienced in practice is more likely to breed cynicism, bitterness and despair rather than concretely situate a real hope.

A manifestation in South Africa of dualistic and idealistic notions of the Church occurs in the seeminingly interminable demands that the Church be an 'alternative society', a 'confessing community'.[36] Notoriously little clarification of the real meaning and possibility of such a demand has occurred, leading frequently to the anomaly in various quarters of fervent resolutions being passed, responsibilities for action assigned, but little further work taking place. What remains are not structures embodying the demands, but documents declaring them. On the other hand, impoverished notions of what the Church as alternative society means have often led to practices which Ernest Baartman (among other Black theologians) labels cheap identification and cheap reconciliation (which may be paralleled with Bonhoeffer's development of the idea of cheap grace during the Third Reich).[37] Sometimes, on the other hand, where there is a desire to avoid cheapness, there is no clear detailing of what costly reconciliation might require.[38]

A great deal of the mediocrity of the Church in its political action, intellectual activity and life-commitment derives from the inability evidenced in all the ways enumerated above:

1   to come to terms with the deepest contradictions in the visible Church,
2   to recognise its intimate connection to the contradictory structures of society (in South Africa, racially discriminatory practices have been partly confronted, but not those other profound structural rifts which this study has attempted to specify),
3   to accept these contradictions as defining the Church *in fact* and not just 'in failure',
4   to analyse the implications of this, and
5   to develop strategic actions realistically capable of confronting them head on.

Consequently, much theological reflection on the contradictory situation of the Church in South Africa speaks of the need for 'prophetic witness' and 'pilgrim service', or of pastoral care situated in social transformation, or of an historical engagement and *metanoia*.[39] Yet seldom does anyone delineate in non-theological, concrete terms, just what implications lie therein for Church structures, policies and practices. Too frequently the Church is implicitly contrasted with the world (or more specifically, the apartheid state). Conflict is situated in that particular opposition, and the contradictions in the Church itself are again and again played down, made the stuff of resolutions alone, or simply side-stepped.[40] Lastly, a tendency to define liberation (which most theologians with whom we are dealing accept in some sense) in abstract, ideal terms, follows on all else.[41]

In contrast to the approaches and concepts considered above, I would stand with TC Oden against an uncritical use of the notion of the 'invisible' Church, and thus against any de-historicised, idealistic or docetic ecclesiology. The traditional doctrine of the invisible Church found in various forms throughout Church history would therefore have to be reinterpreted not merely in terms of a future-orientated, history-bound eschatology as is commonly the practice among many, but also in terms of its possible function as a utopian concept (in the Marxian sense) validating the mission of the visible Church.[42] Our argument up to this point may therefore be summed up in Oden's words:

> Ordinarily theological treatises on the Church dwell at great length upon the non-empirical, non-organisational dimension of the Church: its holiness, its catholicity, etc. Theology has regrettably left the empirical Church to sociology and Church administrations. Our critical need now is to reverse that pattern: to provide a serious theological statement on the visibility of the Church, and to explore its consequences.[43]

The need to recognise the visible Church as the fundamental starting point for an ecclesiology implies too that it is constantly modified by the experiences of its members.[44] In this sense, as Gustafson notes, the Christian community is marked by its 'naturalness': it acts as an agent of social integration and belonging, it meets certain human needs, and it has institutional sanctions for regulating its goals and the means of attaining them.[45] Trutz Rendtorff further suggests that the Church known in history should not be contrasted with an eschatological Church, a Church of origins, a primitive Church or a Reformation Church.[46] Because the memory of actual Church history conjures up its failures, its suspect alliances and its ambiguity, because — as Küng puts it — the Church is historically unavoidably affected by evil and cannot thus take the *status quo* as its yardstick, therefore a contemporary ecclesiological hermeneutic involves not a better interpretation of the Church but a new praxis.[47]

A further implication emerges: the images of the Church in scripture and tradition are multiple; they are frequently out of harmony with each other in their incarnation among various groups of Christians: and they are discarded or rediscovered as time passes and situations change. From an historical material point of view this is not surprising for it demonstrates the practical impossibility of arriving at some 'essential', abstract and universal concept of the Church unrelated to its historical reality. But more than that, it indicates what Dulles concluded in his analysis of models of the Church, namely, that 'within the myriad possibilities left open by scripture and tradition, the Church in every generation has to exercise options'.[48] One need only add, in my view, that these options are not simply a question of the choice of the most appropriate image under particular conditions, but even more so a question of praxis.

We arrive again at where we began, in order once more to connect the demand to recognise the historical, corrupted Church as the 'true' Church, with the realisation that precisely this true Church is fraught with contradiction, and that in a capitalist milieu such contradiction also takes the form of class conflict. To exercise an option then, is to do so within this field in these terms; or as Bonino argues so clearly, the existing ecclesia is 'the field in which the struggle for the Church takes place'. Therefore, 'to belong faithfully to the Church means to claim our place within this field and to engage in the struggle for a true, faithful historical obedience.'[49] One cannot then seek a false (and therefore ideological) reconciliation or fellowship where there is none. One must enter into the contradictions in the acceptance of conflict. One engages in concrete historical praxis within this conflict in order to overcome the contradictions by transforming their conditions. One enters as a Christian, therefore, into a struggle for liberation from domination and oppression not by adding a religious component to that struggle, nor by merely blessing it, but by taking seriously for the Church itself the conditions from which the struggle arises. As unusual as this conclusion may sound to some, it is in fact merely an extension, on the basis of further analysis, of the presently widespread realisation of the need to combat racism in the Church itself. In practical terms, it implies a struggle against structures of domination and a judgement upon the persons who wield those structures. However forcefully the language of fellowship, comradeship and familial relations may be sounded, this language may, and frequently does, hide a lack of what it calls for, thus concealing conflict in the continued interests of domination. This is neither honest nor hopeful.

Finally, notwithstanding the argument that the historical material reality of the Church is the necessary basis for a thorough revisionist ecclesiology, it must also be recognised that the meaning of the Church is not exhausted in its present existence. Its present existence, furthermore, contains images and practical possibilities capable of 'negating its negations'.[50] The doctrinal form in which this truth usually finds expression today is eschatology. We now turn to a consideration of this other side of the coin.

The Church in Anticipation

In a different context from South Africa, Bonino questions Hugo Assman's claim that the true Church is disclosed by the struggle of the poor. This is a relevant question here too:

> Can we rest satisfied with a definition of the Church which coincides entirely with certain — real and important — needs formulated from an extra-ecclesiastical viewpoint? What is the meaning for the world of such a Church (except in a purely pragmatic, practical game)?[51]

In traditional terms, following Irenaeus, one may relate this question to an incarnational Christology. Quoting Iranaeus' central formula: 'He became what we are in order that he might make us what he is', Hendry points out that we confront here an affirmation of an otherwise hidden potential in human agency which can enter into history.[52] Picking up on a clue provided by Paulo Freire, we may relate this potentiality to the notion of praxis. Freire develops the idea that language which historically discloses for a people their conditions of oppression and their possibilities of emancipation is not just a word, but a form of work joining action and reflection. Hence it is also praxis.[53] To translate this into theological discourse, one may begin to speak of the Word of God made flesh in the work of Christ and issuing in a praxis of transforming love.

Then we must ask more specifically, what kind of Christian language appropriately proceeds in this fashion? Who is the historical bearer of that language? How does it relate to the past history of the Church? Here our focus concerns the double characteristic of a Christologically addressed community, as isolated by Moltmann: (1) 'whoever hears you, hears me', and (2) 'what you do to the least, you do to me'. [54] For we are concerned to designate the Church as a community of language (Word and sacrament) and a body of believers expressly tied to an identification with the poor, the captive, the outcast, the oppressed, but without ignoring the reality of fundamental contradictions within the Church.

A particular language shapes the Christian community and thereby establishes its uniqueness. But the meaningfulness of this language lies only in its integration into the life of the members of the community (by which an inter-subjective sociality of a certain kind is established). Gustafson observes four ways in which this may be sociologically observed in the Christian community, namely, in its communication, its interpretation, its understanding and reliving of history, and its commitment in action. The root source of its inter-subjective possibility lies in a common memory stored in scripture and a subsequent tradition. [55] The link of the community's memory to its present intentions is in its 'distinct — and certainly scandalous — claim' that the fullness of humanity is disclosed in Jesus Christ. [56] Even then this 'humanity' only crystallises in the kingdom of God which Jesus announced, thereby shattering the illusions of his society in the impertinence of his proclamation and opening up space for the reconstruction of meaning. [57]

The history of millenarian expectation helps us to grasp more clearly just what such a claim implies when made in an oppressive context. Lanternari shows that millenarian movements expect a world in which the whole human race is fully integrated and free from oppression. [58] Cohn concludes that the picture of salvation coming from these movements is painted as collective, terrestrial, imminent, total and miraculous. Both indicate, however, that these movements usually emerge from crises in traditional life and structures, particularly a threat of destruction, and especially among those most poor, disoriented and therefore relatively powerless. [59]

Such crises, and the contradictions which occasion them, are vividly depicted in language intended to identify and 'gather together' a community with a common experience of suffering and a need for some weapon against anomie. Two examples in South Africa are provided by Enoch Mgijima and Isaiah Shembe. Mgijima, leader of a group forced off their land by processes of proletarianisation, called his group 'the Israelites' on the basis of the struggle of Israel against the land-possessing Midianites and Philistines. His radical conclusion was that Jesus Christ was plainly not the God of the dispossessed; only Jehovah was.[60] Shembe, the famous Zulu prophet, is depicted as standing at the gate of judgement to turn away all white settlers, for they, as the rich, 'have already in their life-time received their good things'. He opens the gate only to his followers.[61]

Apocalyptic language in the millenarian tradition places a heavy emphasis on the radical restoration of history by an external agency. In this respect, an historical materialist viewpoint must regard millenarianism as ideological, for although it represents a marked and powerful cry of the oppressed, it also alienates their action from the real possibilities of history. Not for nothing is the history of such movements marked by cataclysmic disasters rather than triumphant victories. On the other hand, the cosmic drama invoked drives towards a concrete historical specification of the souce of pain and calls, usually through the medium of visions, for the exercise of a practical option aimed at the goal of emancipation.[62] The reversal of the present order is the emphasis, albeit a reversal viewed as a function of faith rather than as a function of human potency (which these groups so badly lack under normal circumstances). Moreover, this reversal embraces not just society, but the established Church of the society.

Apocalyptic thus understood has no intention of being descriptively analytical, nor is it merely a language of 'signs'. Rather it seeks to propagate a pattern of meaning capable or representing reality for a group of people, of orienting them in that reality, and of motivating them to a transformation of it.[63]

Thus, apocalyptic in the New Testament does remind one forcefully that the gospel confronts the powers and principalities on this historical plane, and universally. In this sense apocalyptic, reinterpreted, plays an heuristic role of some importance — an often neglected role.

My argument, therefore, is that eschatology divorced of the intentionality behind apocalyptic is not only unfaithful to a major note in the origins of Christian tradition, but forces it away from history and its contradictions towards some form of an individualist, romanticist or existentialist subjectivism.[64] Not coincidentally then, contemporary political theologies recognise in apocalyptic eschatology a language appropriate to the poor and oppressed and focused on what has yet to occur in human history.[65] Equally its language (especially, Vos notes, the Pauline images of the anti-Christ and the concept of apostasy) warns against taking for granted one's cause, as well as against vague resigned hopes in the gradual amelioration of evil through the mere passage of time.[66] In short, the full force of highly conflictual situations is granted without recourse to cheap solutions.

The understanding of eschatology adopted here assumes the validity of the tension between present-past and future, or in more familiar terms, the tension between the 'already' and the 'not yet' dimension of the New Testament texts on the kingdom of God. In this respect I would argue that the 'already' justifies the notion that the Body of Christ participates in the kingdom of God through its mission, and in so doing 'builds' the kingdom of God within historical material reality. On the other hand, this thrust in Christian history frequently leads to an uncritical assumption that the Church or a group of Christians somehow 'has' the truth, that its/their activity produces the kingdom quite directly, thereby establishing the basis of society. This is the Christendom assumption, which I reject. Consequently, I would regard the eschatological notion of the 'not yet', to be a crucial addition to the 'already', asserting the limit to any claims we may make and in doing so, establishing the principle of self-criticism.

In all these respects then, eschatology informed by the intentionality of apocalyptic may function as the distinctive language of a critically engaged Christian community. Yet there are two problems. Firstly the langauge involved remains fundamentally symbolic and at the same time negative. That is, its concrete, historical impregnation is imprecise and analytically incapable of specification.[67] Secondly, as Moltmann so clearly indicates, the 'signs of the times' when applied to historical realities are not self-evident.[68] In South Africa, for example, the symbol of the anti-Christ is used equally by the ruling regime (against 'communism') and by the ruled (against 'apartheid'). Other criteria than language must be applied. Who then is the historical bearer of the true vision? This would be one form of the question. I shall respond to this question, and with it the issue of past history, via a consideration of the 'committed minority', the memory of suffering, and the concept of a Church-at-the-limits.

What Moltmann refers to as the paradoxical identity of the Church — that it is at once an object of faith and an empirical object — may be understood by recognising that the Christian community is not only a natural community (such as a village might be) but also a covenanted community expressing itself in three forms of action: worship, witness and mission.[69] The aspect of covenanting oneself has an extremely high profile in the tradition and may be regarded as the main door into its historical meaning. What is sociologically clear it that the group of covenanted and committed believers is considerably smaller than the community founded by Christian language.[70]

Here then is one source of the tension in the Church which gives rise either to a wide range of more or less exclusive claims to be the 'true' Church within the Church (a particular Protestant and non-conformist problem), or to an acceptance of the popular base of the Church but under highly centralised, hierarchical controls over a 'truth' the mass are required to accept (a problem of Catholicism). Thus the chief guardians of the faith are on the one hand the self-defined core group of believers, on the other a selected power elite. In both cases they regard themselves as responsible for the orthodoxy of the larger community of Church-goers or nominal Christians.

Overlaying this tension are the social structural conflicts characterising a particular period and place. Here the intensive language of convenant and commitment is often evoked to support contending practices. This in itself disallows any abstract assertion by a particular group that they are the guardians of truth. With this realisation we must consider the relationship between minority and mass.

Segundo argues that 'the most elementary pastoral experience teaches us that mass conduct . . . rejects (participation in an active way). It is looking for security, not responsibility, in its membership of the Church.[71] From a somewhat different angle, Lynch sees in popular church-going, among the bourgeoisie of advanced capitalism at least, an escape from the demands of temporality equivalent to visiting the cinema after a hard day's work: 'Having soaked themselves in time and experience, they feel they are now entitled to something different', something safe and removed from the temporal process.[72] This is natural, and the Church as a natural community cannot seek to by-pass its humanity here. At this level, much of what goes on in Church ritual and liturgy undergirds a 'magical morality': participation in ritual events (eg the eucharist) is regarded as sufficient for the production of moral life. But the moral development of the human being involves a move from this magical morality to a life of action intentionally directed towards specific goals.[73]

At this stage one begins to experience the Christian demands in terms of Durnbaugh's 'believer's Church' — a 'covenanted and disciplined community walking in the way of Jesus Christ'.[74] One becomes part of a 'responsible minority'.[75] One may quite easily overstep the boundaries of the natural community in order to establish an elite, exclusive or sectarian group for the chosen few who hold commitment and convictions over and against the popular base. Yet the popular base is the locus of a people's theology and therefore the real check on all attempts to do theology out of contact with that base. On the other hand, the very notion of a covenant which calls forth a particular people, attacks a simplistic understanding of theology governed by the will of the people without reference to any other authority (the New Testament picture of the people calling for Christ's crucifixion is an original warning against such concepts of people's theology). The problem becomes even more acute when the popular base, as in South Africa, is non-homogeneous and divided by internal contradictions.

Bearing these qualifications in mind, we still need to understand the significance of the 'committed minority', the covenanted groups of Christians for whom the mythos functions as a relatively pervasive primary orientation, and who are a central aspect of the life of the Church. That the extended community who share a Christian language is connected to a smaller 'responsible remnant' is recognised by some through the concept of 'partial identification'. So Rendtorff distinguishes between an identification by the believer with an ecclesiastical tradition (full identification) and the partial identification of one who makes the institutional Church a point of reference only from a critical distance.[76] The role of the latter, the 'committed minority', is affirmed as well as their essential relationship to the popular base. But this provides us with no way of designating what kind of minority the 'committed' are, and in what sense their commitment functions for the edification of the whole.[77] We therefore turn to what it is that the Christian community remembers, to what constitutes its continuing regeneration of the past in order to instruct the present and evoke the future.

The kind of community established and continually enhanced by the fundamental memory of Christ is not found merely where a group of people fervently proclaim the divine name. Rather a consciousness is evolved which has the power to constitute a world, a self, an identity and a developing journey through interiorising other people who have demonstrated the desired way-of-being-in-the-world.[78] Consciousness in this sense is a task, a project and not a state of being. The formulation of consciousness as also an interiorising of other people unites more clearly the social foundation of the psyche with its experienced individuality.[79] Moreover this notion refers to a process of interiorisation that draws on the historical memory of a people. It is in this sense that the memory of Christ drives towards an intentional, committed community.

The central location of this memory for the Church universal and for the ordinary person lies in all its symbolic fruitfulness in the eucharist (notwithstanding the Protestant emphasis on the Word expressed as sermon). The memory uncovered here defines the practical meaning of the term 'committed minority', and its connection to the popular base. But what memory is this? The eucharist meal has been laced with a wide variety of doctrinal flavours. In Gutiérrez's opinion, the fundamental meaning of this memory is in Christ's total giving of himself to others; it is the place, therefore, where mission and the creation of human solidarity simultaneously begin.[80] The Eastern Orthodox understanding of liturgy which aims at holding people to faith in a permanent historic community is substantially the same. In contrast, the tendency in the western Church since Augustine towards a psychologising of faith has tended to make the eucharistic memory somewhat degenerate.[81]

In the context of the Orthodox tradition a richer understanding of liturgy is expounded. Liturgy here *is* the work of the people (*leitourgia* derives from the Greek words *laos*, 'people' and *ergon*, 'work'). The eucharist in this respect centres that work, restores and extends it, so that 'the believers are called to prolong, so to speak, the eucharist so that it penetrates all of their life.'[82] Consequently, one speaks of 'the liturgy after the liturgy' in which the sacrificial memory of Christ is expressed in concrete diakonia. To quote Bishop A Yannoulatos:

> . . . the continuation of liturgy in life means a continuous liberation from the powers of evil that are working inside us, a continual reorientation and openness to insights and efforts aimed at liberating human persons from all demonic structures of injustice, exploitation, agony, loneliness, and at creating real communion of persons in love.[83]

On this understanding another Orthodox bishop claims that 'the altar of the eucharist leads directly to the higher altar of the poor and oppressed: for us there is no theological difficulty here.'[84] Clearly, the eucharist in the Orthodox conception concerns not merely the vicarious sacrifice of Christ, nor a belief by which one is as a result 'ushered in among the saints surrounding the throne of God'. Rather, here Jesus is the 'way' in a dynamic historical sense: there is 'a road which must be walked'.[85] But — and this is crucial — the historical weight of this 'way' as it is expressed in the eucharist is, as Koyama has it, a 'suffering gravity'.[86] In the eucharist one remembers a body broken and blood shed. Thereby the memory acquires flesh: it is embodied only by the responsible Christian who walks the way of the broken and the bleeding, if he or she is not already one of those broken and torn (in which case the eucharist becomes a celebration of hope). Self-evidently, this journey is imbued with emancipatory intention.

At this point we return to the implications of eucharistic practice in respect of historical materialism. Davis' discussion of the importance of remembering those who have suffered adds considerably to an insight into the importance of the eucharistic memory for the Christian community. Referring to a debate between Horkheimer and Benjamin, both members of the Frankfurt School of critical sociology, Davis reports Horkheimer's conviction that 'past injustice will never be made up; the suffering of past generations receives no compensation'. Benjamin in turn sought a concept of history capable of generating a 'basic solidarity with the past generation of the oppressed and slain', a concept grasping history as the history of suffering.[87] Here one is forced to the limit of rationality and thus, as Horkheimer grudgingly acknowledged, to the beginning of theology. Without this memory the sacrifice of the lost generations becomes the occasion for a new practice of domination now resting on what others had suffered for. Thus Davis, following Lenhardt, notes the crucial significance of 'solidarity in remembrance'.[88]

We are now able, on the basis of the location of the Christian *memoria* in the eucharist, to specify more precisely the kind of committed minority which the Christian mythos intends, one whose commitment relates to the edification of the larger community of the Church. The demands of the Christian tradition and the thrust of historical materialism meet in an identification of the poor and the oppressed, the broken and the bleeding, as the locus of transforming action with emancipatory intent. In partial identification with the whole Christian community the committed minority undertakes to engage in an historical task for their sake, as well as for the sake of the poor and oppressed in general. It does so on the basis of a *memoria* injected into the present and directed towards a hopeful future. The historical meaning of the symbolic constructs of liturgy, memory and apocalyptic eschatology are therefore invested in a particular kind of minority among other minorities that may exist in the church. The theological identity of the Church lies in the covenanted, committed minority as 'exemplar' of its faith and practice, in those who salt the total community (with its contradicition and conflicts). This 'salting' can only be conceived of in solidarity with the total community, not in terms of a separate group, an elected privilegium, or a righteous elite.

One vital caution is called for: we cannot establish on this basis a new definition of the 'true' Church abstracted from the real church and its ambiguities. Thus the committed minority is not a particular political grouping nor a fixed body of perons who can be labelled, but is defined in relation to praxis, and therefore in relation to a changing historical experience incapable of final definition and recognisable only in the process. For this reason Rendtorff may say: 'if we take the latest development of theology seriously, then it is clear that we shall not be able to determine the identity of the Church and theology unless first belief in practical terms achieves a wider spread across the world'.[89] We are forced thereby to designate the practical referent of the Christian mythos, the meaning of the Christian-community-in-praxis.

The Church-at-the-limits

> . . . when the Ark of the Covenant is eaten by termites, when the empty tomb is filled with our hermeneutics, when the Kingdom of God is a political product, when the life of Christ is a mere symbol, when the dethroned King takes refuge in speeches, then the dead of night has won the heart and darkened the eyes.
>
> — J Ellul[90]

One major problem of the Church-in-praxis and its critical theologising, as Davis (following Marcel Xhaufflaire) intimates, is its frequent inability to produce a politically coherent theory using its own presuppositions, especially in respect of theoretical, explanatory accounts of the conditions of freedom and oppression. Instead the tendency is to legitimate political interventions already advocated: 'by that very fact its political interventions remain politically incoherent, voluntarist and badly opportunist.'[91] As a result, many Christians commited to an emancipatory struggle with the poor and oppressed find in practice that nothing distinctive exists in being Christian, other than their use of religious language to say what may be said more precisely in sociological or economic terms. A necessary crisis of faith ensues. But there are also those for whom this is not the case even when they have critically reflected upon their faith from practice. What then may be regarded as distinctive, additional, or even corrective for such people in their faith?

We have already gone some way in dealing with this question, via a consideration of the Church as the field in which the struggule for liberation also takes place. Also hinted at, is the distinctive claim that the fullness of humanity is disclosed in Jesus Christ and his proclamation of the kingdom of God. These elements remain rational and reasonable if the assumption is made that the metaphorical language utilised by Christians in fact discloses a prized way-of-being-in-the-world otherwise not available. If not, then the proper response to the language of the Church, its memory, and its intentionality would be rejection, on the grounds that nothing more is disclosed there. But ecclesiological language engaging at the political level does address the 'limits-of' and 'limits-to' the situation in which it exists. Precisely there religious discourse expresses a reorientation on a 'higher' level of meaning, introducing 'impossible' demands, and grounding moral action outside of itself.[92] This occurs in relation to a rich. complex and differentiated memory of suffering and emancipation. Only in this gestalt does the Christian mythos make any special claims, though any particular claim may well not be its exclusive property (eg the claim for justice, for *shalom*, for dignity, etc).

In turn a Christian mythos which has praxis as a meta-criterion of the community it identifies, cannot be regarded as static. Thus, it is not seen as 'founding structures, doctrines or norms, but as launching an historical task drawn and oriented by its final destination.' Because this is not a private task of the Church but an entrance into an already given cosmic task for the world as a whole, any relation in praxis to others who make no Christian claims cannot be aimed at denigrating them or undermining them by some attempt to claim for God a restricted sphere of action. Rather, it is an occasion — as Bonino remarks — for humility and praise, not confusion, as one joins in the struggle for genuine autonomy, responsibility, dignity, and shared dominion.[93] On the other hand, the task is so comprehensive and complete that it may rightly be regarded from a human point of view as a 'limit-of' situation in which the 'limits-to' our resources are quickly apparent, thus giving rise at this juncture to theological discourse.

The Christian mythos then becomes historically meaningful (1) where it grasps — in a metaphorical imagination symbolically rich enough to represent, orientate and transform one's way-of-being-in-the-world — the 'limit-of' a situation and (2) where it is able to integrate the 'limits-to' our potency and action into a practical emancipatory interest already projected in its own symbols (especially the 'kingdom of God').[94] The embodiment of this mythos in a covenanted and committed community gives rise therefore to a Church-at-the-limits in a politically pregnant milieu. It is because this kind of *ecclesia* is what political theology reaches for that its ecclesiology so often enters into a contrast with Christendom concepts of the Church (in which appear a variety of forms of the idea of a society ordered along supposedly Christian lines, or at least inspired in this way).[95]

As many have noted, the project of a Christendom began with Constantine's attempt to establish a Christian commonwealth in the face of growing internal problems of the Republican Romanitas. He thereby sought to add to an already militarised bureaucracy a 'powerful ecclesiastical partner in the new regime'. The Church, increasingly legally recognised as a corporation permitted to accept gifts and legacies, acquired with this an ecclesial model similar to that of the Roman *Civitas*: the *ordo* (clergy) and the *plebs* (laity) were moulded according to the municipal roles of the *curia* (governors) and the *populus* (people).[96] Finally Theodosius transformed the New Republic of Constantine into the Orthodox Empire, thus sealing the direction of the Church for centuries to come.

But, as Segundo remarks, Christendom — despite modern attempts to renew it in revised forms (eg Christian political parties in Europe) — was at root the product of a particular era in human history, a sociologically derived phenomenon.[97] Industrial society, expanding globally, has destroyed the harmony between *ecclesia* and *societas*, making of Christianity in the process 'something it never was — *cultus privatus*', and thus entrusting to religion the 'saving and preserving of personal, individual and private humanity'. As Moltmann notes, the 'sphere of the unburdening of the individual' where the Church is required to cohere a community is separated from the 'realm of practical and businesslike purposes'.

The Church-at-the-limits accepts neither the Christendom model nor the privatised model, entering instead into the historical contradictions of modern society on the side of those who suffer its tyrannies in order to involve itself in the emancipatory transformation of the society. It thereby takes upon itself the full impact of the conflict between the dominant and the dominated. In this sense Moltmann, among others, speaks of an 'Exodus Church', a 'pilgrim people of god'.[98] Here too emerges the Church, to use the language of the Puebla Conference of Latin American bishops, which takes a 'preferential but not exclusive option for the poor'.[99]

A Church of the Poor

Keeping in mind that this Church-at-the-limits is the 'committed minority' of our earlier discussion and that it exists in a larger Christian community divided by the same contradictions which mark its socio-economic context, an option for the poor introduces into the Church at large a prism shattering its supposed purity ('standing above society/political life'). Conflicts otherwise concealed or repressed are revealed in full colour.[100]

In this respect the communication of the gospel has a conscientising function, 'politicising' the Church so that the conscious exercising of an option for the poor becomes possible.[101] This may sound like an appeal to introduce into the Church decisions and choices of an abnormal kind, threatening to destroy the reconciling life of the Church for the sake of predetermined, divisive political projects. But of course some option is always willy-nilly exercised by those who wield the instruments of power in the Church, whether consciously or not (eg in the 'civilising' thrust of the missionary Church in South Africa). The question therefore is not whether the Church makes decisions and choices of this kind or exercises political influence, but in which direction it does so.[102] This is certainly the normal territory within which its synods, assemblies, committees and executives operate. Moreoever, it does not do merely to call for a witness in respect of the poor and oppressed without specifying its content, for thereby 'the Church in anticipation' is not concretely related to 'the Church in contradiction'.[103]

We must agree with Moltmann's claim that the Church will become poor in a spiritual *and* material sense only when and if it 'becomes a Church of the poor, and if the *real* poor find themselves and their hope in the Church'.[104] Similarly we must regard as ideological (in the sense of concealing the interests of the dominant and the real conditions of existence) the claim that JA van Wyk makes in speaking against 'an ideological view of the poor' (by which he appears to mean an identification of the poor in terms of exploitation and marginalisation) and for a concept of poverty that 'reflects man's basic hunger and thirst for God'.[105] Such talk is worse than naive. The emphasis on the real poor is unavoidable in an historical materialist idiom, for only then is an authentic solidarity with the poor and a genuine protest against the conditions of poverty capable of concrete specification.[106] Only there can what Frederick Herzog termed servanthood 'at the boundary of life where no-one else cares' become meaningful.[107]

Moreoever the real situation of poverty, predicated upon exploitation and oppression, cannnot be grasped in abstract terms which assume a situation of open communication and of discourse relatively free from domination. K Nürnberger ascribes to the 'rich' a model of modernisation, to the 'poor' a model of liberation. With that distinction he develops an analysis of the situation of poverty which calls for the rich to share and engage in liberation, the poor to engage in and achieve modernisation. This is a false road, a completely ahistorical approach seemingly oblivious to the realities of power and powerlessness. Thus his conclusion, that 'if Whites would believe in a better distribution and Blacks in a better utilisation we would easily solve the (economic) problem', is the height of abstract philosophical idealism.[108]

Moltmann is much closer to the real situation in his recognition that the liberation of oppressors contradicts their interests and desires, evoking a religious task that transcends all moral power. Consequently, it is the struggle of the poor and oppressed which will force the oppressors to reconsider their position and seek a situation of discourse freed from domination. On the other hand, for the 'rich' person liberation necessarily involves what Moltmann insightfully terms 'the betrayal of the betrayers', a desertion of the cause of one's own position and class, a way of discipleship that may well lead to 'self-denial, suffering and shame' (Mark 8:34).[109] At the same time, voluntary solidarity with the real situation of the poor is capable in itself of introducing freedom into that situation, as DJ Arntz makes particularly clear:

> The really poor man is too poor to free himself from poverty, which he and the generations that follow him regard with a certain fatality.
>
> The man who voluntarily shares the life of the poor therefore acts as a piece of the leaven of freedom in the lives of the poor. Because he chooses his poverty, it does not contain that note of fatality . . . He can draw attention to the breaches of the law, express grievances and find his way for the poor through the bureaucratic maze. A slight improvement may lead to a loss of that sense of fatality among the poor and reveal possibilities which had hitherto been concealed. The man who voluntarily embraces poverty can therefore be a sign giving hope.[110]

Any such solidarity still escapes a discourse free from domination if there is any attempt to use 'instruments of domestication', which in discourse include monologues, slogans, communiques and instructions. An inability to trust the reason of the oppressed prevents one from avoiding a discourse of domination, for then one inevitably takes advantage of the 'emotional dependence of the oppressed — dependence that is the fruit of the concrete situation which surrounds them and which engendered their inauthentic view of the world.'[111] This is so no matter how noble one's good intentions.

Clearly the reinterpretation of the gospel that begins with the struggle of the poor and oppressed presupposes a location in history different from the dominant section of society.[112] For the Church-at-the-limits this necessarily implies:

1   a re-examination of ecclesiastical structures and the life of its members;
2   a condemnation of poverty as anti-evangelical;
3   an effort to understand and criticise the mechanisms which generate poverty and oppression;
4   a support of the aspirations of labourers and peasants and their marginalised dependents;
5   a defence of the fundamental right of these people freely to organise and promote their interests;
6   a promotion of the undeniable values available in the indigenous culture.[113]

These considerations also drive the Church-at-the-limits to develop its practice and accompanying theory where the poor and the oppressed gather together in the name of Christ. Here lies the source for a new ecclesial reality already discovered for example by many Latin Americans in the form of small groups of poor and oppressed Christians whose commitment and involvement in the struggle for their own and other's liberation creates 'centres of communion and participation which produce a Church of the poor, where the real poor find themselves and their hope in the Church.'[114] Here is the sense of the plea for a God 'who respects my traditions as media in His communication with me, the God whom I can experience in the fields, in my hut, on the factory floor, in the homeland-bound bus or train. . .'[115] Here too is the form of a theology born from:

> . . . the songs and hymns of peasants as they till the ground; from the impromptu prayers of Christian parents as they nurse their sick child; from the unorganised sermons of the village catechist; from the charismatic leadership of an illiterate founder of an Independent Church; from the old man who is steeped in traditional religious life. . .[116]

Conclusion

The earlier critical analysis of the Church in relation to the South African political economy has enabled us to diagnose hidden interests and unconscious illusions in its practice and theological reflection, and thus its insertion as a human community into the same contradictions that bedevil

South African society as a whole. By implication a demand for a much clearer and more specific commitment emerged, to be dealt with in terms of the notion of a Church-at-the-limits. In general, however, the Church as a whole, because of the contradictions that afflict it too, and because of its theological confusion and practical mediocrity, is likely to withdraw from its full responsibility, or worse — to sink into a defence of what it already possesses and thereby to ally itself with the dominant powers.

In this context, a contemporary form of apostasy is likely. Apostasy concerns the critical choice, in a situation where one is confronted by contrary demands, as to whether one serves the mission of the Church (manifested for the edification of the whole by the Church-at-the-limits), or not. The choice is thus never personal, merely made in private, but calls one to account for one's actions and one's words. Thus the primary reference point for a concept of apostasy is found in the limit-language of the Lordship of Christ, where an 'impossible demand' confronts one as the occasion for a real option exercised in history. Conversely, the notion of apostasy thereby also says something about the world, declaring a public rejection of those things that destroy the intent of the gospel: where people are broken, where some manipulate others in their image, where the mind and spirit of a people are crushed, where they are dispossessed of their rightful shared-dominion in the world. Consequently, a refusal of apostasy concerns a critical choice and a critical judgement capable of recognising the 'powers and principalities' and their agents and instruments of death, capable of naming — in a specific historical material concreteness — the demons of our time. Apostasy, in contrast, is the desertion of the cause for which Christians have been called and freed, and to which they have committed themselves. The choices in South Africa are particularly stark but a failure of the Church in these choices is likely to bring its own judgement.

The dialectic of apostasy is completed by the notion of edification, the 'making holy' of the Christian community whereby its testimony to the generative existence of a liberated and liberating life through Christ in the midst of the world is intensified and given body and blood in praxis. Edification of the body thus correctly emerges out of the commitment which apostasy betrays. Those who live towards this reality, whose behaviour and action as far as may be humanly expected is congruent with what they claim to honour, are on their way to overcoming for themselves and for others the madness of our time of which Boris Pasternak wrote: '. . . what people say is different from what they do'. Their testimony to the transforming power of God where people are dispossessed of their dignity and shared-dominion, their testimony to the gift of life (in its earthiest sense) which animates the struggle, is the mark of the Church. In that context liturgia, diakonia, koinonia, and other activities of the Church will surely evince a vitality and reality which are sorely lacking in the congregations which bear the mark of the affluent, the powerful and the privileged.

> 'Salt is good; but if salt has lost its taste;
> how shall its saltness be restored?
> It is fit neither for the land nor for the dunghill;
> men throw it away.'

(Luke 14:34—5, RSV)

Notes

1 JM Gustafson (1961), p5.

2 *Ibid,* p7.

3 G Ebeling (1979), p78.

4 See J Moltmann (1977), p18; H Küng (1968) p4. Küng believes that 'every age has its own image of the Church, arising out of a particular historical situation; in every age a particular view of the Church is expressed by the Church in practice, and given conceptual form, *post hoc* or *ante hoc*, by the theologians of the age.'

5 H Küng (1968), p5. This kind of fact alone makes meaningful the desire of New Testament scholars to ascertain the *Sitz im Leben* of biblical pericopae, though few have gone far enough in considering the sociology and political economy of Israel/the Roman Empire of the time.

6 A Dumas (1978), p20.

7 G Ebeling (1979), p106; JM Gustafson (1961), p ix.

8 JW de Gruchy, JTSA, no8, September 1974, p43.

9 T Rendtorff, 'The Problem of Revelation in the Concept of the Church', in M Douglas Meeks (1974), p150.

10 J Moltmann, 'The Rose in the Cross of the Present', (1971), p141; also M Douglas Meeks (1974), p150.

11 B Goba, 'Towards a Black Ecclesiology', *Missionalia,* vol 9, no2, August 1981, p55.

12 *Ibid,* p50.

13 K Nürnberger (1979), p19.

14 Some theologians link racism to modern economic imperialism, among them J Cone (see for example, 'Black Theology and the Black Church', in GH Anderson and TF Stransky, 1979, p131), as well as Latin American liberation theologians whose analyses of international economic forces are relevant to South Africa. Some feminist theology analysing sexism now heads in similar directions, though the impact of such theology in South Africa is yet small (see for example ES Fiorenza, 'Feminist Theology', in *ibid,* p195; also C Davis, 1980, p11).

15 RH Tawney (1926), p272.

16 JW de Gruchy (1979), p215—16. See also PE Hoffman, in 'The Origin and Nature

of Marxism as a Challenge to the Church', *Missionalia,* vol 6, no2, August 1978: he is more aware of the issues involved, recognising the worth and complexity of Marxism, and thus pointing in the direction of the Church's need to understand its challenge.

17 See F Houtart, 'Extra-Ecclesial Interests and Maintaining the Status Quo of the Churches', in JB Metz (1970), pp15—19.

18 We take this to be one sense in which JL Segundo (1973), p118ff, among other Latin Americans, suggests that economic development challenges the Church.

19 Z Kameeta, 'The Liberated Church and True Freedom', in T Sundermeier (1975), p124; also MS Mogoba, 'The Church in Future South Africa', in *SACC Conference Papers,* 1975, p49ff; E Mosothoane, 'Toward a Theology for Southern Africa', *Missionalia,* vol 9, no 2, August 1981, p101; C Desmond (1978), Chapter 4, who discusses the issue in terms of 'religious schizophrenia'.

20 P Randall (1972), pp61, 67 & 69ff.

21 See R Moore (1974), pp26—7, on Methodism and the working class. A rather explicit statement along the lines indicated is to be found in the report of the CPSA 'Commission on the Church and the Nation' which met from 1946—9, in which the Church made clear that '. . . contrary to some social theorists, we do believe in the organic nature of society which implies a co-ordination of the interests of the state, the community as a whole, employers and employees in the questions concerning wages and conditions of work.' See the Commission Records 1946/9, Diocese of Johannesburg, CPSA archives.

22 See also C Davis (1980), p53.

23 P Randall (1971)m p12ff.

24 *Ibid,* pp110—112.

25 The understanding of the Church as a sign of the kingdom is by now almost universally a consensus in theology in Protestant, Roman Catholic and Orthodox traditions, in South Africa as well. See for example, conciliar statements of Vatican II; the Conference of Latin American Bishops at Puebla (J Eagleson and P Scharper, 1979, p15); G Gutiérrez (1973), p261; I Bria (1980), pp8—9 and 237; J Moltmann (1967), p325 and (1977), p293; W Pannenberg (1969a), pp73 & 77; A Biéler (1974), pp84—5; DJ Bosch, *Missionalia,* vol 5 no 2, August 1977, p16; JW de Gruchy, JTSA, no 8, September 1974, p42.

26 It need hardly be said that drawing an implication such as this from historical materialism is an extension of the Marxian method, and not something Marx personally would ever have pursued. However, the grounds for doing so have been discussed in Chapter 8, which obviously revises aspects of classical Marxism. See M Bonino (1975), p154; also G Gutiérrez (1973), p276.

28 M Bonino (1975), p159.

29 J Moltmann (1977), p334.

30 R Rouse and SC Neill (1967), pp154 & 248 *passim.*

31 DF Durnbaugh (1968), p9ff.

32 A Dulles (1976), p35ff.

33 H Küng (1968), p17.

34 Probably dozens of examples could be listed. Two that come close to being idealist in my opinion are JG Davies (1954), for example on p83; and W Pannenberg (1969a), Chapter II. Similarly, one may go further back to the 'father of modern theology', Friedrich Schleiermacher, who in Trutz Rendtorff's opinion 'does not refer to definite, concrete historical problems, but to the mere existence of the

Church'; see W Pannenberg (1969b), p164.

35 A Biéler (1974), p78ff & p89ff.

36 For example, E Mosothoane, quoting S Gqubule, in 'Toward a Theology for Southern Africa', *Missionalia*, vol 9, no 2, August 1981, p106; also JW de Gruchy, 'The Identity of the Church in South Africa', JTSA, no 8, September 1974, p49.

37 EN Baartman, 'The Significance of the Development of Black Consciousness for the Church', JTSA, no 2, March 1973, pp22ff.

38 For example, JW de Gruchy (1979), p235; also S Govender, 'Reconciling Mission in the Contemporary South African Situation of Cultural Pluralism and Identity', *Missionalia*, vol 7, no 2, August 1979, p89.

39 See respectively, DJ Bosch, 'The Church in South Africa Tomorrow', SACC Conference Papers (1975), p33ff; B Goba, 'The Role of the Black Church in the Process of Healing Human Brokenness', JTSA, no 28, September 1979; and JW de Gruchy, 'English-speaking South Africans and Civil Religion', JTSA, no 19, June 1977, p50ff; also in 'The Identity of the Church in South Africa', JTSA, no 8, September 1974, p47ff.

40 For example D Hurley's article on 'An Ecclesiology of Confrontation', in K Nürnberger (1979), p361, criticised by Nürnberger for precisely this reason. Nürnberger himself points to the need to deal instead with the confrontation within the Church of different ideologies, as he puts it: see p361fn.

41 So for example, DJ Bosch claims that the only definition of true liberation is 'shalom, biblical peace'. That this is not definition at all (or at most a merely nominal definition), is clear. It is rather an image, capable to be sure of directing a definition, yet still requiring its content to be given. But this does not appear necessary to Bosch here. See 'The Church and the Liberation of Peoples', *Misionalia*, vol 5, no 2, August 1977, p39.

42 TC Oden (1970), pp20—1 & p69.

43 *Ibid*, p27.

44 See A Dulles (1976), p187.

45 JM Gustafson (1961), pp15—27.

46 T Rendtorff, 'The Problem of Revelation in the Concept of the Church', in W Pannenberg (1969b), p177.

47 H Küng (1968), p28; JB Metz (1971), p11.

48 A Dulles (1976), p188.

49 M Bonino (1975), p170.

50 V Lossky (1976), p175ff.

51 M Bonino (1975), p163.

52 GS Hendry (1959), pp10—11; M Bonino (1975), p164 also points to the source of this conception in Iranaeus.

53 P Freire (1971), p75fn. The notion of language as praxis is a commonly explored theme of neo—Marxian thinkers today, among them Jürgen Habermas.

54 J Moltmann (1975), pp116—7; also G Gutiérrrez (1973), p14.

55 JM Gustafson (1961), pp10—13, 45 & 73.

56 M Bonino (1975), p167.

57 See a provocative discussion on this in D McGaughey (1983), pp316—40.

58 V Lanternari (1963), p x.

59 N Cohn (1970), p1, pp52ff; and also pp281—2.

60 Mgijima and the Israelites, as was mentioned in Part One, were the victims of the

'Bulhoek Massacre'.

61 *Ibid,* p291. M West, 'People of the Spirit', in JTSA, no 7, June 1974, pp28—9, notes also the importance of Spirit experiences to those otherwise deprivated and powerless, for their comfort and healing.

62 See AN Wilder, 'The Rhetoric of Ancient and Modern Apocaplyptic', in *Interpretation,* vol XXV, 1971, p453. The 'strikingly rational element in apocalyptic vis-a-vis the desire to know and understand the world and its history' is uncovered by W Zimmerli (1968), p138.

63 DS Russell (1978), p43, is therefore accurate in describing Christian apocalyptic as essentially kerygmatic.

64 Johannes Weiss' conclusions (see 1971, pp129—31) still stand today in this respect despite occasional attempts to dispute them, none to my knowledge having succeeded in substantially undermining them. One author who does not accept the apocalyptic framework as true to the original thrust of the gospel is WG Kümmel (1957), p155; see also AN Wilder *op cit*, p453.

65 A Dumas (1978), p7.

66 G Vos (1972), p135.

67 *Ibid,* p22; and JM Gustafson (1961), p86ff.

68 J Moltmann (1977), p41ff.

69 *Ibid,* p22; and JM Gustafson (1961), p86ff.

70 *Ibid,* p93.

71 JL Segundo (1977), p200.

72 W Lynch (1960), p59.

73 JL Segundo (1973), p51. One may refer to this as the call to *Mündigkeit*, that is, full autonomy and social responsibility as a human being.

74 DF Durnbaugh (1968), p33.

75 JL Segundo (1977), p204; also S Hauerwas (1974), on J Howard Yoder's ecclesiology, pp211—1, *passim*.

76 T Rendtorff, 'Christianity without the Church', in JB Metz (1971), p57ff; also H Schlette, 'On So-called Partial Identification with the Church', in *ibid*, pp44—8.

77 The mark of edification is for Paul of course, one crucial test on whether any role is valid: see especially I Cor 13 & 14.

78 In another context this aspect of personhood, grounded in a Meadian notion of Sociality-in-process, finds eloquent expression in R Snyder (1977), p35. An interesting reference to the African sense of *ubuntu* ('humanity') which illustrates one meaning of this sociality-in-process through the historical interiorisation of the other, is found in a criticism of the 1930—2 Native Economic Commission Report. Here Rev C Callaway described *ubuntu* in terms of the recall of 'the Great Chiefs, the heroes of the past, the exploits of brave men, the tradition of the tribe, the great bond of social fellowship', these being an essential heritage of each person (see Papers, Dr AB Xuma, 1 March 1933).

79 This refers to the potential for a historical material development of psychology in George Herbert Mead's work.

80 G Gutiérrez (1973), p262.

81 See A Schmeman, 'The Missionary Imperative in the Orthodox Tradition', in GH

Anderson (1961), p255.

82 I Bria (1980), p61.

83 *Ibid,* p64; also A Yannoulatos, 'Discovering the Orthodox Missionary Ethos', *ibid,* p28.

84 I am indebted here to a conversation with Bishop Georg Khodr, Metropolitan of Mount Lebanon, in December 1980.

85 R Snyder (1977), pp48—9.

86 K Koyama (1974), p3. Koyama develops this image in a Japanese context by uniting two Japanese words, *tsutsumu* (to enfold) and *tsurasa* (feel pain for the sake of others).

87 C Davis (1980), pp142—3.

88 *Ibid,* p145. Note that African ancestor veneration comes very close to this limit-experience of memory, and may thereby have a powerful role to play in generating an African theology linked to a liberative praxis. Some brief comments in this direction are made by B Goba, 'An African Christian Theology', JTSA, no 26, March 1975, p10; see also B Goba, 'Towards a Black Ecclesiology', *Missionalia*, vol 9 no 2, August 1981, p55. The Orthodox use of ikons also functions to regenerate the memory of those who have exemplified the sacrificial life in the Christian tradition, in order to press the believer to renewed commitment and action.

89 T Rendtorff, 'Christianity without the Church', in JB Metz (1971), p60.

90 J Ellul (1977), p155.

91 C Davis (1980), pp60—1.

92 *Ibid,* p134; also JL Segundo (1973), p57, who responds to much the same issue, and develops the idea of 'self-giving' as a 'limit-of' possibility, by which the 'scope of love' is extended beyond what may be rationally grounded (though such love may nevertheless be reasonable for the person/people concerned).

93 M Bonino (1976), p156 & p168. In this sense also, R Vidales, in R Gibellini (1979), p38, refers to a 'new ecclesiology' which established fellowship not just with believers but also non-believers.

94 This latter gives rise to many attempts to understand Christian praxis in terms of 'anticipating' or 'building' the kingdom of God.

95 See for example G Gutiérrez (1973), p53ff.

96 CN Cochrane (1940), pp179, 205 & 219.

97 JL Segundo (1973), pp44—7.

98 J Moltmann (1967), pp304—11 *passim,* & pp316—7.

99 See J Eagleson and P Scharper (1979), p262ff. In one form or another, the demand to make a conscious choice in relating to oppression and its conditions, is also expressed by Black theologians in South Africa, among others, A Boesak (1976); and D Tutu, 'Mission in the Old and New Testaments' in M Nash (1977). The Eastern Orthodox Church has also recently made clear its support for a preferential option for the poor and oppressed: see the text of Report no 4, 'Confessing Christ Today', Bucharest, June 1974, in I Bria (1980), p228.

100 A point the Puebla Conference also recognised: See J Eagleson and P Scharper, *loc cit.*

101 G Gutiérrez (1973), p269.

102 *Ibid,* p267. The idea prevalent among many in the English-speaking churches that they have no political influence is itself a sign of ideological captivity, for it really only signifies that, for whatever good or bad reasons, they are withdrawn from praxis.

103 For example, JW de Gruchy (1979), p255, makes such a call without any specifics, while at the same time finding the opportunity to be quite specific about the witness of the Church to the state. The result of this procedure is evident in his repetition of the axiom that the church must support the state in the task of maintaining order, without any real consideration of that to which much of the rest of his book testifies, namely, that the state is marked profoundly by disorder, at least from the point of view of the dispossessed and disinherited bulk of the population.

104 J Moltmann (1977), p356.

105 JA van Wyk, 'Latin American Protestant Theology of Liberation', *Missionalia,* vol 5 no 2, August 1977, p91.

106 See G Gutiérrez (1973), pp287ff; here we also criticise the notion of P Bigo (1977), p125, that 'evangelical poverty' cannot be defined in sociological terms.

107 F Herzog (1972), p181.

108 K Nürnberger (1978), p226; also 'Reconciliation in a Situation of Severe Economic Discrepancies', *Missionalia,* vol 7 no 2, August 1979, pp59ff, where similar ideas are put forward.

109 J Moltmann, 'The Liberation of Oppressors', JTSA, no 26 March 1979, p25 & p35.

110 DJ Arntz, 'Is there a New Openness to the Church's Charismatic Testimony?' in JB Metz (1971), p88.

111 P Freire (1971), pp52—3 *passim.*

112 G Gutiérrez and R Shaull (1977), p75.

113 I am indebted here to the proclamations of the Puebla Conference of Latin American Bishops: see J Eagleson and P Scharper (1979), p267.

114 *Ibid,* p204 & pp211—13.

115 C Ramusi, 'Church and Homelands', in T Sundermeier (1975), p122.

116 JS Mbiti, 'Theological Impotence', in GH Anderson and TF Stransky (1976), p15.

APPENDIX A

Synoptic Chart of South African History, 1903—1928

Selected events indicating matters of concern for the anlysis of political economy in the designated period

KEY

— (underlining) key event

• organisation or body established

--- period during which event pertains

DATE	EXTERNAL EVENTS	POLITICS	ECONOMY	LABOUR ACTION	RESISTANCE
1903	MARCH: Inter-colonial Conference.	FEB: J Chamberlain tours Cape Colony. SANAC (Lagden) begins.	Customs Union formed Gold mining: expansion in output and profit. Recession begins. Drought.		SA Native Congress: memo to Sec of State for Colonies on political discrimination. Herero uprising.
1904		Natal Locations Act. NOV: •Tvl Progressive Assoc. Chamber of Mines interests (P Fitzpatrick and G Farrar). •Tvl Labour Party DEC: •Tvl Responsible Govt Assoc (diamond interests).	Ordinance 17: controls access of black workers to Tvl & reserves jobs. Labour importation Ord. (Tvl): Chinese labour for mines. 4778 factories in the four colonies: Goods valued at 19,3m. Begin period relative apathy in Trade Unions.		•Natal Native Congress •Orange River Colony Native Vigilance Assoc. •Tvl Congress. •Bapedi Union. •Basuto Assoc. Dr A Abdurahman on CT City Council.

1905	DEC: Britain: Liberal Party in power.	JAN: *'Het-Volk' (L Botha) MAR: Tvl granted representative govt JUL: *'Oranje Unie' AUG: *Political Labour League of WTLC (Pres WH Andrews). 'Afrikaanse Taal' movement Schools Boards Act (Cape) — excludes 'Coloureds'.	Natal enacts Poll Tax £1 per head. Natal: Delimitation Comm releases 2.6m ex 6.5m Zulu land effectively for settler purchase.		*African People's Org'n in Cape (Dr Abdurahman).
1906		JAN: Smuts to London: Lobbies for Tvl Responsible Govt. Tvl granted self-govt. L Botha Cabinet.	Mines fully productive after war: Labour—163 000 *Tvl Land Bank. WNLA crisis. Tvl Indigency Commission.		Zulu Poll Tax Rebellion (Bambata): killed— 30 Militia/3000 blacks. 1st Indian passive resistance campaign: against extension of pass laws. *Ilanga Nase Natal (J Dube).
1907	World Trade Recession	OFS granted self-govt.	Importation of Chinese labour stopped (but used until 1910). *First General Workers Union.	4 000 white mine-workers strike.	2nd Indian passive resistance campaign. Gandhi's 1st Satyagraha campaign.
1908		National Convention: Durban	Report of Tvl Indigency Comm on squatters.		Indians burn passes in Jhb. Dinuzulu on trial. *Cape Native Convention. (T Jabavu).
1909	AUG: SA Act passed in Britain	National Convention: Cape Town National Convention: Bfn. *SA Labour Party.	Tvl Industrial Disputes Prevention Act. 6 894 miles of rail in SA.	APR/MAY: Railwaymen's strike (white).	MAR: APO meeting on National Conv — against SA Nat Cong meeting on Nat Conv — against. *Ohlange Institute in Natal. (J Dube). DEC: SA Socialist Federation.
1910	1st International Missionary Conf. (Edinburgh: John Mott).	MAY: (31st) UNION of SA JUL: Socialist Party, (shortlived).			Rubusana & Abdurahman elected to Cape Prov Council.

DATE	EXTERNAL EVENTS	POLITICS	ECONOMY	LABOUR ACTION	RESISTANCE
1911	Universal Races Congress, London: Jabavu & Rubusana present.		Mines & Works Act no 12: (i) job reservation (blasting cert)— job colour bar. (ii) strikes by African contract workers outlawed.	Jhb Tramwaymen's strike, (JWW)	'Native Union' proposed by Pixley ka i Seme.
1912		Miner's Phthisis Act. Botha resigns, forms govt with Hertzog. Union Defence Act. Govt Commission to investigate 'black peril'.	325 000 miners, of which whites — 36 000. •Land Bank. •Native Recruiting Corp		Jan: (8th) •SA Native National Congress (later ANC). •Later ANC). APR: •SA Races Congress opposition to SANNC, (T Jabavu). MAY: •U/d Socialist Party •Abantu-Batho (SANNC) •SA Teachers' League
1913		Hertzog forms National Party. Commission on Assaults on Women: proposes separate residential areas.	LAND ACT. SEPT: Economic Commission to investigate workers' grievances.	JULY: Miner's strike: riots, 18 000 workers. 'The Workers' Charter' publ (white grievances). Newcastle: Indian coalminers strike.	African women protest in Bfn against extension of Pass Laws in OFS. Natal Indians march into Tvl.
1914	AUG: (4th) World War 1 begins.	JAN: (14th) Martial Law •National Party Riotous Assemblies Act Commission on TB— proposes segregated areas. SEPT: (10th) Union joins War: 91 vs 12 votes. Military expedition to German SWA.	Union Income Tax begun. 'Gold-mining: contraction & crisis.	JAN: (8th): Industrial disturbances on Rand. African strike, OFS at Jagersfontein. (1914) 12 strikes.	JAN: (16th): Smuts and Gandhi meet. JULY: Gandhi leaves SA. SANNC delegation to colonial Sec & House of Commons, Britain. T Jabavu opposes Rutusana in Cape Prov Council election — both lose. •War on War League (Jones, Bunting and Wade). Afrikaner Rebellion.
1915		(Surrender of German forces in SWA).			•International Socialist League: left-wing break from SA Labour Party.

1916	Union expeditionary force to German East Africa. •SA Native College at Fort Hare. •Die Burger Smuts in Imperial War Cabinet, Britain.	Beaumont Commission: 'Native Lands Comm' — on enlargement of reserves.	100 000 'Poor Whites'		
1917	Russian Revolution.	Native Administration Bill: segregated political institutions based on Lagden Commission principles and Glen Grey system of District Councils.	•Industrial Development Corp.	JAN: White mine-workers' strike at Van Rhyn Deep: against semi-skilled employment of blacks.	•Industrial Workers of Africa (ex ISL).
1918	NOV: (11th) Armistice.	•Afrikaner Broederbond SEPT/OCT: Influenza epidemic.	Status Quo Agreement: Chamber of Mines & White TU's. 488 000 farm workers.	'Bucket strike' in Jhb. Africans boycott food in Rand compounds (high prices).	SANNC protest against conviction of sanitary workers under Masters & Servants Act.
1919		AUG: Botha dies, Smuts PM — Mandate over SWA		MAR: Bfn wage strike (Msimang). OCT: CT dock strike (ICU). (1919) 47 strikes.	MAR: Rand Pass Campaign •ICU in CT (Kadalie). African delegation (SANNC) to Versailles. •Bantu Union (Meschach Pelem)).
1920	Lenin's 'Colonial Thesis' publ.	MAR: General election: Nat Party largest—44 seats. •1820 Memorial Settlers' Assoc (inc Selbourne, Milner, Smuts). Native Affairs Act: based on Lagden principles.	•SA Reserve Bank NOV: 7 gold mines working at loss or marginal profit. DEC: 15 mines failing	FEB: African miners' strike: 40–70 000. OCT: Municipal workers' strike, PE: ICWU 21 killed. (1920) 66 strikes.	MAY: ICWU (Kadalie) launched nationally. •SA Indian Congress
1921	Post-War Depression. 2nd Pan African Congress, London J Dube present.	SAP & Unionist Party merge uniting capital interests. FEB: Special General Election, new SAP win. JULY: •Communist Party ex ISL.	est 120 000 'Poor Whites' est 120 000 'Poor Whites'		MAY: Bulhoek Massacre of 'Israelites' at Ntabalenga. Wellington Buthelezi: anti-settler campaign (millenarian). •Joint Councils of Africans and Europeans, Jhb.

DATE	EXTERNAL EVENTS	POLITICS	ECONOMY	LABOUR ACTION	RESISTANCE
1922	Britain returns to Gold standard at pre-war parity— 35% drop in price.	MAR: (10th): Martial Law Martial Law Commission	Mines lay-off 2 000 white workers. Apprenticeship Act: effectively limits skilled training to whites.	JAN: (8th). Strike ballot. (10th): Strike of white workers on gold mines, power station, engineering. MAR: (5th): General Strike. (7th): 1st assaults on Africans. (14th): Uprising quelled.	Delegation to London, Chief Sobhuza II of Swazi against incorporation into SA. Bondelswarts Rebellion: SWA.
1923		APR: Hertzog Creswell electoral pact. Native Urban Areas Act: 'Stallard doctrine', locations policy and systemisation of migratory labour.	Drought Investigation Comm •ESCOM AUG: Hildick-Smith case: test of job colour bar.		SANNC renamed ANC, adopts 'Bill of Rights •Workers Herald (ICU).
1924		APR: (5th) Smuts resigns, JUNE: (30h) Election: PACT Govt under Hertzog.	Industrial Conciliation Act: Africans not defined as 'employees' JUL: Civilised Labour Policy: favours whites workers. NOV: Mining Regulation Comm to investigate job colour bars.		•SA Assoc of Employee's Organisations
1926	Imperial Conf (London). Balfour Declaration. Le Zoute Conf	Hertzog at Imperial Conf 'Hertzog Bills': Representation of Natives/Natives (Councils) Act/Native Lands Act/ 'Colour Bar' Act, Conf between SA and Indian govts: re status of Indians in SA.	MAY: Mines and Works Amendment Act: colour bar in mining.		•SA Trade Union Congress ex SAAEO. Kadalie arrested in Natal. ICU expels communist members.

1927	Congress of Oppressed Nationalities (Brussels).	Native Administration Act: extended Natal colonial/tribal systems to Union. Immorality Act. Nationality and Flag Act	Agricultural sector income drop: falls between 1927/8 & 1932/3 by 42%.	Coal Strike, N. Natal. JUN: African dock workers' strike, Durban. JUL: Railway goods yard strike, Jhb.	*1st African TU's on Rand. JUN: ICU at zenith: Kadalie goes to Europe. 1st non-European conf Kimberley (ANC/APO/ICU & SA Indian Congress).
1928	Butler Reports to ILO on Labour in SA.	Labour Party split: Creswell/Madley.	*ISCOR.	African Diamond Diggers strike at Lichtenburg: 30 000 workers.	JAN: SATUC rejects ICU affiliation. MAR: *SA Fed of non-European TUs: parallel unions. *SA Worker MAY: ICU yase Natal formed by Champion. WG Ballinger arrives to advise ICU.

APPENDIX B

Statistical Tables

TABLE 8
Religious Affiliations of Africans, 1911 and 1936

	Number	
	1911	1936
Dutch Reformed	71 422	154 180
Anglican	170 704	407 528
Presbyterian	68 211	108 094
Congregational	95 706	57 054
Methodist	451 746	795 369
Lutheran	144 244	307 387
Roman Catholic	24 058	232 905
Apostolic		13 003
Other Christian	27 615	62 691
African Independent Churches		1 089 479
Islam	1 896	1 440
Other and Unspecified	1 301	37 959
No religion	2 962 103	3 329 600
Total	4 019 006	6 596 689

	Distribution over Denominations (%)	
	1911	1936
Dutch Reformed	1,8	2,3
Anglican	4,2	6,2
Presbyterian	1,7	1,6
Congregational	2,4	0,8
Methodist	11,2	12,1
Lutheran	3,6	4,7
Roman Catholic	0,6	3,5
Apostolic		0,2
Other Christian	0,7	1,0
African Independent Churches		16,5
Islam	0,1	
Other and Unspecified		0,6
No religion	73,7	50,5
Total	100,0	100,0

Figures taken from Population Census, 1960, Sample Tabulation, No. 6, pp2, 16, 25, 29. The rest are taken from Union Statistics for Fifty Years, ppA-26-A-29.
Tables from Oxford History of South Africa, Vol II, p475.

Note that between them the Anglican and Methodist churches include no less than 79% of the African affiliated population out of those churches defined as 'English-speaking'.

APPENDIX C

Data on Missions

Table 9: Statistics on Mission in South Africa, 1904

Work Commenced	Society	Field(s)	European Workers	Native Workers	Stations	Out-stations	Communicants	Baptised	Adherents
1737	Moravian Church	Cape Province, Native Territories	89	513	23	139	6 331	19 338	21 595
1799	London Missionary Society	Cape Province, Bechuanaland	50	126	41	141	21 250	21 250	75 344
1814	Wesleyan Missionary Society	British South Africa	102	1873	5?	1853	96 489	170 953	361 606
1820	United Free Church of Scotland	Native Territories, Natal	123	856	28	509	15 994	19 411	35 039
1824	Dutch Reformed Church	British South Africa	225	457	92	56	31 270	31 270	137 295
1829	Paris Evangelical Missionary Soc	Basutoland, Barotsiland	43	445	15	210	17 160	17 160	24 460
1829	Rhenish Missionary Society	German SW Africa, Cape Province	64	79	35	28	15 969	15 969	35 106
1834	Berlin Missionary Society	Cape Province, OFS, Natal, Tvl	103	649	55	249	23 853	48 360	48 360
1835	American Board Mission	Natal, Rhodesia	41	560	15	27	5 532	5 532	19 711
1835	Church of England	British South Africa	177	910	134	301	43 403	156 059	206 501
1844	Norwegian Missionary Society	Natal, Zululand	31	58	12	63	2 231	3 842	5 089
1854	Hermannsburg Mission	Natal, Transvaal	51	518	47	133	22 760	22 760	67 184
1869	Swiss Romande Mission	Tvl, Portuguese East Africa	73	81	14	65	1 992	1 992	4 462
1870	Finnish Mission	Ovamboland	37	35	8	15	708	1 772	2 529
1873	Church of Norway Mission	Zululand, Natal	19	29	5	31	761	1 845	2 800

Work Commenced	Society	Field(s)	European Workers	Native Workers	Stations	Out-stations	Communicants	Baptised	Adherents
1876	Church of Sweden Mission	Natal, Zululand, Rhodesia	28	82	6	60	1 281	2 735	5 124
1885	Free Methodist Church Mission	Natal	18	26	6	28	329	329	2 120
1889	South Africa General Mission	Native Territories, Natal, Swaziland	61	57	25	50	948	1 254	5 000
1890	Swedish Zulu Mission (Holiness Union)	Natal	9	3	2	8	122	122	160
1890	Salvation Army	British South Africa	33	56	33	27	1 763	1 763	7 523
1890	Hanoverian Free Church Mission	Transvaal	17	55	9	34	5 110	5 119	20 000
1892	Scandanavian Alliance Mission	Natal	7	3	2	8	122	122	160
1892	Scandanavian Independent Baptist Union	Natal	10	70	2	—	350	350	945
1892	SA Baptist Missionary Society	Kafaria	11	5	4	28	625	625	2 795
1896	SA Compounds & Interior Missions	Johannesburg, Portuguese East Africa	23	46	14	23	1 000	1450	3 550
1896	Hephzibah Faith Missionary Assoc	Natal, Johannesburg	9	20	3	1	40	40	160
1898	Brethren in Christ Mission	Rhodesia	11	7	4	3	106	106	266
1899	Methodist Episcopal Church	Rhodesia	18	47	3	14	1 245	1 245	6 498
1899	Norwegian Free Mission	Natal	5	2	1	—	42	42	71
1904	Presbyterian Church of SA	Transvaal, Rhodesia	2	7	2	20	750	750	1 750
			1490	7619	693	4124	319 596	563 566	1 095 680

Table 10
Missionary Expansion, Statistics 1850 and 1911

	1850	*1911*
Missionary Bodies	11	30+
Missionary Personnel	150	1650

(Figures from JH du Plessis, 1911, p104)

Table 11
Institutions of the SA Missionary Society, 1908

1 Training Institution for Coloured Teachers and Evangelists, Cape Town
2 Heald Town Training Institution
3 Ayliff Instituition (girls)
4 Lessington Training and Industrial School (girls; closed in 1908)
5 Lamlough Training and Industrial School (girls)
6 Clarkesbury Training and Industrial Scholl (boys)
7 Shawbury Training and Industrial School (girls)
8 Pondoland Training and Industrial School (boys)
9 Bensonville Training and Industrial School (boys)
10 Edendale Training and Industrial School (boys)
11 Indalem Training and Industrial School (girls)
12 Butterworth Mission Training School (boys)

(Data from the 27th SA Missionary Society Report, 1908)

Table 12
1st General Missionary Conference, 1904: Societies Present

American Zulu Mission
Baptist
Berlin Evangelical Society
Berlin Evangelical Society for German East Africa
Brethren
Brethren in Christ
Church of Norway Mission
CPSA
Church of Sweden Mission
Dutch Reformed Church
East Central Africa Mission
Free Methodist
Hanoverian Mission
London Missionary Society
Methodist Episcopelian
Moravian Mission
Paris Evangelical Mission
Presbyterian Church of SA
SA Compounds Mission
SA General Mission
Society of Friends
Swedish Mission
United Free Church of Scotland
Wesleyan Mission

Table 13
Data on Basis and Structure of the General Missionary Conference

1 Conference met from 1904—1932
2 Individual representation
3 During its 28 years, 41 societies and churches were represented, but only 6 of those at all Conferences
4 The aims of the Conference were:
   a. to promote co-operation and brotherly feeling between different missionary societies;
   b. to labour for the most speedy and effective evangelisation of the native races of SA;
   c. to enlighten public opinion on Christian mission;
   d. to watch over the interests of the native races, and where necessary to influence legislation on their behalf;
   e. to keep ever in view the goal of establishing self-supporting and self-propagating Native Churches in SA.

(From the General Missionary Conferences of SA Summary, p144)

Bibliography

Archival Material

(a) Church of the Province of SA: Books

Bantu-European Student Christian Conference, *Christian Students and Modern SA.*
CAWOOD, Lesley, *The Churches and Race Relations in SA.*
Christian Council of SA, *The Christian Citizen in a Multi-Racial Society.*
Christian Council of SA, *Christian Reconstruction in SA.*
COTTON, WA, *The Race Problem in SA.*
CRIPPS, Arthur S, *An Africa for Africans; a plea . . .*
ELLISON, John (ed), *Church and Empire.*
TAYLOR, JD, *Christianity and the Natives of SA: Year Book of SA Missions*
LEWIS, C and EDWARDS, GE, *Historical Records of the CPSA.*
PATON, A, *Apartheid and the Archbishop.*

Minutes and Documents

CPSA — Memo (BB Burnett) 1960.
   — Scrapbooks (1961—74).
   — Commission on Compositions of Trusts Board (1973)
   — Diocese of Cape Town, St Mary's Church, Woodstock: '95 Thes
   — Diocese of Johannesburg, Scrapbook (1961—72).
   — Diocese of Johannesburg, Cathedral Records (1853—1971).

— Diocese of Johannesburg, Commission on the Church and the Nation (1941—50).
— Diocese of Pretoria, Diocesan Board of Missions and Minutes (1905—21).
— Diocese of Pretoria, Native Conference: Minutes (1915—24).
— Diocese of St John's, Scrapbook (1902—22).
— Diocese of St John's, St Barnabas and St Cuthbert's Missions.
— Provincial Board of Missions, 1903.
— Records, 1940—1.
— Provincial Misssionary Conference (1906—38) Minutes.
— Women Missionaries, 1913.
— Women's Missionary Auxiliary, Minutes and Records (1910—28).
Anglican Women's Fellowship, Records (1964—76).
CPSA — Church Missionary Society: Records (1914—76).
— Diocese of Cape Town: Records (1847—1964).
— Diocese of Damaraland: Records (1970—3).
— Diocese of Pretoria: Press Cuttings (1892—1935).
— Diocese of St John's: Notes (1976).
— Provincial Letter Books (1921—59).
— Provincial Minutes Books (1870—1976).
— Provincial Standing Commission Records (1910—70).
— Women's Central Missionary Commission Minutes (1922—3).
— Diocesan Synods: Cape Town, Bloemfontein, Natal, St John's, Johannesburg, Pretoria, Grahamstown.

Other Manuscripts and Documents

African Bishops, Letters (1889—1934).
BOYS, John, 'Steadfast in Faith: Work of CPSA', 1963, Ts.
BROOKES, EH, 'Universal Church in its SA Setting', Mimeograph.
CAMERON, George H, 'SA Revisited', 1929, Ts.
CARTER, Bishop WM, Papers (1891—1930).
CLAYTON, GH, Papers (1864—1923).
GAUL, Bishop WT, Scrapbook (1874—1931).
Gray Centenary, 5 Lectures on Anglican History, Ts.
KARNEY, Bishop ABL, Papers (1922—35).
PAGE, BT, 'Outline History of Church of Province', Ts.
PALMER, Rev WA, Scrapbook/Album (1925—45).
PARKER, Bishop W, 'Missionary Work in CPSA, 1910—1957'.
PARKER, Bishop W, Scrapbook (1920—53).
SA Church Institute, London, Minutes and Papers (1914—30).
WOOD, Rev CT, Papers (1930—72).
YATES, Rev RF, Papers (1930—72).
ETHERIDGE, Bishop EH, Memoirs (1900—54), Ts.
MERRIMAN, John X, Letter to Archbishop, Cape Town, 1915.
Multi-Racial Conference of SA, Records (1957—8).
PAGE, Bishop EF, Papers (1898—1963).
BUCKLE, HO, Letter, 1922, Rand Strike, Ts.

GANDHI, MK, Draft chapters, 'Satyagraha in SA', Ts/Ms Con.
HILLS, W, Papers and Diaries (1878—1960).
LAIDLER, PW, Papers (1841—1936), Scrapbook (1909—19).
NORTON, Rev WA, Papers (1918—28).
SACC, Records (1923—72).
XUMA, Dr AB, Papers (1918—60).
Baptist Union of SA, Records (1913—74).
BUNTING, SP, Papers (1922—45).
CALATA, Rev JA, Address, 1939, Ts.
COPE, RK, Papers incl on 1907/13/22 Strikes.
LAGDEN, Sir GY, Papers (1877—1934), incl SANAC Report.
Martial Law Commission, Verbatim Record, 1922.
National European-Bantu Conference Papers, 1933.

Periodicals/Journals

The Church Missionary Review, 1971, CMS, London.
The East and The West, 1903—1922.
CR (Community of the Resurrection), 1907—24.
The Mission Field (SPG Monthly, London), 1909—24.
'With One Accord' — Unified Statement, 1933.
The Kingdom (Pretoria Diocese Magazine 1904: 'The Anglican') 1904—23.
The Watchman (Johannesburg Diocese Magazine) 1922—3.
The Transvaal Missions Quarterly, 1924—5.
The Net (Zululand Missionary Association Quarterly), 1918—22.
The Church Chronicle (CPSA Newspaper), 1909—28, TCC.
The Church Times, London, Various 1922—32.

Pamphlets

BIRTWHISTLE, NA, 'Colour: Problem of Racial Discrimination', 1954.
CALLAWAY, G, 'The National Problem in SA. . .', 1926.
CHESTER-MASTER, Colonel R, 'The Work of Churches in SA', 1908.
CAMERON, W, 'The Work of Churches in SA', 1908.
Church of Scotland, Foreign Missions Commission.
CPSA, Diocese of Johannesburg, 'The Church and the Nation', 1943 (Clayton)
CROKAT, W, 'Government in the English Church'.
DEBENHAM, M, 'Bantu, Boers and Briton: . . .', 1924.
GIBSON, AGS, 'The Native Question', 1897.
International Missionary Council, 1952, 'Missionary Church'.
LAVIS, Bishop SW, 'Christian Ideals and Social Order'.
LEE, Bishop AW, 'Christianity and the Bantu: . . .'
VICTOR, O, 'A Large Room' (Pretoria/Johannesburg Diocese work) 1926.
WAGGETT, PN, 'Church Affairs in SA' (WWI —).
WEBB, Bishop AB, 'Some 'Questions on . . .SA', 1900.
WEBB, Bishop AB, 'Some Social Forces . . . in SA', 1894/5.

WEBB, Bishop AB,' Principles of Missions', 1897.
RAYNES, Father R, 'Christian Liberalism . . .', 1955.
Christian Council of Rhodesia, 'Church and Human Relations', 1965.
CARTER, Archibishop WM, Letter, 1920.
CARTER, Archbishop WM, Charges to Cape Town Diocesan Synod, 1914—19.
KEY, Bishop B, Charge to Diocesan Synod, St John's, 1897.

(b) Methodist Church: Books

CALDERWOOD, Rev H, *Caffres and Caffre Missions*.
EDMUNDS, Arthur, *A Great Adv: Story of Founding of Methodism in SA*.
EVELEIGH, W, *Settlers and Methodism: 1820—1920*.
SMITH, Edwin, *The Christian Mission in Africa* (Le Zoute Conference).
DEVITT, Napier, *Memoirs of a Magistrate*.
BRADY, JE, *Trekking for Souls* (Oblate Mission).
EVELEIGH, W, *The Story of a Century: 1923—1923*.

Manuscripts and Documents

BLENCOWE, Rev G, Letters.
BUCHANAN, M, Essay.
CRAGG, Rev AW, Journals.
DUGMORE, DP, Thesis.
HORNABROOK, Rev RF, Cuttings.
HURCOMBE, Rev EH, Notebook.
LOWE, Rev G, Diaries.
MEARA, Rev W, Notes and Papers.
Methodist Historical Society of SA, Journals.
MOSELEY, Rev GC, Diaries.
MSIMANG, B, Manuscripts.
GLADWIN, FP, Manuscripts.
MATHABATHE, S, Manuscripts.
Women's Auxiliary, Documents.
General Missiological Conference of SA, Documents.

Periodicals and Reports

Advance (Primitive Methodist Church) (1902—32).
Forward (Wesleyan Methodist Church) (1925—28).
The Methodist Churchman (1905—30), TMC.
Methodist Recorder (London).
The Rand Methodist (Journal, Johannesburg).

The Transvaal Methodist (Parish-based).
SA Outlook (Lovedale), SAO (CE).
Methodist Church: Conference Brochures.
Methodist Church: Minutes of Conference (1905—30).
Methodist Church: SA Missionary Society Reports (1904—27).
Methodist Church: Women's Auxiliary General Report.
Methodist Church: Transvaal and Swaziland District Directory (1915—29).
Primitive Methodist Year Book (London).
Transvaal Missionary Association (Reports).
Methodist Church: Missionary Report on Indians, 1914.
Methodist Church: Bloemfontein Circuit, Quarterly.

Pamphlets

ATKINS, WC, 'Cash Value of National Education'.
BALLINGER, WG, 'Race and Economics in SA'.
MASON, Rev F, 'National Policy in Natal, 1906'
EVELEIGH, Rev W, 'Some Notable Men' ex 'A Short List of SA Methodists', 1913.
RIDER, Rev WW, 'A Wonderful Century'.
Methodist Church: CCD 'Methodism and Social Questions', CCD.
Methodist Church: Missionary Department, 'Circuits of Methodist Churches' (Map).
Methodist Church: Witwatersrand Methodist Mission.
Primitive Methodist Missionary Society: Report of Deputation to South and Central Africa.

Theory and Historical Analysis

ARMSTRONG, A (1973), *The Church of England, The Methodists and Society: 1700—1850*. London: University of London Press.
ASHLEY, MJ (1980), 'Universes in Collision: Xhosa, Missionaries and Education in 19th Century South Africa'. *JTSA no 32*.
BEINART, W (1982), *The Political Economy of Pondoland: 1860 to 1930*. Johannesburg: Ravan Press.
BERGER, P (ed) (1969), *Marxism and Sociology: Views from Eastern Europe*. Appleton-Century-Crofts, Meredith Corp.
BLOOM, H (1982), *Transvaal Episode*. Cape Town: David Philip. (Original publication: 1956).
BONNER, PL (ed) (1979), *orking Papers in Southern African Studies*. Johannesburg: African Studies Institute.
— (1980), 'The Transvaal Native Congress 1917 —1920: the Radicalisation of the Black Petty Bourgeoisie on the Rand'. Johannesburg: African Studies Institute, University of the Witwatersrand.
— (1981) (ed), *Working Papers in Southern African Studies*, Volume II. Johannesburg: Ravan Press.

BOTTOMORE, T (1975), *Marxist Sociology.* London: Macmillan Press.

BOTTOMORE, T and NISBET, R (1978), *A History of Sociological Analyses.* London: Heinemann.

BOUDON, R (1980), *The Crisis in Sociology: Problems of Sociological Epistemology.* London: MacMillan Press. (First published in French, 1971).

BOZZOLI, B (1973/4), 'Ideology and the Manufacturing Class in SA; 1907—26.' London: Institute for Commonwealth Studies.

BROOKES, E (1974), *White Rule in SA: 1830—1910.* Pietermaritzburg: University of Natal Press.

BROWN, WR (1960), *The Catholic Church in SA.* London: Burns and Oates. (Center for Cultural Studies).

Centre for Cultural Studies, (1978) *On Ideology.* London: CCS, University of Birmingham, publ Hutchinson & Co.

COCK, J (1980), *Maids and Madams.* Johannesburg: Ravan Press.

CONNERTON, P (ed) (1976) *Critical Sociology.* Harmondsworth: Penguin Books.

COOPER, F (1981), 'Peasants, Capitalists and Historians'. *Journal of Southern African Studies,* vol 7.

CUBER, JF (1959), *Sociology: A Synopsis of Principles.* New York: Appleton-Century-Crofts.

DAVENPORT, TRH (1977), *South Africa: A Modern History.* Johannesburg: MacMillan SA.

DAVIES, R, KAPLAN, D and O'MEARA, D (1976), 'Class Struggle and the Periodisation of the State in South Africa'. *Review of Political Economy,* vol 7, September.

DAVIES, R (1979), *Capital, State and White Labour: 1900—1960.* Sussex: Harvester Press.

DE GRUCHY, JW (1979), *The Church Struggle in South Africa.* Grand Rapids: Eerdmans.

DE KIEWIET, CW (1937), *The Imperial Factor in South Africa.* London: Cambridge University Press.

— (1941), *A History of South Africa: Social and Economic.* London: Oxford University Press.

DELIUS, P (1981), 'From Refuge to Resistance: Botsabelo, Mafolofolo and Johannes Dinkwanyane', Johannesburg: African Studies Institute, University of the Witwatersrand.

DENOON, D (1972), *Southern African Since 1800.* London: Longmans.

DE VILLIERS A (ed) (1976), *English-speaking South Africa Today: Proceedings of the National Conference, July 1974.* London: Oxford University Press.

DE VRIES, JL (1978), *Mission and Colonialism in Namibia.* Johannesburg: Ravan Press.

DURKHEIM, E (1938), *The Rules of Sociological Method.* New York: The Free Press.

DU PLESSIS, JH (1911), *A History of Christian Missions in SA.* Cape Town: C Struik (originally publ Longmans, Green & Co, London).

EDGAR, B (1974/5), 'Garveyism in Africa: Dr Wellington and the "American Movement" in the Transkei, 1925—40'. London: Institute for Commonwealth Studies.'

FLORIN, H (1967), *Lutherans in SA.* London: Penguin Books.

FREEDMAN, R (ed) (1961), *Marx on Economics.* London: Penguin Books.

GALLAGHER, J and ROBINSON, R (1968), *Africa and the Victorians: the Climax of Imperialism.* New York: Anchor Books, Morgan and Scott.

GERDENER, GBA (1958), *Recent Developments in the South African Mission Field.* London: Marshall, Morgan and Scott.

GIDDENS, A (1971), *Capitalism and Modern Social Theory.* Cambridge: Cambridge University Press.

— (1976), *New Rules of Sociological Method: A Positive Critique of Interpretative Sociologies.* London: Hutchinson.

GUY, J (1982), *The Destruction of the Zulu Kingdom: the Civil War in Zululand, 1879—1884.* Johannesburg: Ravan Press.

HABERMAS, J (1970), *Toward a Rational Society.* Boston: Beacon Press.

— (1971), *Knowledge and Human Interests.* Boston: Beacon Press.

— (1974), *Theory and Practice.* London: Heinemann.

— (1976), *Legitimation Crisis.* London: Hutchinson.

— (1979), *Communication and the Evolution of Society.* London: Heinemann.

HATTERSLEY, AF (1969), *An Illustrated Social History of SA.* Cape Town: AA Balkema.

HEGEDÜS, A (1977), *The Structure of Socialist Society.* New York: St Martin's Press (original title: *A szocialists társadalom struktúrájáról, 1966).*

HEWSON, LA (1950), *An Introduction to South African Methodists.* Cape Town: Standard Press.

HINCHLIFF, P (1963), *The Anglican Church in SA.* London: Darton, Longman and Todd.

— (1968) *The Church in South Africa.* London: SPCK.

HIRSCH, ED Jr (1967), *Validity in Interpretation.* London: Yale University Press.

HOFMEYR, J (1979), *Religion in the Interpretation of Experience.* Unpubl doctoral dissertation: University of Cape Town.

HOUGHTON, DH (1967), *The South African Economy.* Cape Town: Oxford University Press.

HOWARD, D (1977), *The Marxian Legacy.* London: MacMillan Press.

HUGHES, EJ (1944), *The Church and the Liberal Society.* Notre Dame: University of Notre Dame Press.

(Institute for Commonwealth Studies Essays) (var), Institute for Commonwealth Studies on the Societies of Southern Africa in the 19th and 20th Centuries. University of London.

INNES, D and PLAUT, M (1977/8), 'Class Struggle and Economic Development in SA: the Inter-war Years'. London: Institute for Commonwealth Studies.

JAY, M (1973), *The Dialectical Imagination.* London: Heinemann.

JOHNSTONE, FA (1976), *Class, Race and Gold.* London: Routledge and Kegan Paul.

— (1978), 'The Labour History of the Witwatersrand in the Context of South African Studies, and with Reflection on the New School'. *Social Dynamics,* vol 4, pt 2: University of Cape Town.

KALLAWAY, P and ADLER, T (eds) (1978), *Contemporary Southern African Studies: Research Papers,* 2 vols. Johannesburg: Faculty of Education, University of the Witwatersrand.

KAMPHAUSEN, E (1976), *Anfänge der Kirchlichen Unabhängigkeitsbewegung in Südafrika: Gesichte und Theologie der Äthiopischen Bewegung, 1872—1912.* Frankfurt: Peter Lang.

KARIS, T and CARTER, G (1972), *From Protest to Challenge: A Documentary History of African Politics in SA: 1882—1964.* Stanford: Hoover Institution Press.

KATZ, E (1976), *A Trade Union Aristocracy.* Johannesburg: African Studies Institute,

University of the Witwatersrand.

KUHN, T (1962), *The Structure of Scientific Revolutions.* Chicago: University of Chicago Press.

LARRAIN, J (1979), *The Concept of Ideology.* London: Hutchinson.

LEFEBVRE, H (1968), *The Sociology of Marx,* London: Allen Lane, The Penguin Press (French original in 1966).

LEVISON, AB (1974), *Knowledge and Society.* New York: The Bobs-Merrill Co.

LEWIS, J (1975), *Max Weber and Value-Free Sociology.* London: Lawrence and Wishart.

LINDEN, I (1980), *The Catholic Church and the Struggle for Zimbabwe.* London: Dartman, Longman and Todd.

LONERGAN, B (1957), *Insight: A Study of Human Understanding.* London, Darton, Longman and Todd.

MAJEKE, N (1952), *The Role of Missionaries in Conquest.* Johannesburg: Society of Young Africa.

MANNHEIM, MK (1936), *Ideology and Utopia.* London: Routledge and Kegan Paul.

MANNING, DJ (1976), *Liberalism.* London: JM Dent and Sons.

MARX, K and ENGELS, F (1970), *The German Ideology.* London: JM Dent and Sons.

MCCARTHY, T (1978), *The Critical Theory of Jürgen Habermas.* London: Hutchinson and Co.

MCLELLAN, D (1971), *The Thought of Karl Marx.* London: MacMillan Press.

— (1979), *Marxism after Marx.* London: MacMillan Press.

MCQUARRIE, D (ed) (1978), *Marx, Sociology, Social Change, Capitalism.* London: Quintet Books.

MEMMI, A (1965), *The Colonizer and the Colonized.* New York: Condor Books, Orion Press.

MOHUN, S (1979), 'Ideology, Knowledge and Neoclassical Economics: Some Elements of a Marxist Account'. In *Issues in Political Economy: a Critical Approach,* Francis Green and Peter Nore (eds). London: MacMillan Press.

MOLTENO, F (1977), 'Historical Significance of the Bantustan Strategy'. *Social Dynamics,* vol3, pt 2.

MOORE, R (1974), *Pit-men, Preachers and Politics: the Effects of Methodism in a Durham Mining Community.* London: Cambridge University Press.

MURRAY, C (1981), *Families Divided: the Impact of Migrant Labour in Lesotho.* Johannesburg: Ravan Press.

NASH, M (ed) (1977), *Out of the Dust: the Moratorium Debate.* Johannesburg: South African Council of Churches.

O'QUIGLEY, A (197?), 'The 1913 and 1914 White Workers' Strikes'. Johannesburg: African Studies Institute, University of the Witwatersrand.

PARSONS, QN (1969/70), 'Independency and Ethiopianism among the Tswana in the 19th and 20th Centuries'. London: Institute for Commonwealth Studies.

PATON, A (1973), *Apartheid and the Archbishop.* Cape Town: David Philip.

PEARSON, P (1975), 'Authority and Control in a SA Goldmine Compound', Johannesburg: African Studies Institute, University of the Witwatersrand.

PEIRES, JB (1981), *The House of Phalo: a History of the Xhosa People in the Days of their Independence.* Johannesburg: Ravan Press.

PYRAH, GB (1955), *Imperial Policy and SA: 1902—10.* London: Oxford University Press.

RANDALL, P (1982), *Little England on the Veld: the English Private School System in*

South Africa. Johannesburg: Ravan Press.

RANGER, T (1978), 'Growing from the Roots: Reflection on Peasant Research in Central and Southern Africa'. *Journal of Southern African Studies,* vol 5.

SALES, J (1971), *The Planting of the Churches in South Africa.* Grand Rapids: Eerdmans.

SAUNDERS, CC (1969/70), 'The New African Elite in the Eastern Cape and Some Late 19th Century Origins of African Nationalism'. London: Institute for Commonwealth Studies.

SCHLEMMER, L and WEBSTER, E (eds), *Change, Reform and Economic Growth in SA.* Johannesburg: Ravan Press.

SCHULTZ, HJ (1972), *English Liberalism and the State: Individualism or Collectivism?* Massachusettes: DC Heath and Co.

SCHROYER, T ((1973), *The Critique of Domination.* Boston: Beacon Press.

SIMONDS, AP (1978), *Karl Mannheim's Sociology of Knowledge.* Oxford: Clarendon Press.

SIMONS, HJ and RE (1969), *Class and Colour in SA: 1850—1950.* Harmondsworth: Penguin Books.

SKEATS, HS and MIALL, CS (1891), *History of the Free Churches of England: 1688—1891.* London: Alexander and Shepheard.

STONE, J (1973), *Colonist or Uitlander? A Study of the British Immigrant in SA.* London: Oxford University Press.

SUNDKLER, BGM (1961), *Bantu Prophets in SA.* London: Oxford University Press (2nd ed).

TAWNEY, RH (1926), *Religion and the Rise of Capitalism.* Harmondsworth: Penguin Books.

THOMSON, D (1950), *England in the 19th Century.* London: Pelican Books.

THOMPSON, EP (1968), *The Making of the English Working Class.* Harmondsworth: Penguin Books.

TICKTIN, D (1976), 'The White Labour Movement in SA, 1902—1910, and Working Class Solidarity'. Johannesburg: African Studies Institute, University of the Witwatersrand.

TRAPIDO, S (1972/3), 'Liberalism in the Cape in the 19th and 20th Centuries'. London: Institute for Commonwealth Studies.

— (1977), 'Landlord and Tenant in a Colonial Economy: the Transvaal, 1880—1910'. Johannesburg: African Studies Institute, University of the Witwatersrand.

TREVELYAN, GM (1964), *Illustrated English Social History: no 4.* Harmondsworth: Pelican Books.

VAN DEN BERGHE, P (1967), *South Africa: A Study in Conflict.* Berkeley: University of California Press.

VAN ONSELEN, C (1974/5), 'Randlords and Rotgut, 1886—1903'. London: Institute for Commonwealth Studies.

— (1975/6), 'SA's Lumpenproletarian Army: "Umkosi wa Ntaba" — "The Regiment of the Hills", 1890—1920'. London: Institute for Commonwealth Studies.

— (1982a), *Studies in the Social and Economic History of the Witwatersrand, 1886—1914:* vol 1, New Babylon. Johannesburg: Ravan Press.

— (1982b)*Studies in the Social and Economic History of the Witwatersrand, 1886—1914:* vol 2, New Ninevah. Johannesburg: Ravan Press.

VERRYN, TD (1971), *A History of the Order of Ethiopia,* Transvaal: Central Mission Press.

VILAKAZI, A (1962), *Zulu Transformations: A Study in the Dynamics of Social Change.* Pietermaritzburg: University of Natal Press.

WALSHE, P (1971), *The Rise of African Nationalism in South Africa: the African National Congress, 1912—1952;* Berkeley: University of California Press.

WEBSTER, E (ed) (1978), *Essays in Southern African Labour History.* Johannesburg: Ravan Press.

WELSH, D (1971), *The Roots of Segregation: 1845—1910;* London: Oxford University Press.

WILLIAMS, R (1961), *Culture and Society: 1780—1950;* Harmondsworth: Penguin Books.

WILSON, M and THOMPSON, L (eds) (1971), *The Oxford History of South Africa,* vol II: 1870—1966. London: Oxford University Press.

WILSON, F (1972), *Labour in the SA Gold Mines: 1911—1969.* London: Cambridge University Press.

WRIGHT, HM (1977), *The Burden of the Present: Liberal-Radical Controversy over Southern Africa History.* Cape Town: David Philip.

YOUNG, GW (1964), *Victorian England: Portrait of an Age.* New York: Oxford University Press, Galaxy Book.

Theological Material

ALVES, RA (1969), *A Theology of Hope.* New York: Corpus Books.

— (1972), *Tomorrow's Child.* London: SPCK.

ANDERSON, GH (ed) (1961), *The Theology of the Christian Mission.* Nashville: Abingdon Press.

ANDERSON, GH and STRANSKY, TF (eds) (1976), *Mission Trends no 3: Third World Theologies.* New York: Paulist Press.

— (1979), *Mission Trends no 4: Liberation Theologies.* New York: Paulist Press.

ASSMAN, H (1975), *Practical Theology of Liberation.* London: Search Press.

BARTH, K (1933), *The Epistle to the Romans.* London: Oxford University Press.

BIÉLER, A (1974), *The Politics of Hope.* Grand Rapids: Eerdmans.

BIGO, P (1977), *The Church and Third World Revolution.* New York: Orbis Books.

BOESAK, A (1976), *Farewell to Innocence.* Kampen: Uitgeversmaatschappij JH Kok.

BONINO, JM (1975), *Revolutionary Theology Comes of Age.* London: SPCK.

BRAATEN, CE (1974), *Eschatology and Ethics.* Minneapolis: Augsburg Publishing House.

BRIA, I (ed) (1980), *Martyria Mission: the Witness of the Orthodox Churches Today.* Geneva: World Council of Churches.

BURRIDGE, K (1971), *New Heaven, New Earth: A Study of Millenarian Activities.* Oxford: Basil Blackwell.

CARTER, J (1963), *Methods of Mission in Southern Africa* London: SPCK.

Christian Centre, The (1977), *Church, Society, Liberation, Hope.* Windhoek: The Christian Centre.

COCHRANE, CN (1940), *Christianity and Classical Culture.* London: Oxford University Press.

COHN, N (1970), *The Pursuit of the Millenium*. New York: Oxford University Press.

DAVIES, JG (1954), *The Spirit, the Church and the Sacraments*. London: The Faith Press.

DAVIS, C (1980), *Theology and Political Society*. London: Cambridge University Press.

DESMOND, C (1978), *Christians or Capitalists? Christianity and Politics in South Africa*. London: Bowerdean Press.

DULLES, A (1976), *Models of the Church*. Dublin: Gill and MacMillan.

DUMAS, A (1978), *Political Theology and the Life of the Church*. London: SCM Press.

DURNBAUGH, DF (1968), *The Believer's Church; the History and Character of Radical Protestantism*. London: Collier-MacMillan.

EAGLESON, J and SCHARPER, P (eds) (1979), *Puebla and Beyond*. New York: Orbis Books.

EBELING, G (1971), *Introduction to a Theological Theory of Language*. Philadelphia: Fortress Press.

— (1979), *The Study of Theology*. London: Collins.

ELIADE, M and KITAGAWA, JM (eds) (1959), *The History of Religions: Essays in Methodology*. Chicago: University of Chicago Press.

ELLACURIA, I (1976), *Freedom Made Flesh*. New York: Orbis Books.

ELLUL, J (1977), *Hope in Time of Abandonment*. New York: Seabury Press.

FERRÉ, F (1970), *Language, Logic and God*, London: Collins-Fontana.

FIERRO, A (1977), *The Militant Gospel*. New York: Orbis Books.

FREIRE, P (1971), *Pedagogy of the Oppressed*. New York: Herder and Herder.

FROSTIN, P (1978), *Materialismus, Ideologie, Religion: Die materialistische Religionskritik bei Karl Marx*. Lund: CWK Gleerup.

GEERTZ, G (1973) *The Interpretation of Cultures*. New York: Basic Books.

GIBELLINI, R (1979), *Frontiers of Theology in Latin America*. New York: Orbis Books.

GILKEY, L (1976), *Reaping the Whirlwind: A Christian Interpretation of History*. New York: Seabury Press.

GUSTAFSON, JM (1961), *Treasure in Earthern Vessels: the Church as a Human Community*. New York: Harper and Bros.

— (1975), *Can Ethics be Christian?* Berkeley: University of California Press.

GUTIÉRREZ, G (1973), *A Theology of Liberation*. London: SCM Press.

GUTIÉRREZ, G and SHAULL, R (1977), *Liberation and Change*. Atlanta: John Knox Press.

HAUERWAS, S (1974), *Vision and Virtue*. Notre Dame: University of Notre Dame Press.

HENDRY, GS (1959), *The Gospel of the Incarnation*. London: SCM Press.

HERZOG, F (1972), *Liberation Theology: Liberation in the Light of the Fourth Gospel*. New York: Seabury Press.

JENNINGS, TW (1976), *Introduction to Theology*. Philadelphia: Fortress Press.

JOHANSON, B (ed) (1975), *The Church in SA Today and Tomorrow*. Johannesburg: South African Council of Churches.

KÄSEMAN, E (1969), *Jesus Means Freedom*. London: SCM Press.

KOYAMA, K (1974), *Waterbuffalo Theology*. London: SCM Press.

KÜMMEL, WG (1957), *Promise and Fulfilment*. London: SCM Press.

KÜNG, H (1968), *The Church*. London: Search Press.

LANTERNARI, V (1963), *The Religions of the Oppressed*. New York: Alfred A Knopf, Mentor Books.

LOSSKY, V (1976), *The Mystical Theology of the Eastern Church*. New York: St Vladimir's Press.

LYNCH, WF (1960), *Christ and Apollo*, New York: Sheed and Ward.

— (1965), *Images of Hope*. Indiana: University of Notre Dame Press.

MCGAUGHEY, DR (1983), *On the Soteriological Significance of the Symbol of the Kingdom of God in the Language of the Historical Jesus*. University of Chicago: unpubl dissertation.

MEEKS, MD (1974), *Origins of the Theology of Hope*. Philadelphia: Fortress Press.

MELAND, B (1953), *Faith and Culture*. Carbondale: Southern Illinois University Press.

METZ, JB (ed) (1971), *Perspectives of a Political Ecclesiology*. New York: Herder and Herder.

MOLTMANN, J (1967), *Theology of Hope*. New York: Harper and Row.

— (1971), *Hope and Planning*. London: SCM Press.

— (1975), *The Experiment Hope*. Philadelphia: Fortress Press.

— (1977), *The Church in the Power of the Spirit*. London: SCM Press.

NIEBUHR, HR (1943), *Radical Monotheism and Western Culture*. New York: Harper and Row.

— (1963), *The Responsible Self*. New York: Harper and Row.

NÜRNBERGER, K (1978), *Affluence, Poverty and the Word of God*. Durban: Lutheran Publishing House.

— (1979), *Ideologies of Change in SA and the Power of the Gospel*. Mapumulo: Missiological Institute.

ODEN, TC (1970), *Beyond Revolution: A Response to the Underground Church*. Philadelphia: Westminster Press.

PANNENBERG, W (1968), *Jesus — God and Man*. Philadelphia: Westminster Press.

— (1969a), *Theology and the Kingdom of God*. Philadelphia: Westminster Press.

— (1969b) (ed), *Revelation as History*. London: Sheed and Ward.

PELIKAN, J (1974), *The Spirit of Eastern Christendom (600—1700), vol 2, The Christian Tradition*. Chicago: University of Chicago Press.

RANDALL, P (1971), *Power, Privilege and Poverty: Report of the Spro-cas Economic Commission*. Johannesburg: Spro-cas.

— (1972), *Apartheid and the Church*. Johannesburg: Spro-cas.

RICOEUR, P (1967), *The Symbolism of Evil*. Boston: Beacon Press.

— (1974a), *The Conflict of Interpretations*. Evanston: Northwestern University Press.

— (1974b), *Political and Social Essays* (ed D Stewart and J Bien). Athens, Ohio: Ohio University Press.

— (1977), *The Rule of Metaphor*. London: Routledge and Kegan Paul. (Trans R Czerny, original in French, 1975).

ROUSE, R and NEILL, S (1954), *A History of the Ecumenical Movement: 1517—1948*. London: SPCK.

RUSSELL, DS (1978), *Apocalyptic Ancient and Modern*. London: SCM Press.

SCHLEIERMACHER, F (1970), *Brief Outline on the Study of Theology*. Richmond: John Knox Press.

SEGUNDO, JL (1973), *The Community Called Church, vol 1: A Theology for Artisans of a New Humanity*. New York: Orbis Books.

— (1977), *The Liberation of Theology*. Dublin: Gill and MacMillan.

SNYDER, R (1977), 'Boisen's Understanding of Religious Experience with Implications for Therapy and for a Pastor's Work with a Congregation'. *Chicago Theological Seminary Register,* vol LXVII, no 1, Winter 1977.

SUNDERMEIER, T (ed) (1975), *Church and Nationalism in SA*. Johannesburg: Ravan Press.

THIESSEN, G (1978), *The First Followers of Jesus*. London: SCM Press.

TILLICH, P (1977), *The Socialist Decision*. New York: Harper and Row.

VOS, G (1972), *The Pauline Eschatology*. Grand Rapids: Eerdmans.

WEISS, J (1971), *Jesus' Proclamation of the Kingdom of God*. London: SCM Press (English translation).

ZIMMERLI, W (1968), *Man and His Hope in the Old Testament*. London: SCM Press.

Index